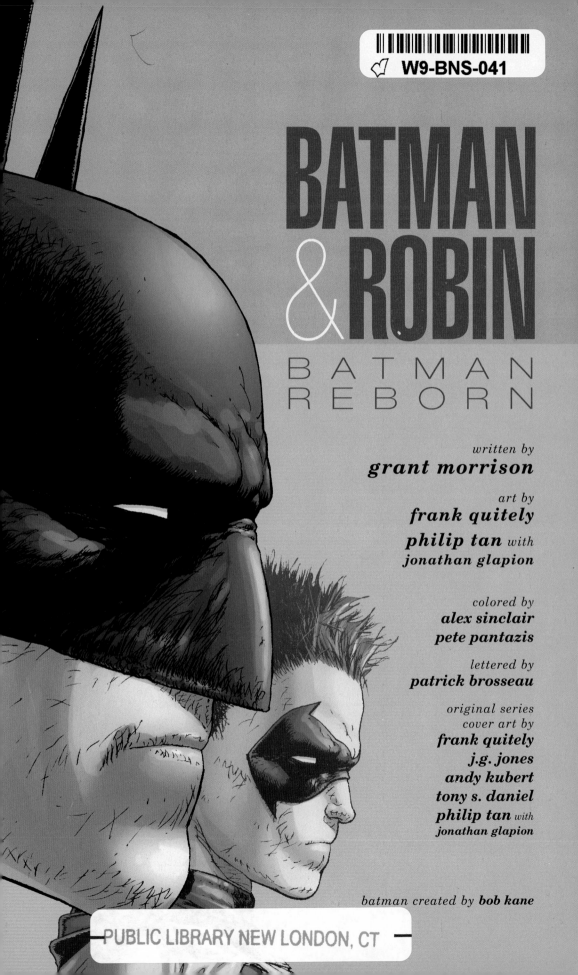

BATMAN & ROBIN

BATMAN REBORN

written by
grant morrison

art by
frank quitely

philip tan with
jonathan glapion

colored by
alex sinclair
pete pantazis

lettered by
patrick brosseau

original series
cover art by
frank quitely
j.g. jones
andy kubert
tony s. daniel
philip tan with
jonathan glapion

batman created by **bob kane**

MIKE MARTS Editor – Original Series
JANELLE SIEGEL Assistant Editor – Original Series
SCOTT NYBAKKEN Editor
ROBBIN BROSTERMAN Design Director – Books
CURTIS KING JR. Publication Design

BOB HARRAS Senior VP – Editor-in-Chief, DC Comics

DIANE NELSON President
DAN DIDIO and JIM LEE Co-Publishers
GEOFF JOHNS Chief Creative Officer
AMIT DESAI Senior VP – Marketing and Franchise Management
AMY GENKINS Senior VP – Business and Legal Affairs
NAIRI GARDINER Senior VP – Finance
JEFF BOISON VP – Publishing Planning
MARK CHIARELLO VP – Art Direction and Design
JOHN CUNNINGHAM VP – Marketing
TERRI CUNNINGHAM VP – Editorial Administration
LARRY GANEM VP – Talent Relations and Services
ALISON GILL Senior VP – Manufacturing and Operations
HANK KANALZ Senior VP – Vertigo and Integrated Publishing
JAY KOGAN VP – Business and Legal Affairs, Publishing
JACK MAHAN VP – Business Affairs, Talent
NICK NAPOLITANO VP – Manufacturing Administration
SUE POHJA VP – Book Sales
FRED RUIZ VP – Manufacturing Operations
COURTNEY SIMMONS Senior VP – Publicity
BOB WAYNE Senior VP – Sales

Cover art by Frank Quitely.
Cover color by Alex Sinclair.

BATMAN AND ROBIN: BATMAN REBORN

DC Comics, 4000 Warner Blvd., Burbank, CA 91522.
A Warner Bros. Entertainment Company.
Printed by Solisco Printers, Scott, QC, Canada. 6/03/15. Fifth Printing.
ISBN: 978-1-4012-2987-0

Library of Congress Cataloging-in-Publication Data
Morrison, Grant.
  Batman and Robin : Batman reborn / Grant Morrison, Frank Quitely, Philip Tan.
    p. cm.
  ISBN 978-1-4012-2987-0
1. Graphic novels. I. Quitely, Frank, 1968- II. Tan, Philip, 1978- III. Title. IV. Title: Batman reborn.
  PN6728.B36M6726 2012
  741.5'973—dc23

SUSTAINABLE FORESTRY INITIATIVE

Certified Chain of Custody
Promoting Sustainable Forestry
www.sfiprogram.org
SFI-01368

This Label only applies to the text section

CONTENTS

BATMAN & ROBIN
BATMAN REBORN

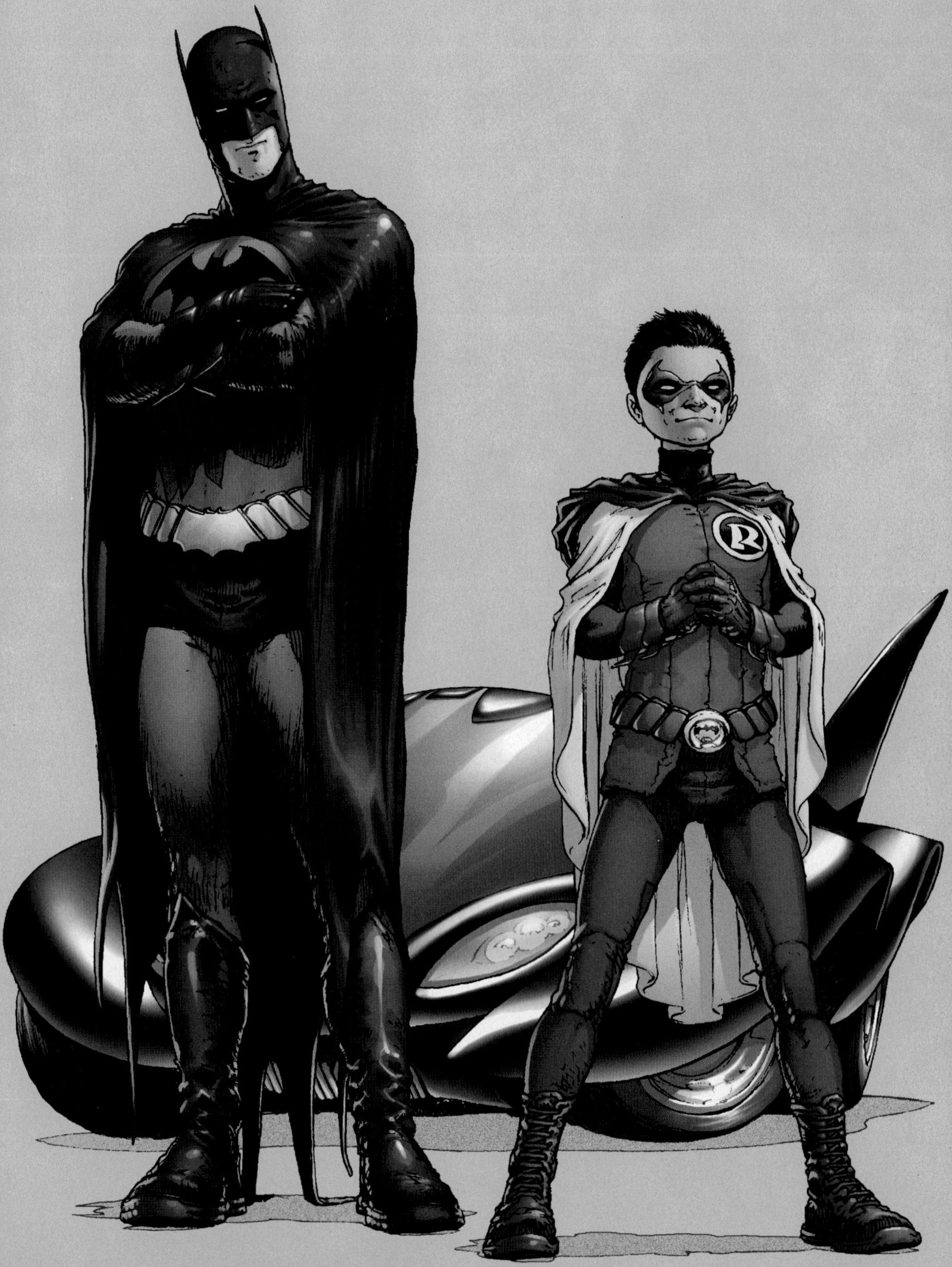

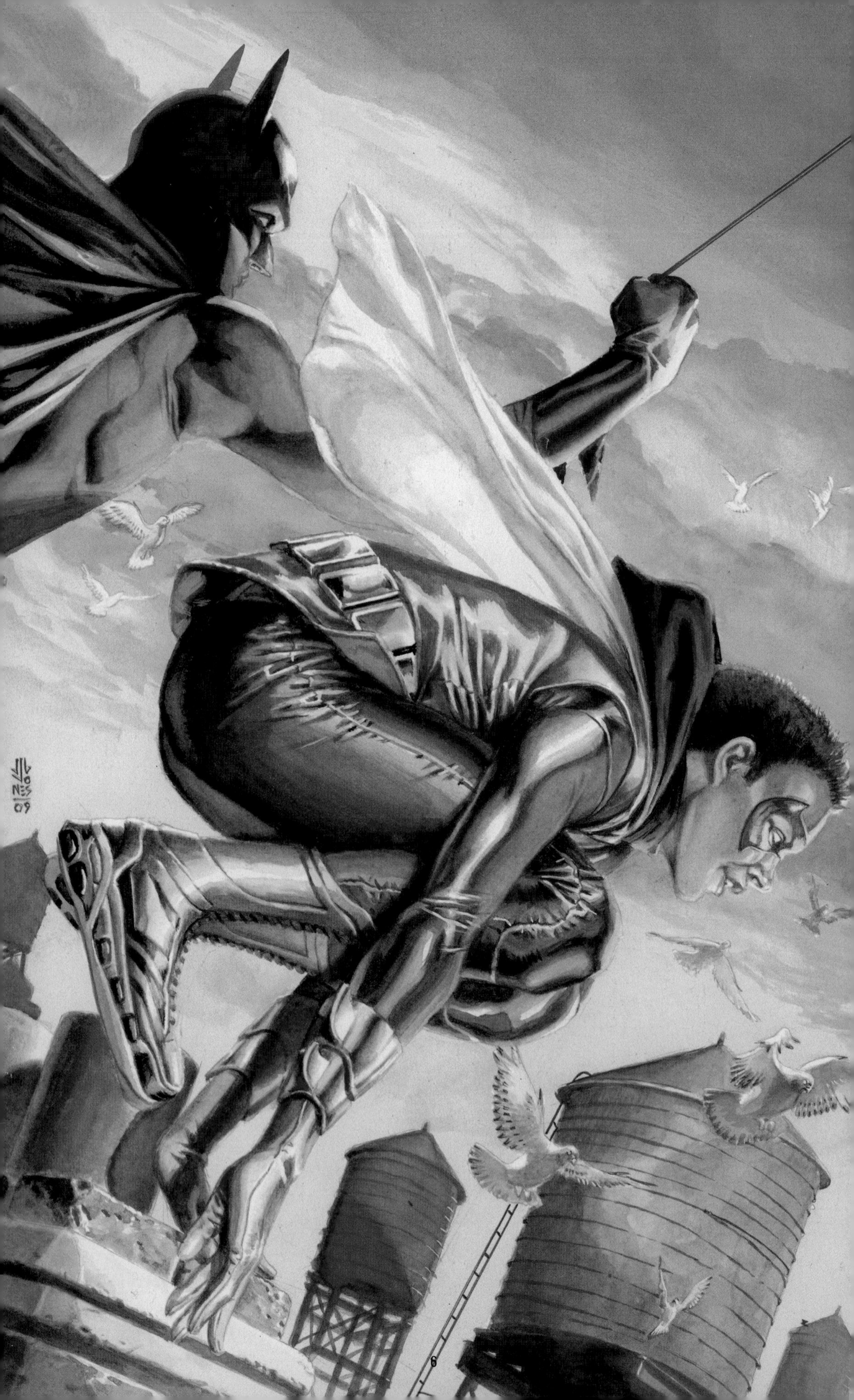

YOU SAID THIS WOULD BE *EASY!*

A SIMPLE *EXCHANGE,* YOU SAID!

LEV, *SHUSH.*

~*HEKK!*~ WHY THE *PANIC?*

THE MINGERS CAN'T *CATCH* US NOW!

THEY'D NEED *WINGS* TO CHASE OLD *TOAD!*

NO.

THEY'D HAVE TO BE *BATMAN*--AND BATMAN'S AS *DEAD* AS THE SKY IS *BLACK!*

BELTS, GENTLEMEN, PLEASE!

SAFETY FIRST!

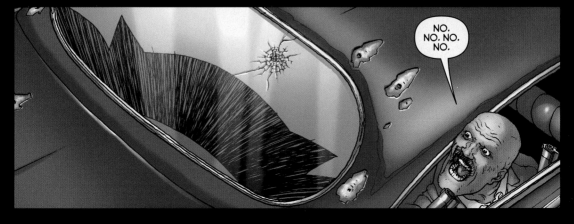

NO. NO. NO. NO.

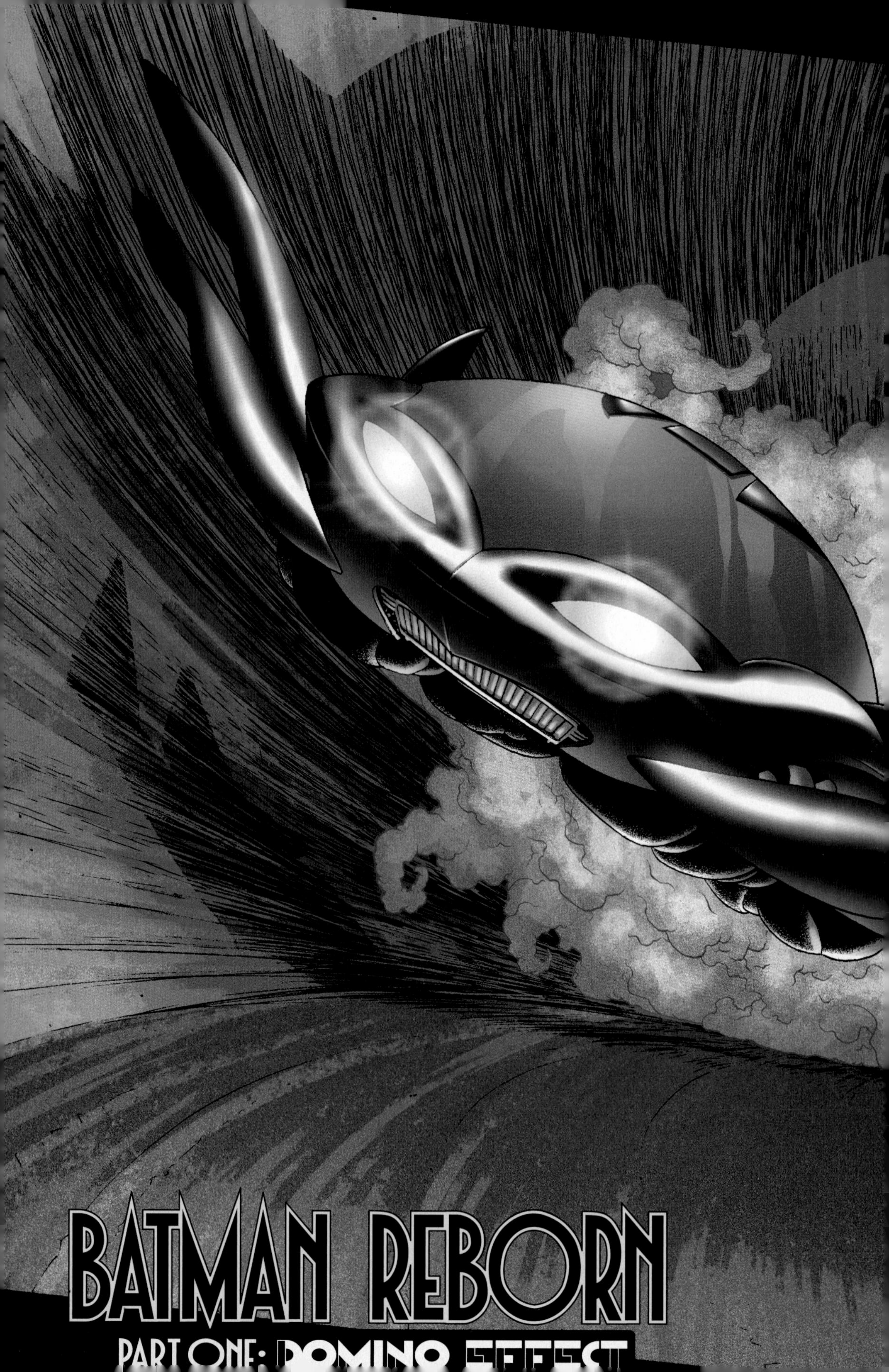
BATMAN REBORN
PART ONE: DOMINO EFFECT

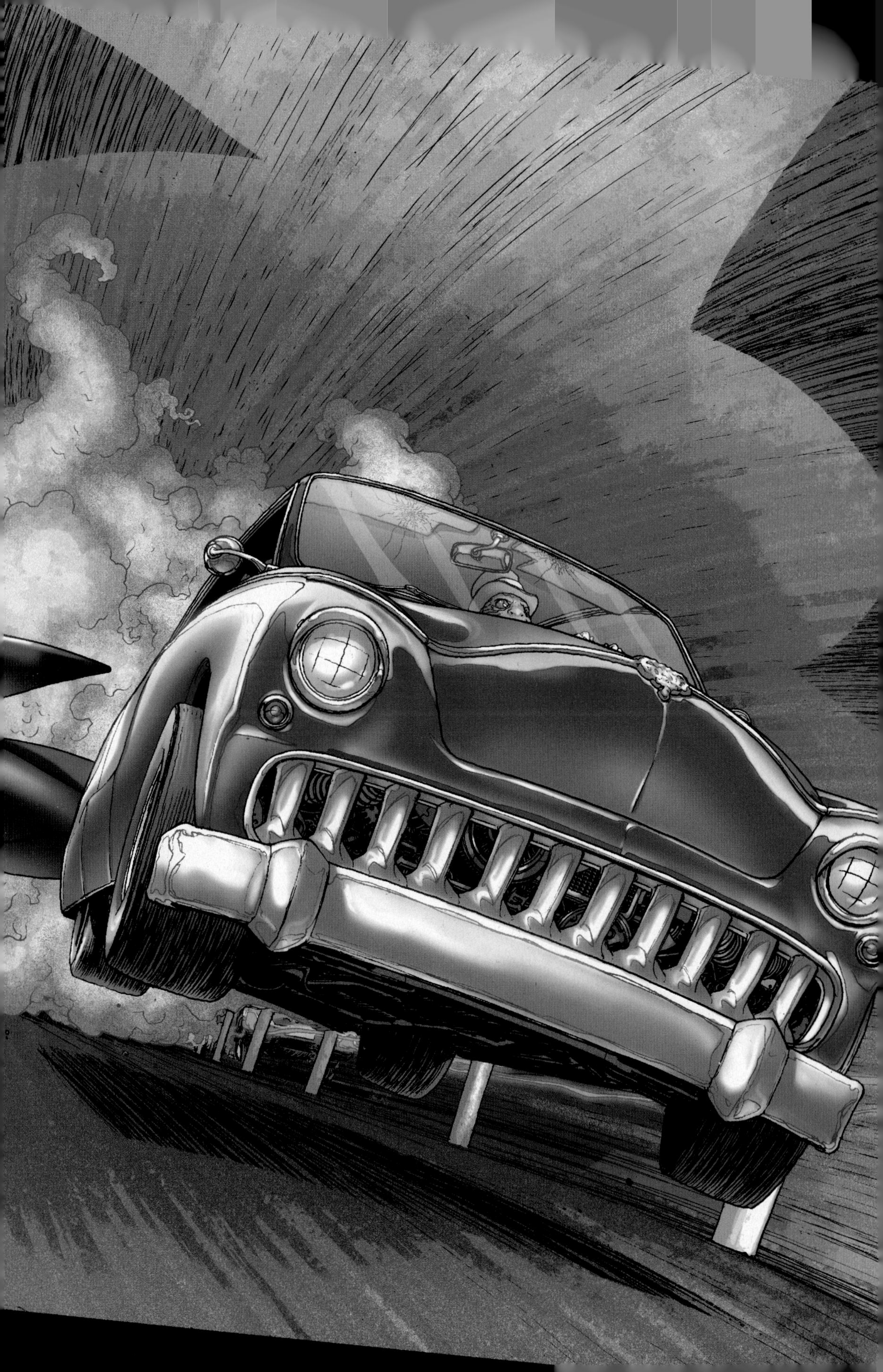

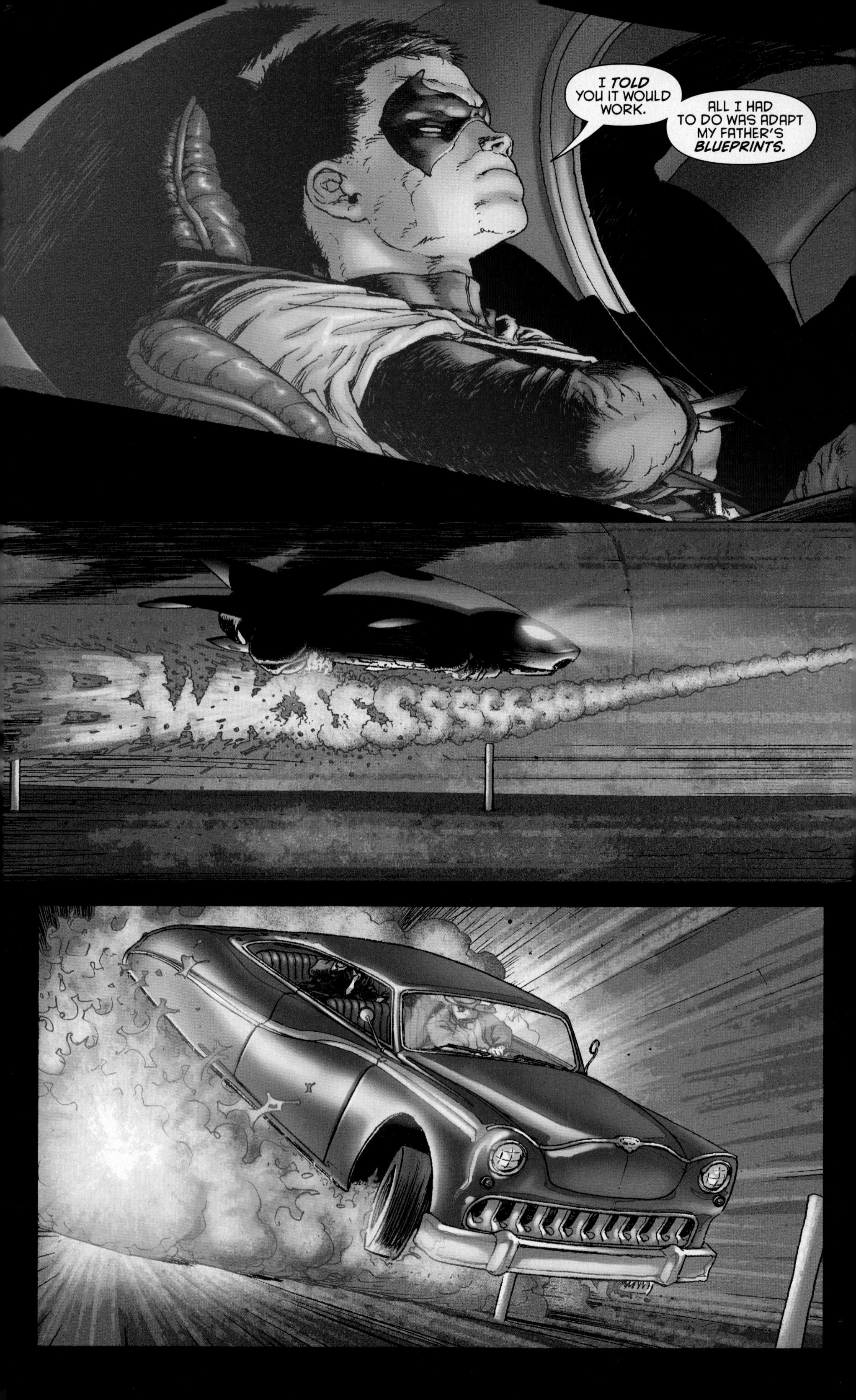
I TOLD YOU IT WOULD WORK.
ALL I HAD TO DO WAS ADAPT MY FATHER'S BLUEPRINTS.

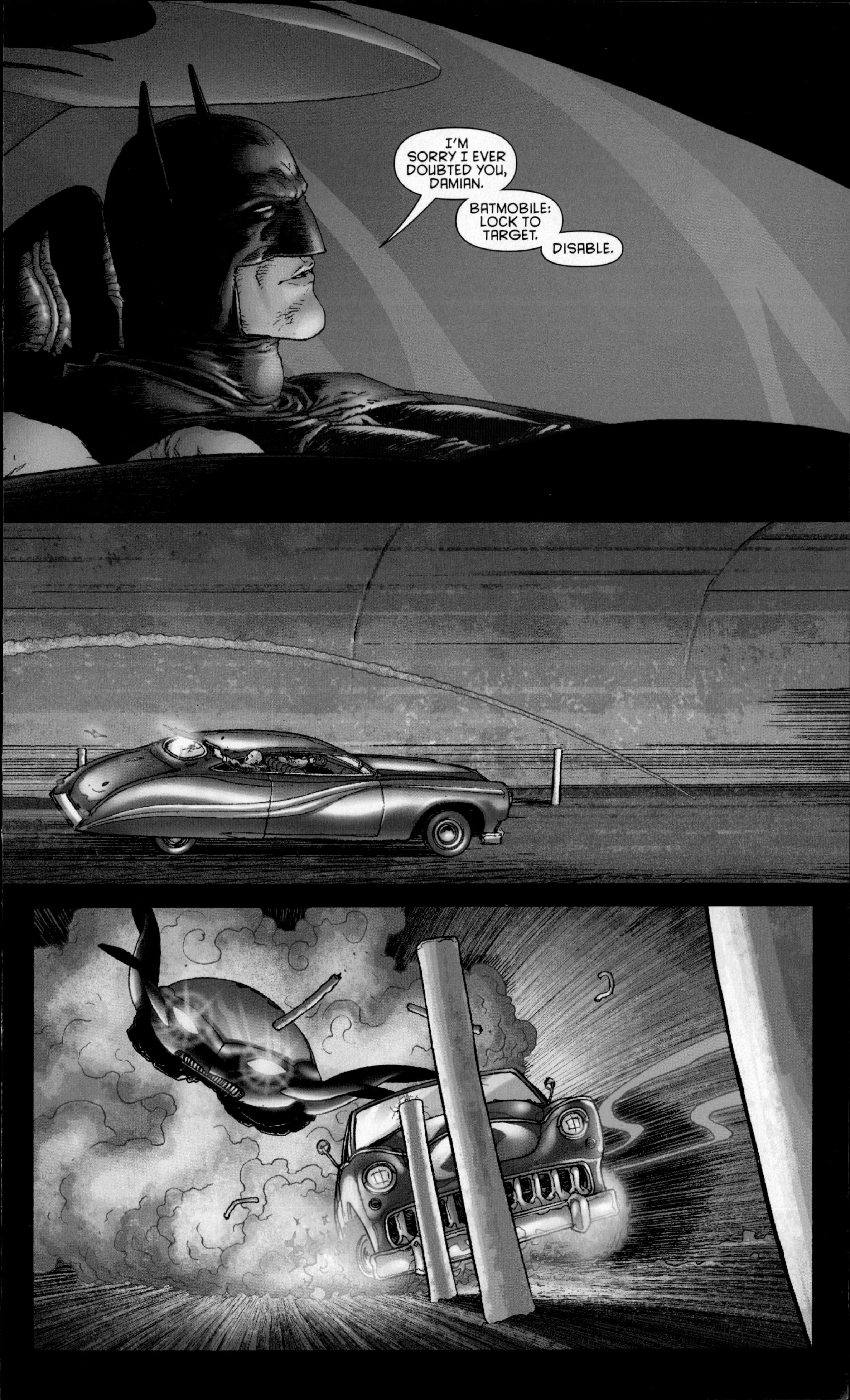
I'M SORRY I EVER DOUBTED YOU, DAMIAN.
BATMOBILE: LOCK TO TARGET.
DISABLE.

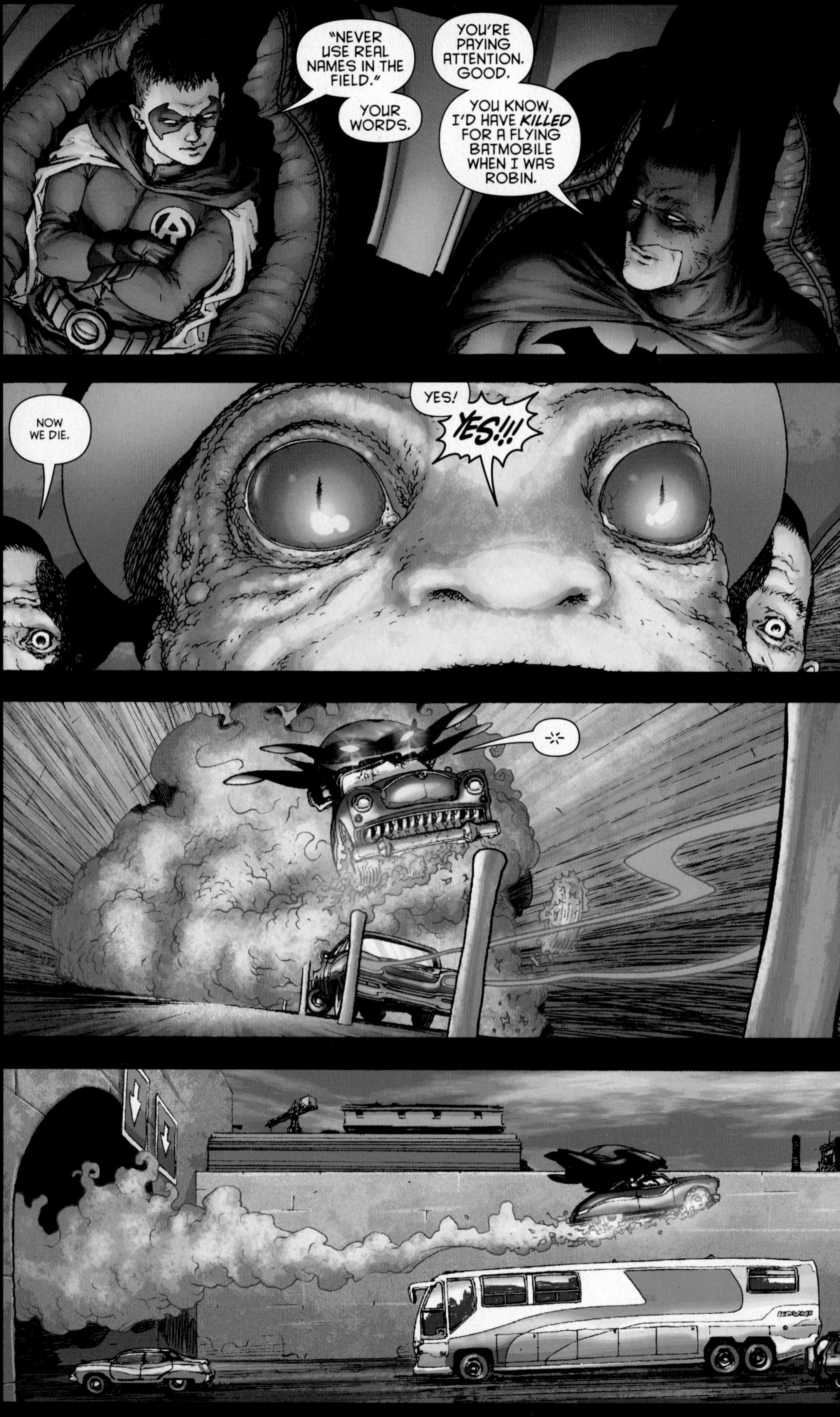
"NEVER USE REAL NAMES IN THE FIELD."
YOUR WORDS.
YOU'RE PAYING ATTENTION. GOOD.
YOU KNOW, I'D HAVE KILLED FOR A FLYING BATMOBILE WHEN I WAS ROBIN.
NOW WE DIE.
YES!
YES!!!

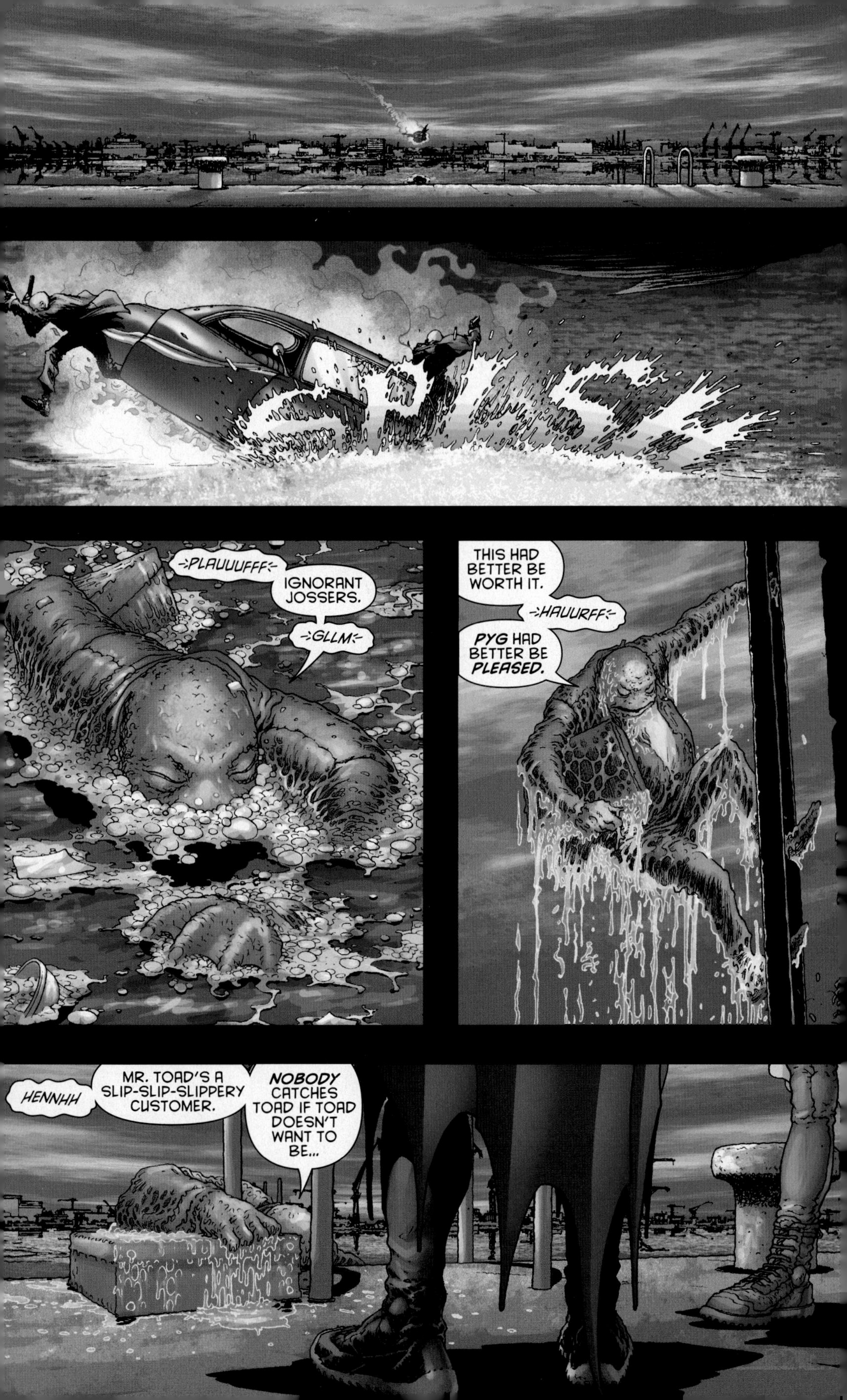
-PLAUUUFFF-
IGNORANT JOSSERS.
-GLLM-
THIS HAD BETTER BE WORTH IT.
-HAUURFF-
PYG HAD BETTER BE PLEASED.
HENNHH
MR. TOAD'S A SLIP-SLIP-SLIPPERY CUSTOMER.
NOBODY CATCHES TOAD IF TOAD DOESN'T WANT TO BE...

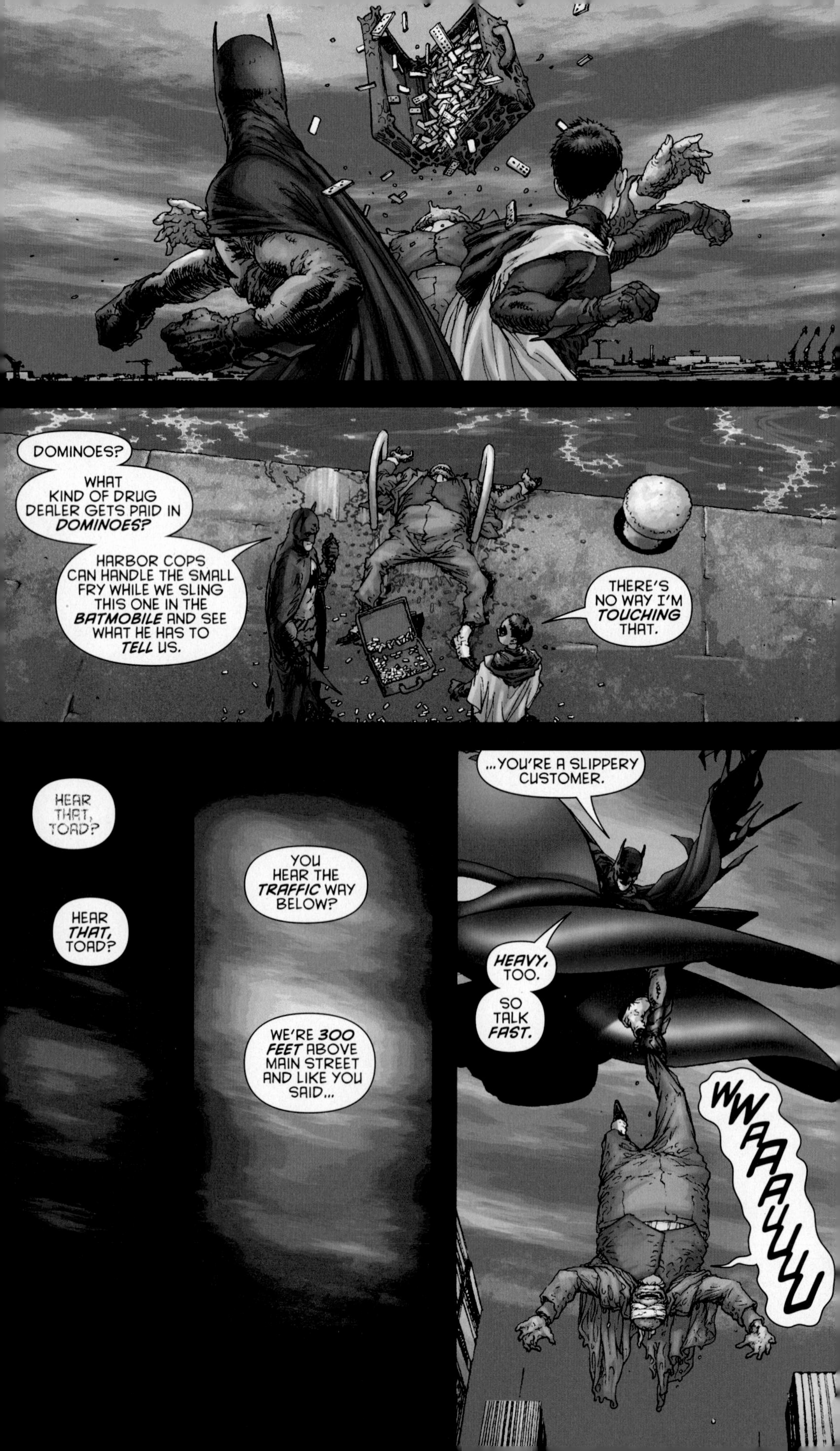
DOMINOES?
WHAT KIND OF DRUG DEALER GETS PAID IN *DOMINOES?*
HARBOR COPS CAN HANDLE THE SMALL FRY WHILE WE SLING THIS ONE IN THE *BATMOBILE* AND SEE WHAT HE HAS TO *TELL* US.
THERE'S NO WAY I'M *TOUCHING* THAT.
HEAR THAT, TOAD?
HEAR *THAT,* TOAD?
YOU HEAR THE *TRAFFIC* WAY BELOW?
WE'RE *300 FEET* ABOVE MAIN STREET AND LIKE YOU SAID...
...YOU'RE A SLIPPERY CUSTOMER.
HEAVY, TOO.
SO TALK *FAST.*
WWAAAAUUUU

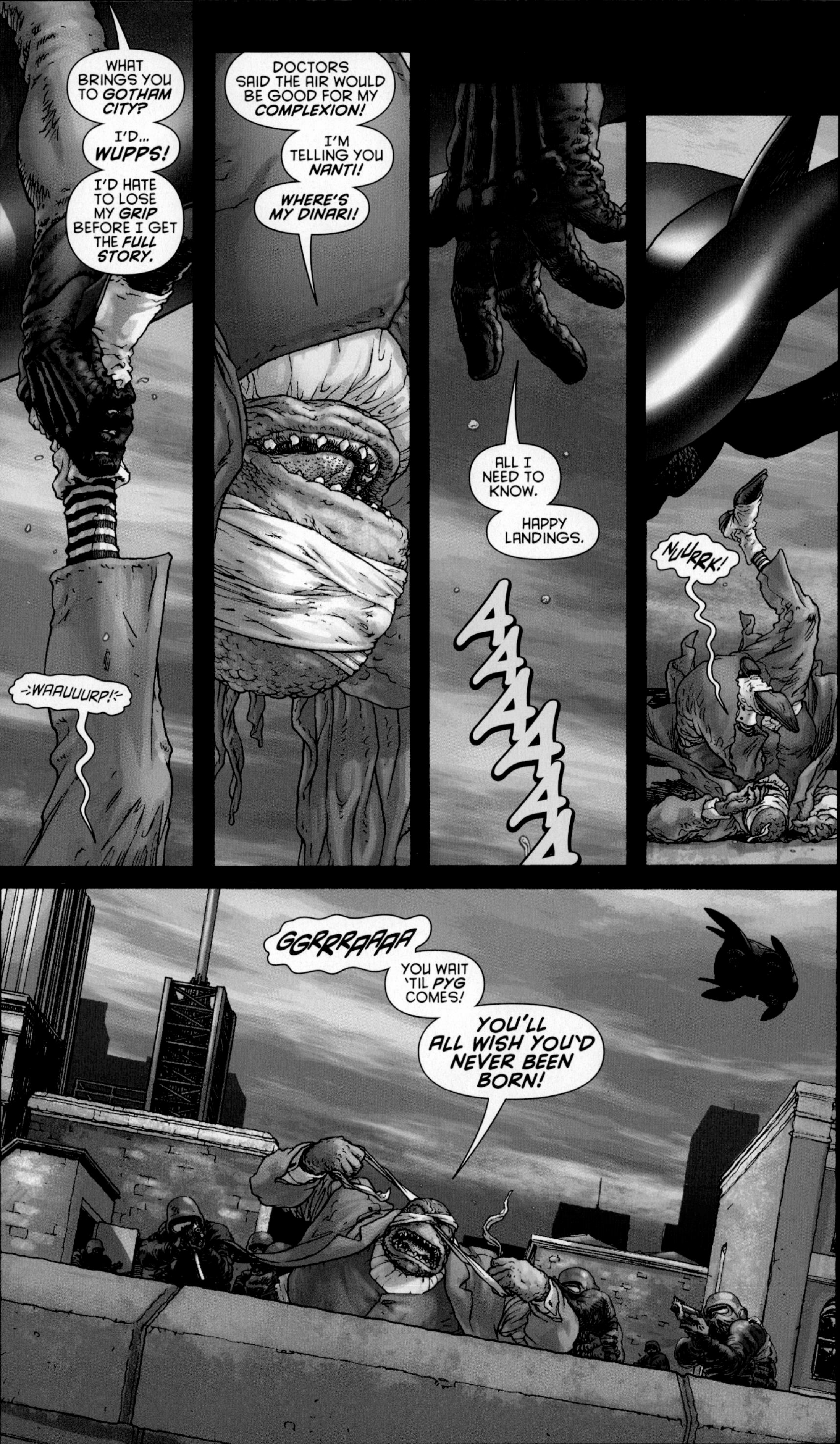

WHAT BRINGS YOU TO GOTHAM CITY?
I'D... WUPPS!
I'D HATE TO LOSE MY GRIP BEFORE I GET THE FULL STORY.
WAAUUURP!
DOCTORS SAID THE AIR WOULD BE GOOD FOR MY COMPLEXION!
I'M TELLING YOU NANTI!
WHERE'S MY DINARI!
ALL I NEED TO KNOW.
HAPPY LANDINGS.
AAAAAA
NUURRK!
GGRRRAAAA
YOU WAIT 'TIL PYG COMES!
YOU'LL ALL WISH YOU'D NEVER BEEN BORN!

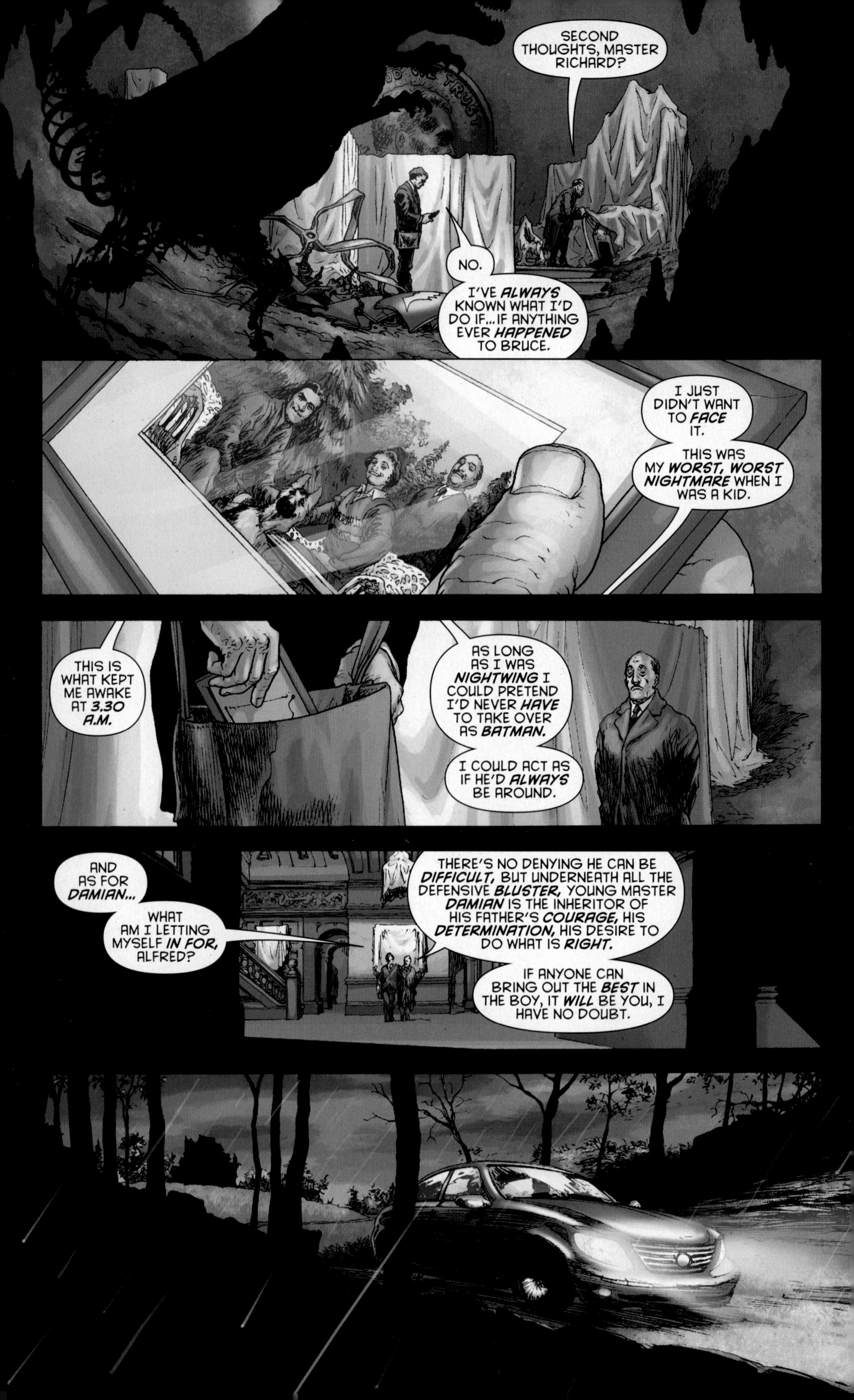
SECOND THOUGHTS, MASTER RICHARD?
NO.
I'VE ALWAYS KNOWN WHAT I'D DO IF...IF ANYTHING EVER HAPPENED TO BRUCE.
I JUST DIDN'T WANT TO FACE IT.
THIS WAS MY WORST, WORST NIGHTMARE WHEN I WAS A KID.
THIS IS WHAT KEPT ME AWAKE AT 3.30 A.M.
AS LONG AS I WAS NIGHTWING I COULD PRETEND I'D NEVER HAVE TO TAKE OVER AS BATMAN.
I COULD ACT AS IF HE'D ALWAYS BE AROUND.
AND AS FOR DAMIAN...
WHAT AM I LETTING MYSELF IN FOR, ALFRED?
THERE'S NO DENYING HE CAN BE DIFFICULT, BUT UNDERNEATH ALL THE DEFENSIVE BLUSTER, YOUNG MASTER DAMIAN IS THE INHERITOR OF HIS FATHER'S COURAGE, HIS DETERMINATION, HIS DESIRE TO DO WHAT IS RIGHT.
IF ANYONE CAN BRING OUT THE BEST IN THE BOY, IT WILL BE YOU, I HAVE NO DOUBT.

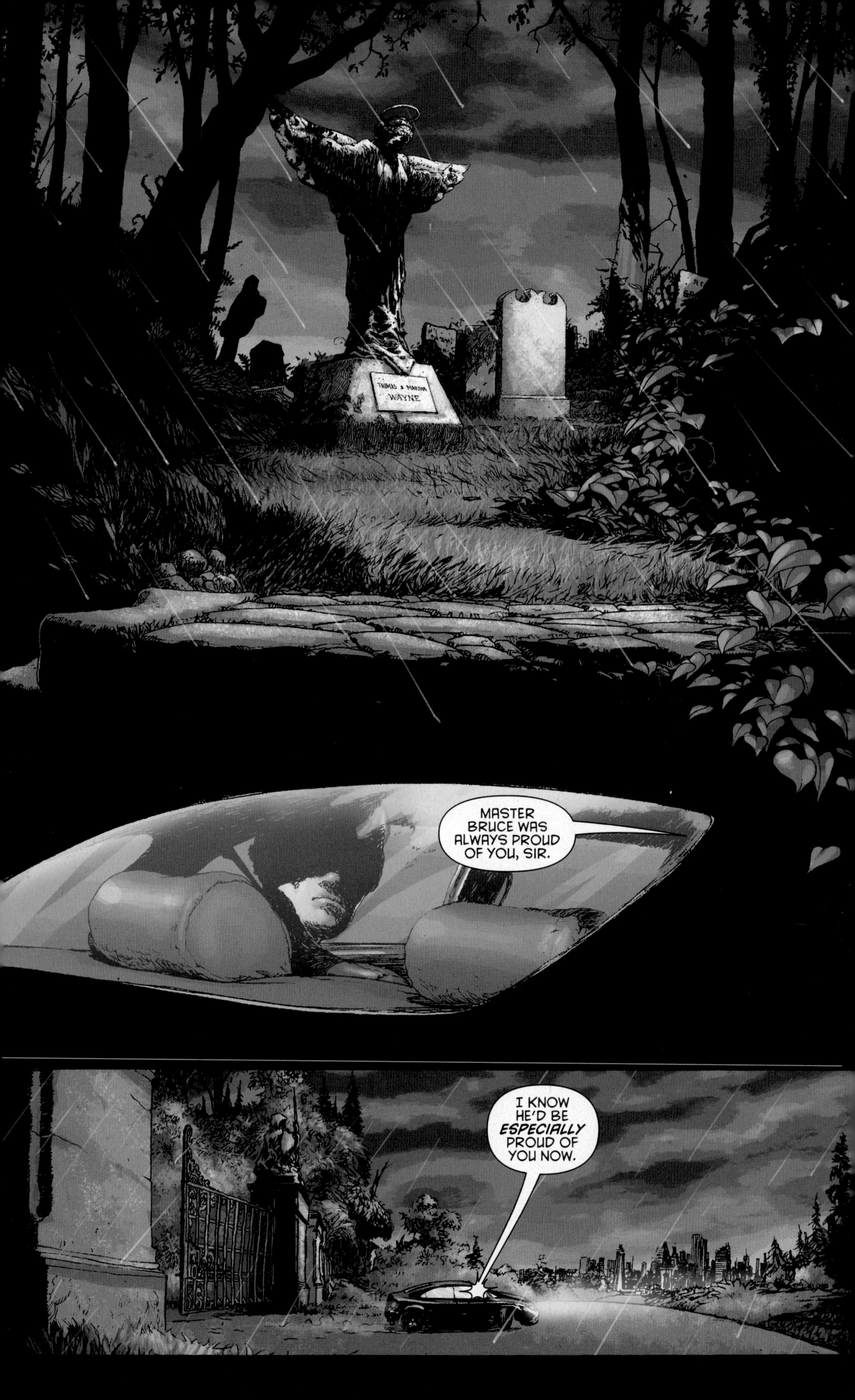
THOMAS & MARTHA WAYNE
MASTER BRUCE WAS ALWAYS PROUD OF YOU, SIR.
I KNOW HE'D BE *ESPECIALLY* PROUD OF YOU NOW.

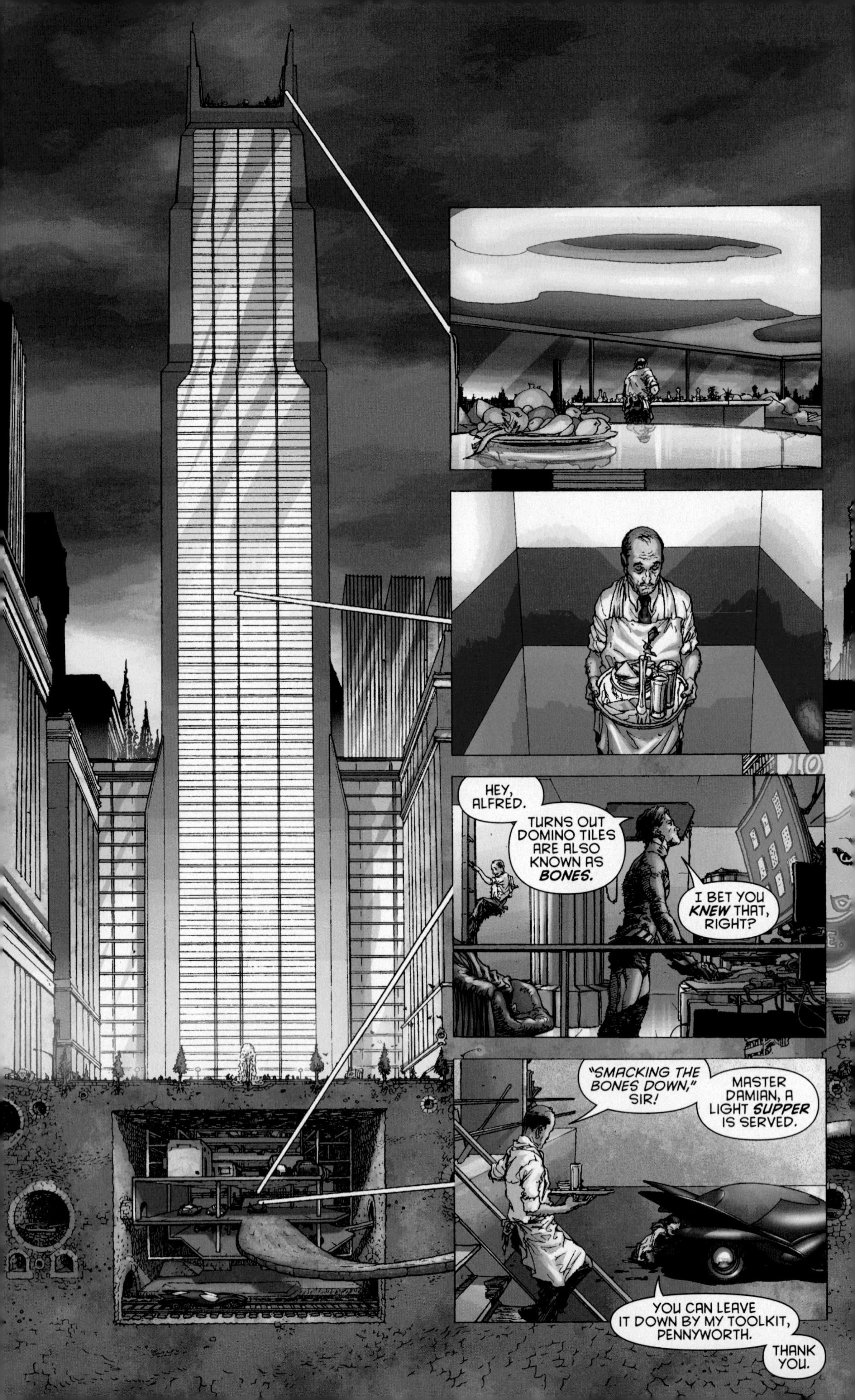
HEY, ALFRED.
TURNS OUT DOMINO TILES ARE ALSO KNOWN AS BONES.
I BET YOU KNEW THAT, RIGHT?
"SMACKING THE BONES DOWN," SIR!
MASTER DAMIAN, A LIGHT SUPPER IS SERVED.
YOU CAN LEAVE IT DOWN BY MY TOOLKIT, PENNYWORTH.
THANK YOU.

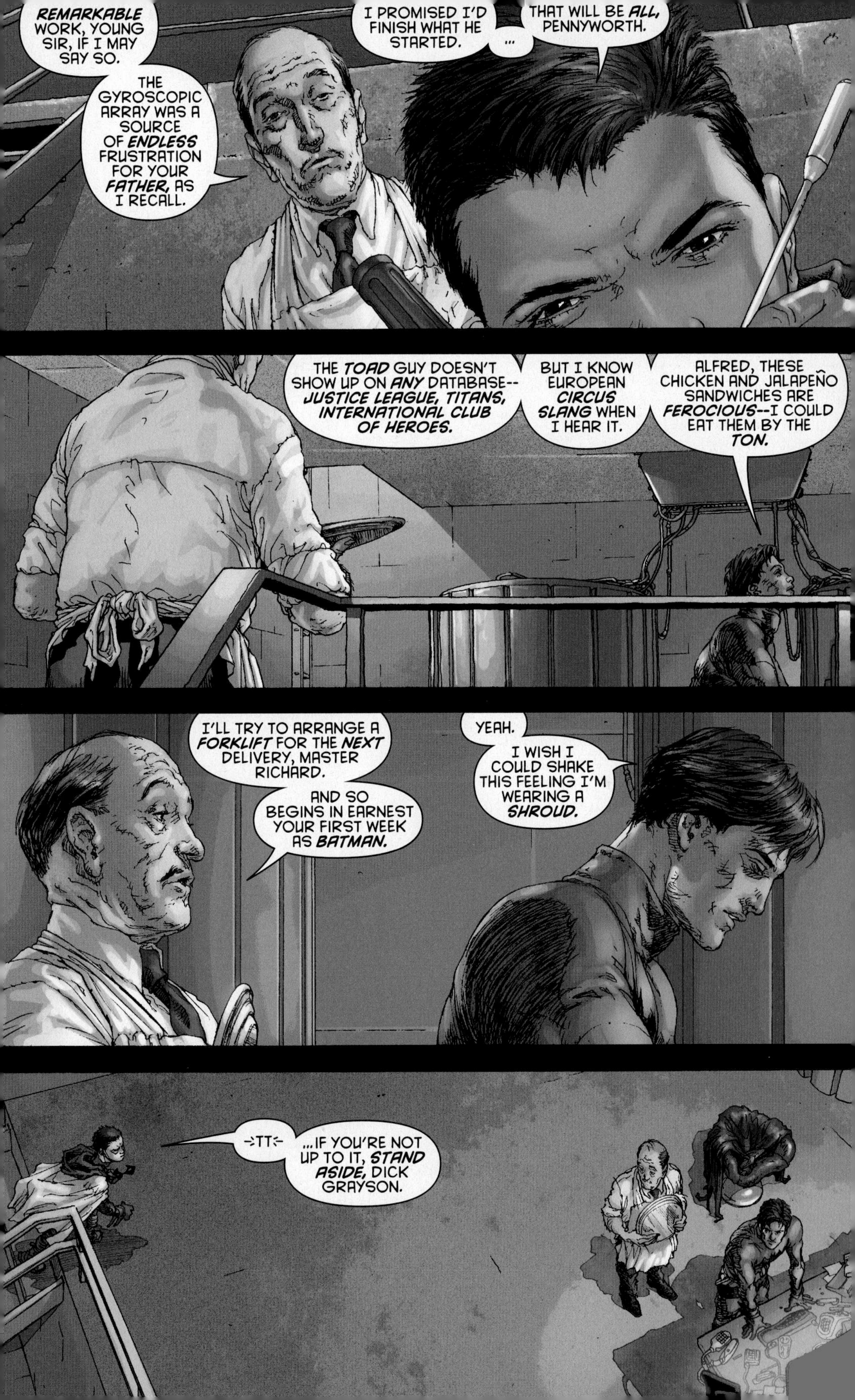
REMARKABLE WORK, YOUNG SIR, IF I MAY SAY SO.
THE GYROSCOPIC ARRAY WAS A SOURCE OF ENDLESS FRUSTRATION FOR YOUR FATHER, AS I RECALL.
I PROMISED I'D FINISH WHAT HE STARTED.
...
THAT WILL BE ALL, PENNYWORTH.
THE TOAD GUY DOESN'T SHOW UP ON ANY DATABASE-- JUSTICE LEAGUE, TITANS, INTERNATIONAL CLUB OF HEROES.
BUT I KNOW EUROPEAN CIRCUS SLANG WHEN I HEAR IT.
ALFRED, THESE CHICKEN AND JALAPEÑO SANDWICHES ARE FEROCIOUS--I COULD EAT THEM BY THE TON.
I'LL TRY TO ARRANGE A FORKLIFT FOR THE NEXT DELIVERY, MASTER RICHARD.
AND SO BEGINS IN EARNEST YOUR FIRST WEEK AS BATMAN.
YEAH.
I WISH I COULD SHAKE THIS FEELING I'M WEARING A SHROUD.
-TT-
...IF YOU'RE NOT UP TO IT, STAND ASIDE, DICK GRAYSON.

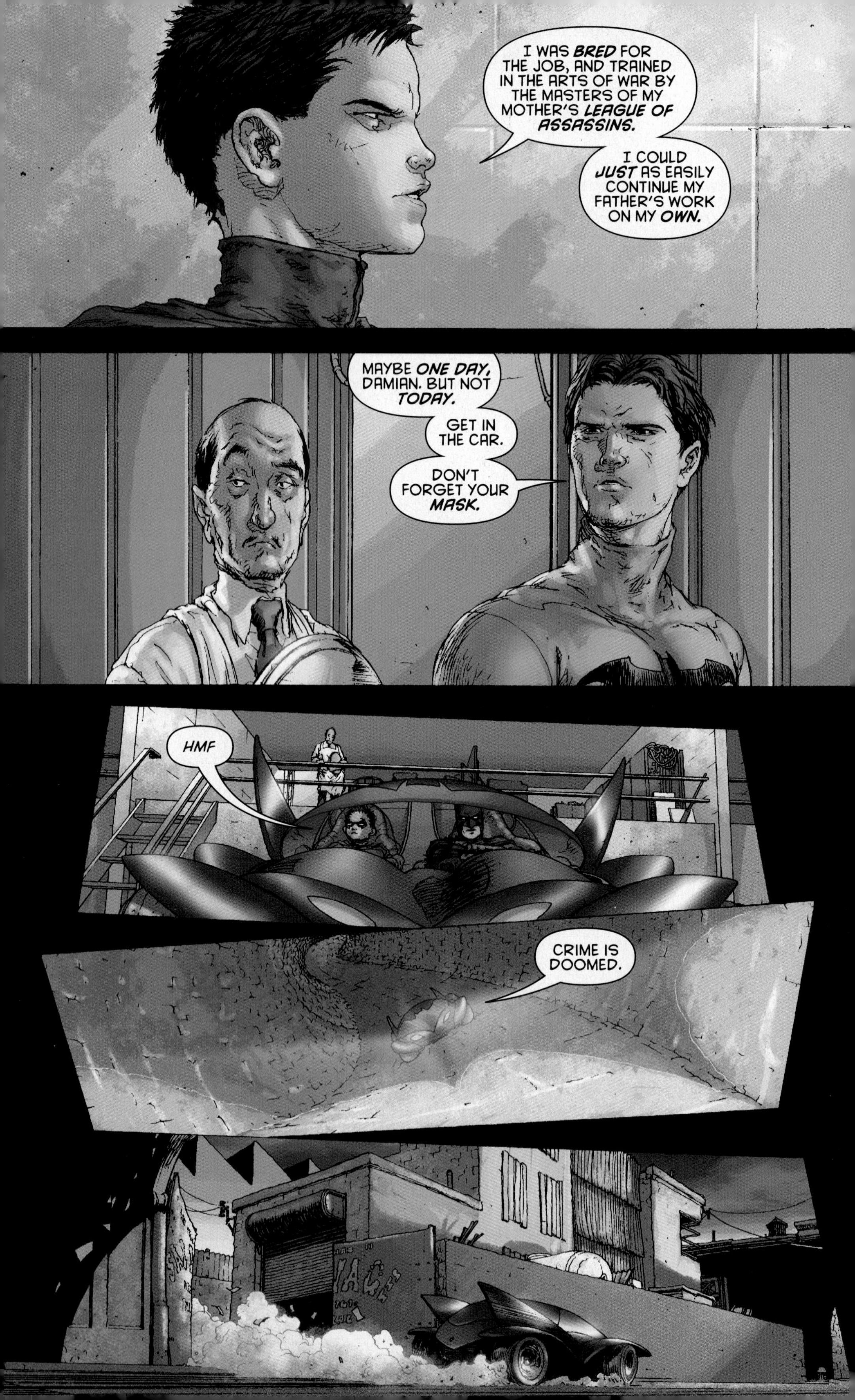
I WAS BRED FOR THE JOB, AND TRAINED IN THE ARTS OF WAR BY THE MASTERS OF MY MOTHER'S LEAGUE OF ASSASSINS.
I COULD JUST AS EASILY CONTINUE MY FATHER'S WORK ON MY OWN.
MAYBE ONE DAY, DAMIAN. BUT NOT TODAY.
GET IN THE CAR.
DON'T FORGET YOUR MASK.
HMF
CRIME IS DOOMED.

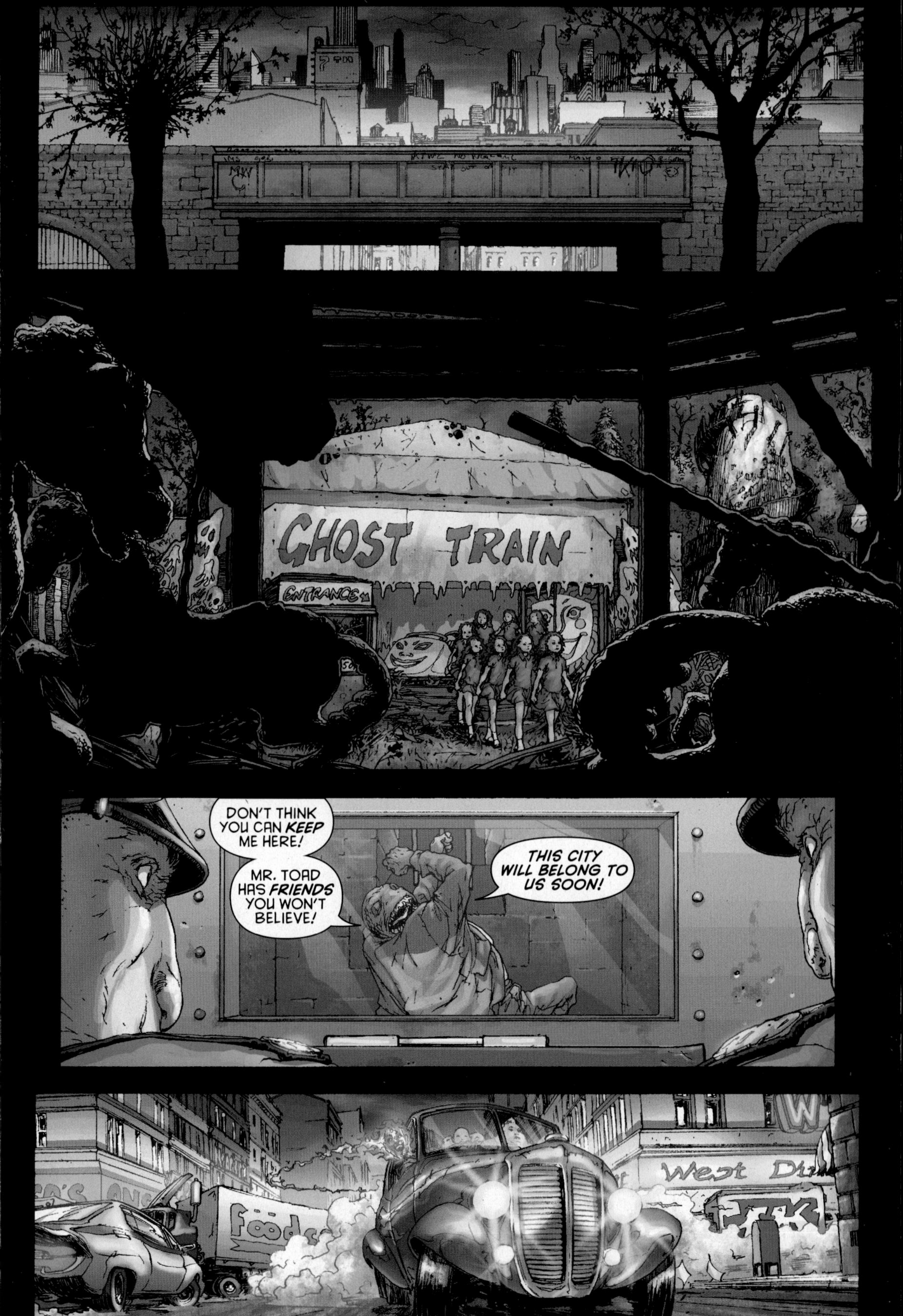
GHOST TRAIN
ENTRANCE
DON'T THINK YOU CAN KEEP ME HERE!
MR. TOAD HAS FRIENDS YOU WON'T BELIEVE!
THIS CITY WILL BELONG TO US SOON!
Foods
West

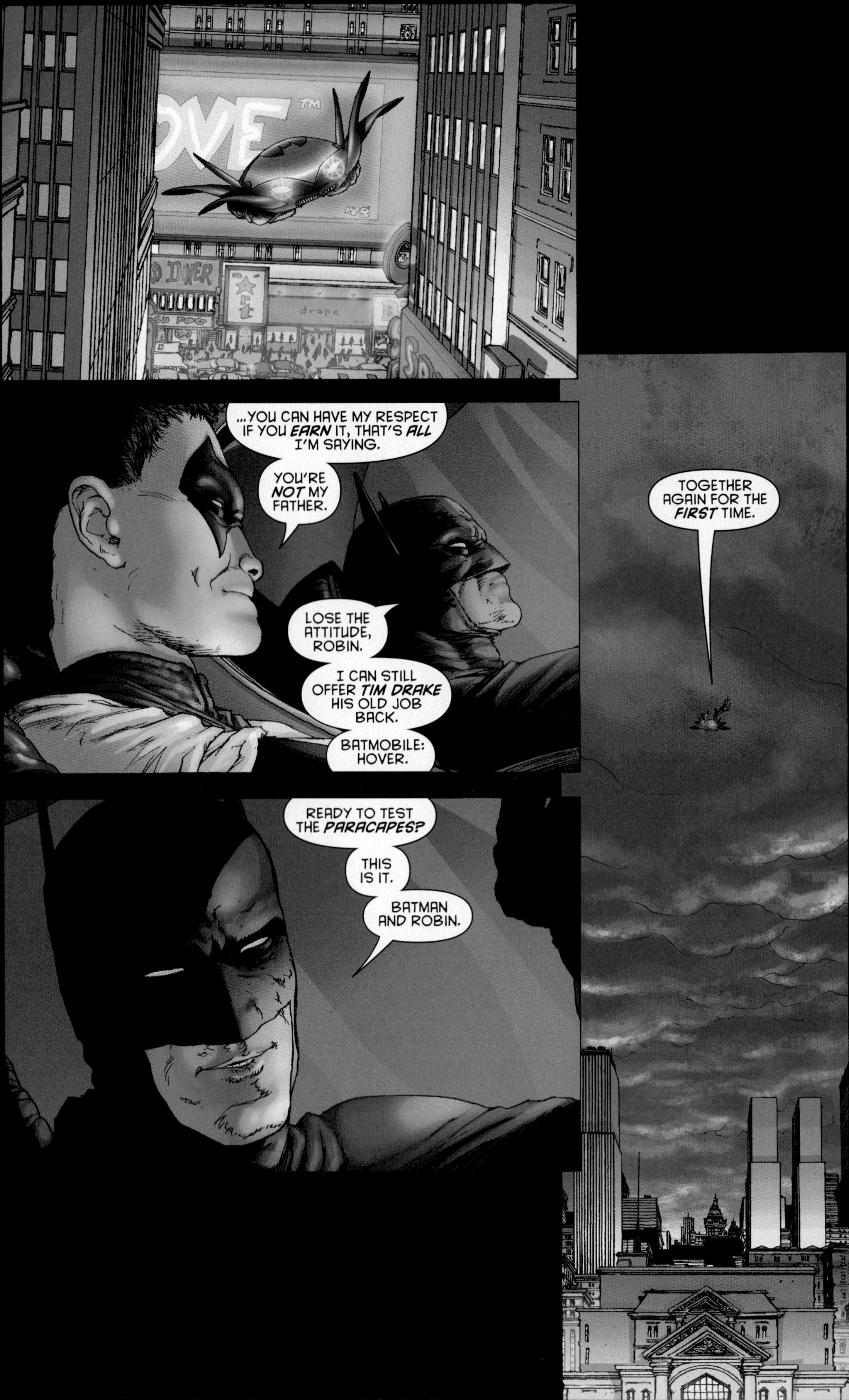
...YOU CAN HAVE MY RESPECT IF YOU EARN IT, THAT'S ALL I'M SAYING.
YOU'RE NOT MY FATHER.
LOSE THE ATTITUDE, ROBIN.
I CAN STILL OFFER TIM DRAKE HIS OLD JOB BACK.
BATMOBILE: HOVER.
TOGETHER AGAIN FOR THE FIRST TIME.
READY TO TEST THE PARACAPES?
THIS IS IT.
BATMAN AND ROBIN.

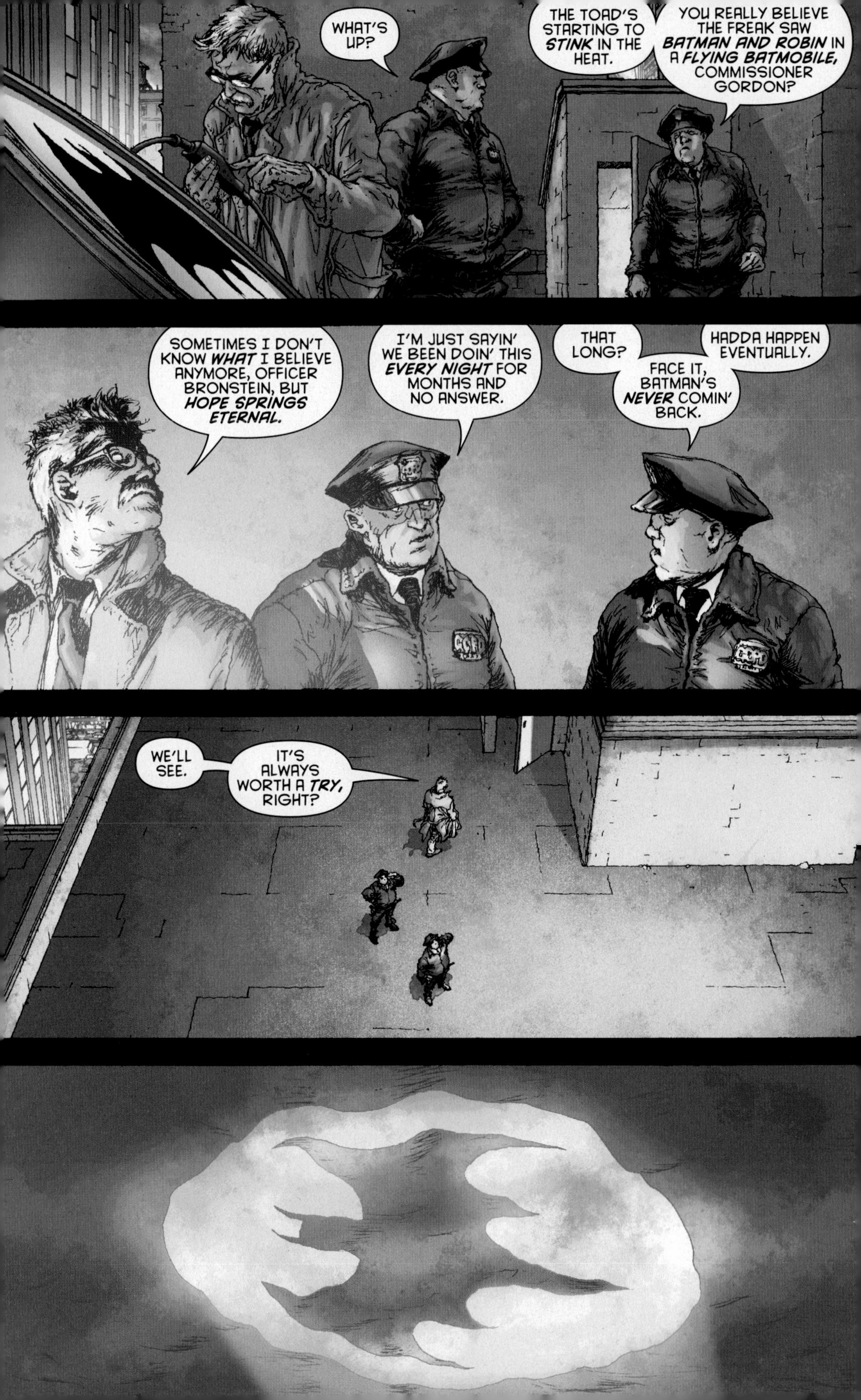
WHAT'S UP?
THE TOAD'S STARTING TO STINK IN THE HEAT.
YOU REALLY BELIEVE THE FREAK SAW BATMAN AND ROBIN IN A FLYING BATMOBILE, COMMISSIONER GORDON?
SOMETIMES I DON'T KNOW WHAT I BELIEVE ANYMORE, OFFICER BRONSTEIN, BUT HOPE SPRINGS ETERNAL.
I'M JUST SAYIN' WE BEEN DOIN' THIS EVERY NIGHT FOR MONTHS AND NO ANSWER.
THAT LONG?
HADDA HAPPEN EVENTUALLY.
FACE IT, BATMAN'S NEVER COMIN' BACK.
WE'LL SEE.
IT'S ALWAYS WORTH A TRY, RIGHT?

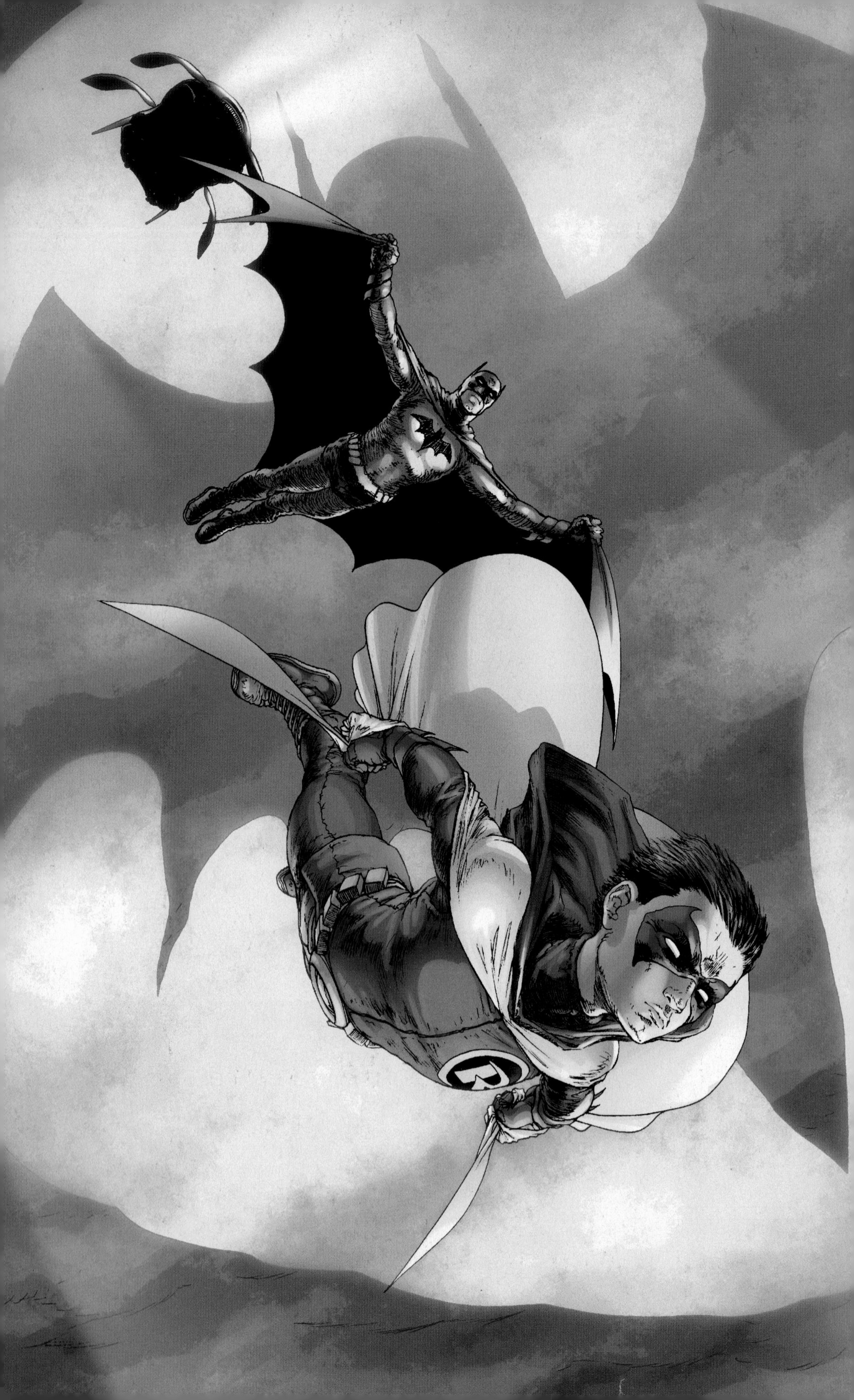

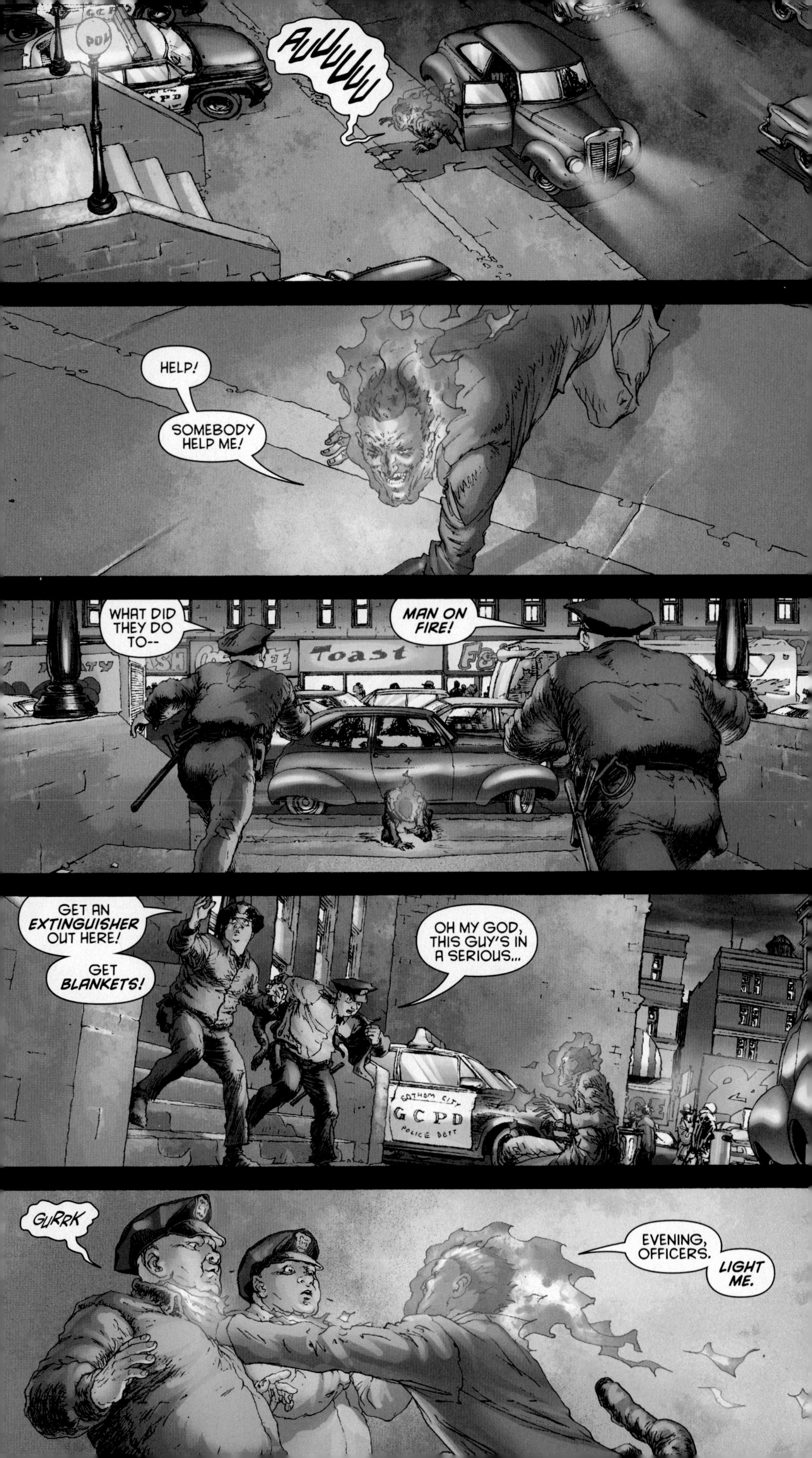
AUUUUUU
HELP!
SOMEBODY HELP ME!
WHAT DID THEY DO TO--
MAN ON FIRE!
GET AN EXTINGUISHER OUT HERE!
GET BLANKETS!
OH MY GOD, THIS GUY'S IN A SERIOUS...
GURRK
EVENING, OFFICERS.
LIGHT ME.

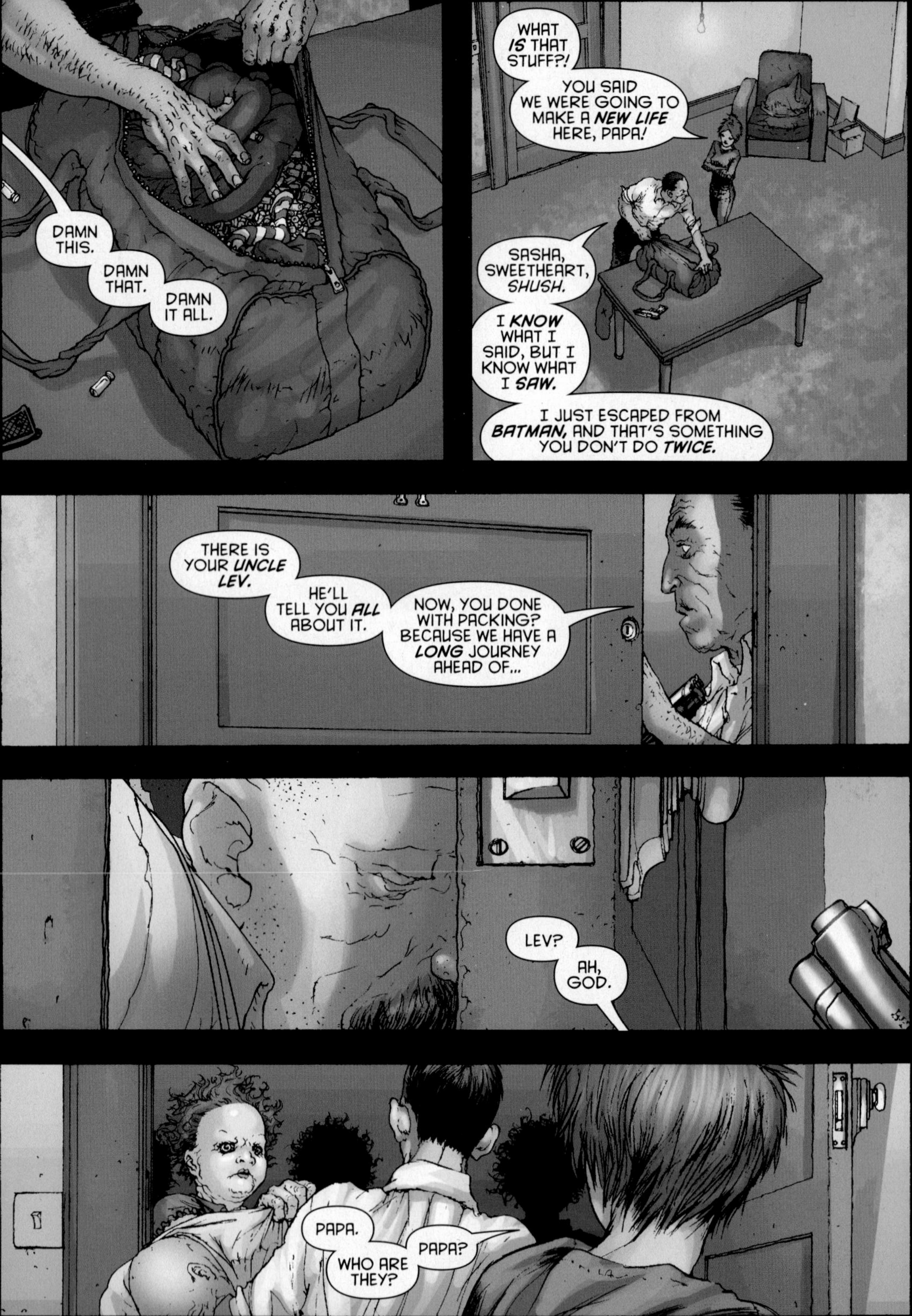
DAMN THIS.
DAMN THAT.
DAMN IT ALL.
WHAT IS THAT STUFF?!
YOU SAID WE WERE GOING TO MAKE A NEW LIFE HERE, PAPA!
SASHA, SWEETHEART, SHUSH.
I KNOW WHAT I SAID, BUT I KNOW WHAT I SAW.
I JUST ESCAPED FROM BATMAN, AND THAT'S SOMETHING YOU DON'T DO TWICE.
THERE IS YOUR UNCLE LEV.
HE'LL TELL YOU ALL ABOUT IT.
NOW, YOU DONE WITH PACKING? BECAUSE WE HAVE A LONG JOURNEY AHEAD OF...
LEV?
AH, GOD.
PAPA.
PAPA?
WHO ARE THEY?

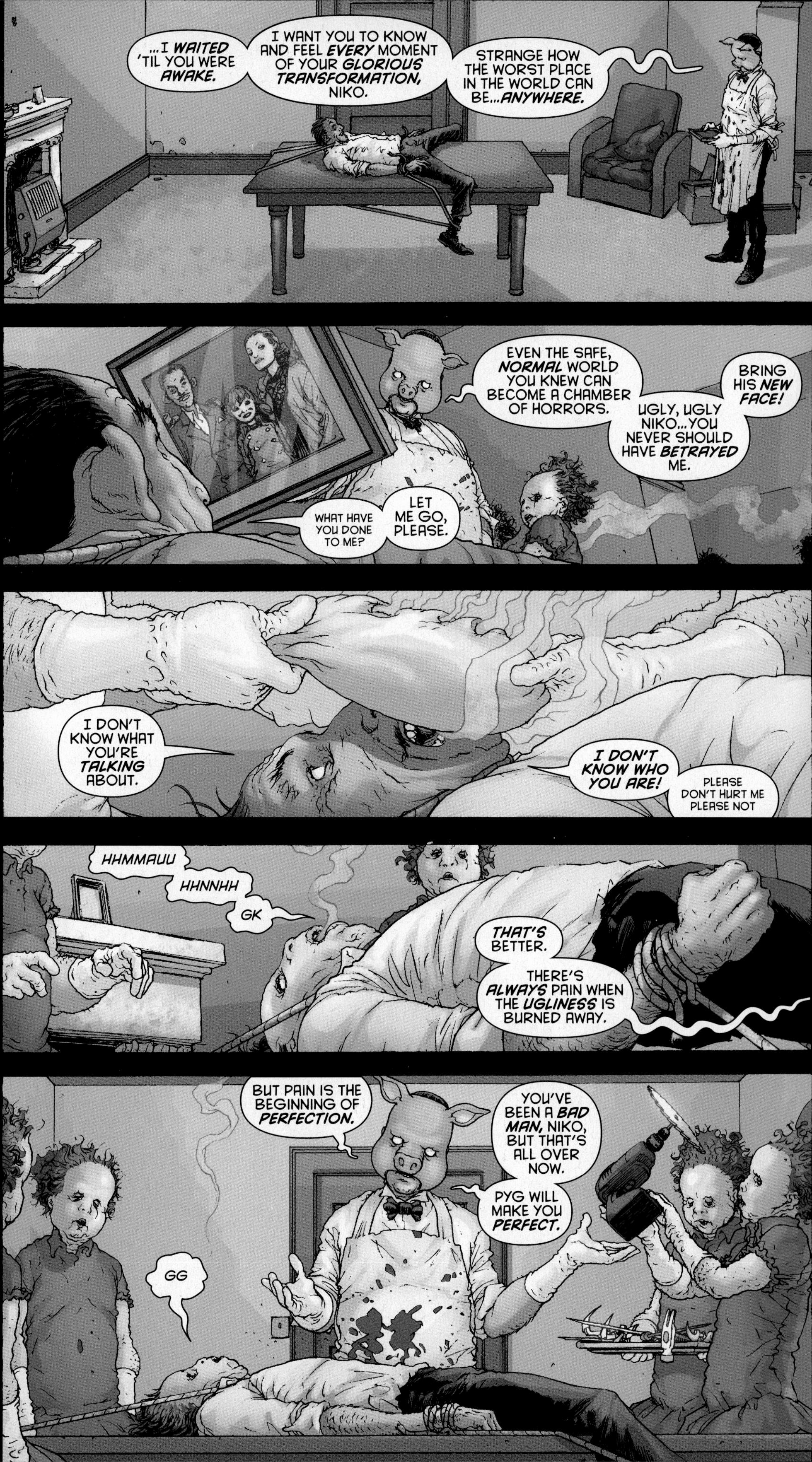
...I WAITED 'TIL YOU WERE AWAKE.
I WANT YOU TO KNOW AND FEEL EVERY MOMENT OF YOUR GLORIOUS TRANSFORMATION, NIKO.
STRANGE HOW THE WORST PLACE IN THE WORLD CAN BE...ANYWHERE.
EVEN THE SAFE, NORMAL WORLD YOU KNEW CAN BECOME A CHAMBER OF HORRORS.
BRING HIS NEW FACE!
UGLY, UGLY NIKO...YOU NEVER SHOULD HAVE BETRAYED ME.
LET ME GO, PLEASE.
WHAT HAVE YOU DONE TO ME?
I DON'T KNOW WHAT YOU'RE TALKING ABOUT.
I DON'T KNOW WHO YOU ARE!
PLEASE DON'T HURT ME PLEASE NOT
HHMMAUU
HHNNHH
GK
THAT'S BETTER.
THERE'S ALWAYS PAIN WHEN THE UGLINESS IS BURNED AWAY.
BUT PAIN IS THE BEGINNING OF PERFECTION.
YOU'VE BEEN A BAD MAN, NIKO, BUT THAT'S ALL OVER NOW.
PYG WILL MAKE YOU PERFECT.
GG

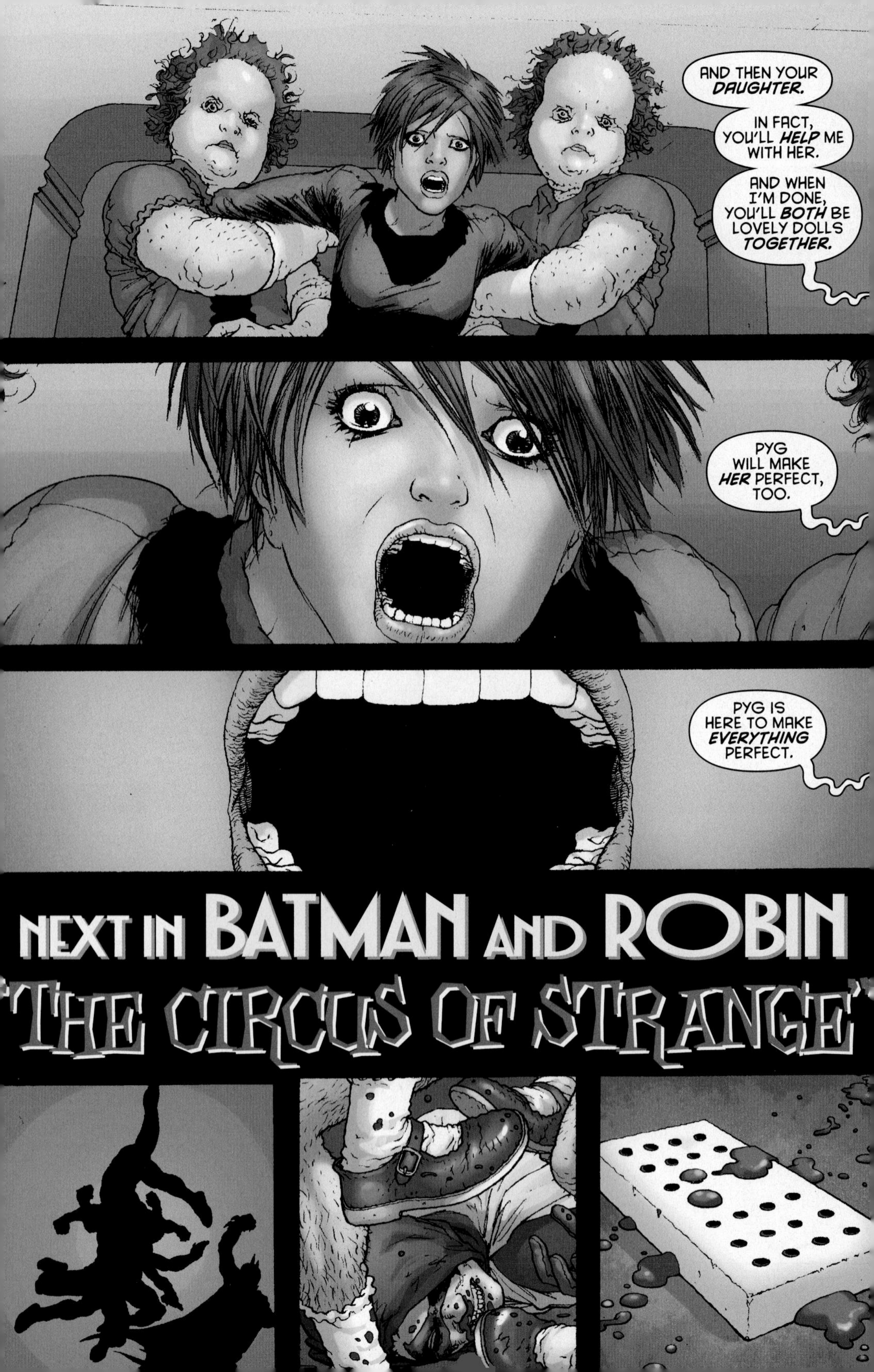
AND THEN YOUR DAUGHTER.
IN FACT, YOU'LL HELP ME WITH HER.
AND WHEN I'M DONE, YOU'LL BOTH BE LOVELY DOLLS TOGETHER.
PYG WILL MAKE HER PERFECT, TOO.
PYG IS HERE TO MAKE EVERYTHING PERFECT.
NEXT IN BATMAN AND ROBIN
"THE CIRCUS OF STRANGE"

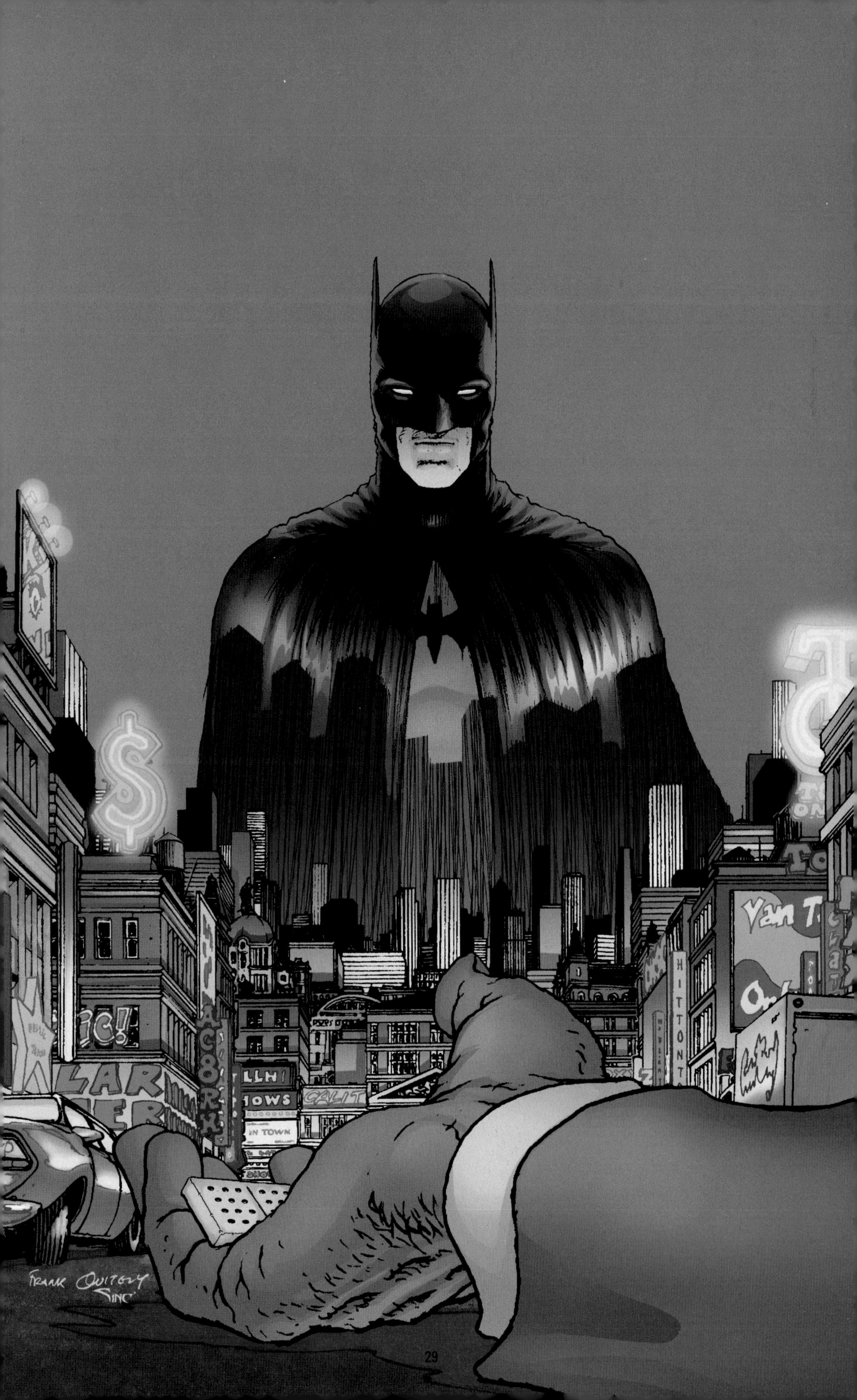

$
Van T
HITTONTA
IN TOWN
FRANK QUITELY
SINC

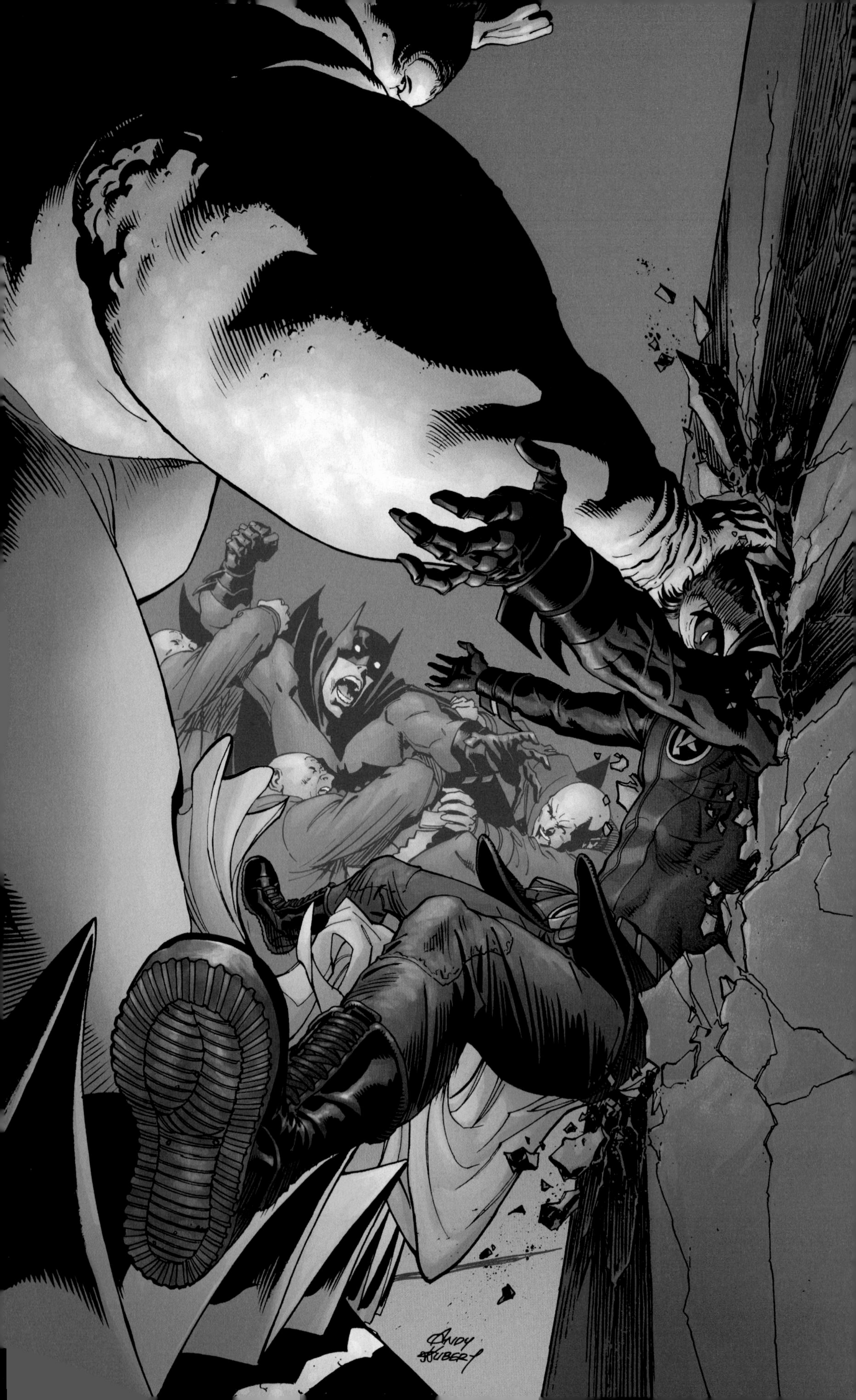
ANDY KUBERT

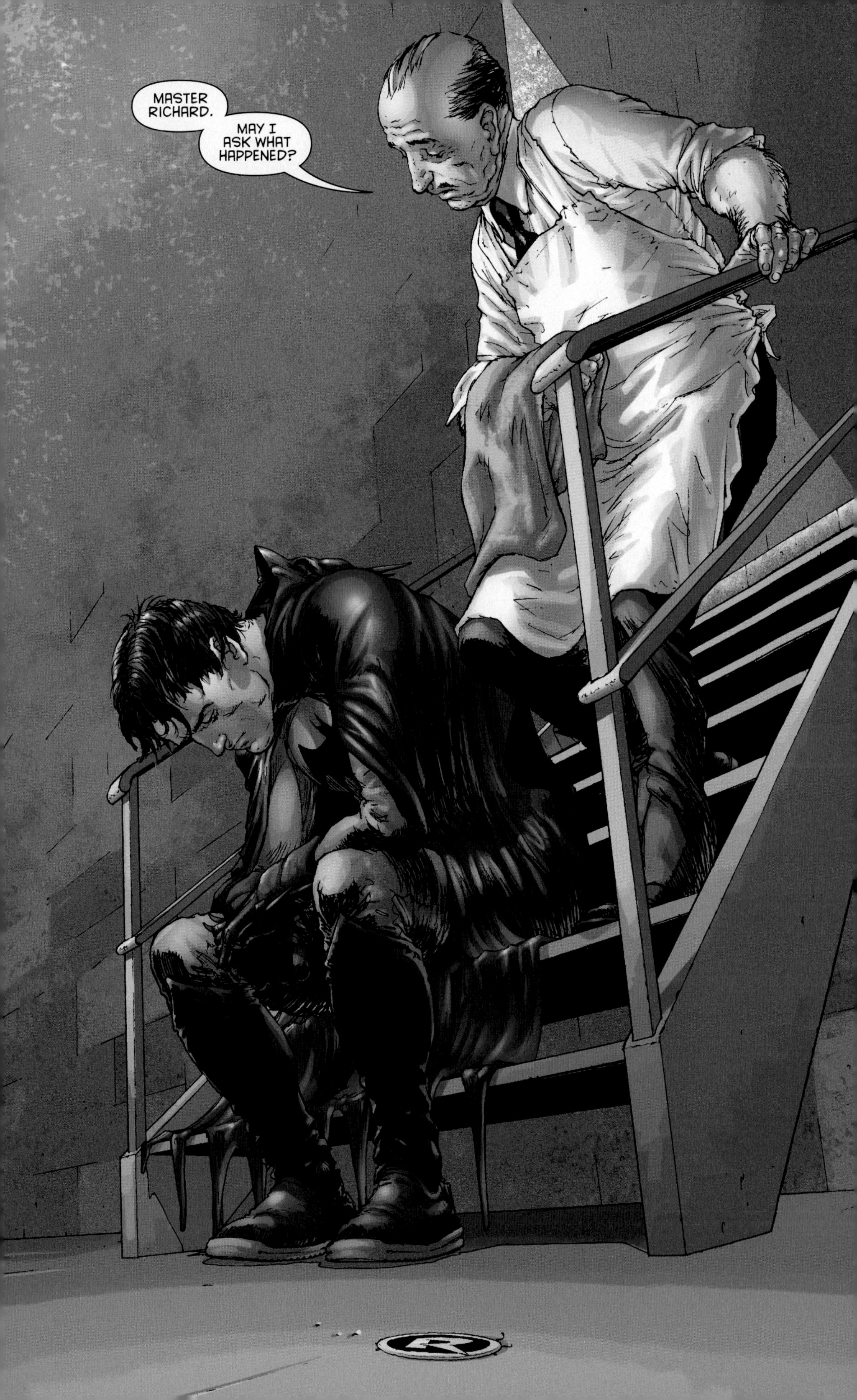
MASTER RICHARD.
MAY I ASK WHAT HAPPENED?

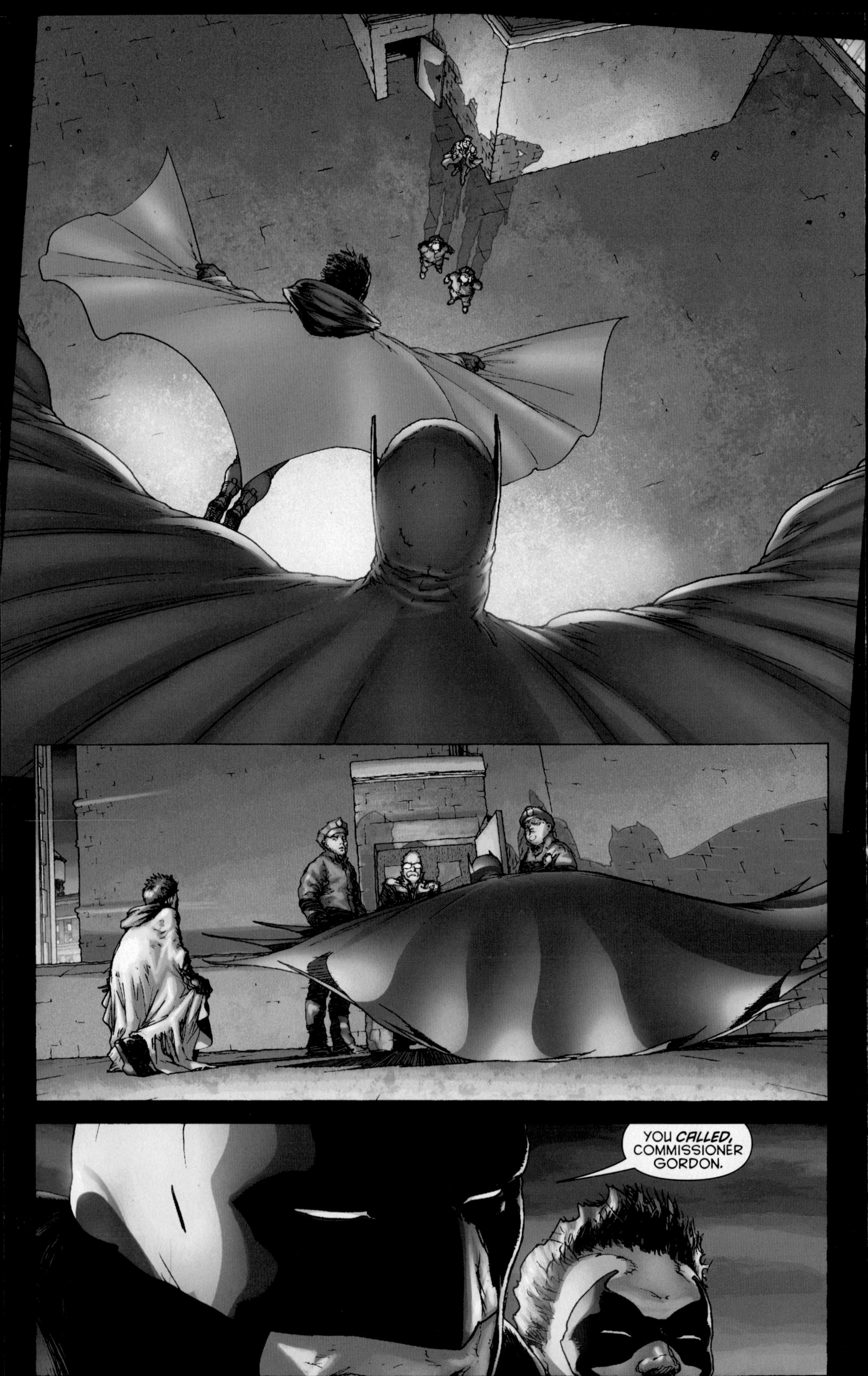
YOU CALLED, COMMISSIONER GORDON.

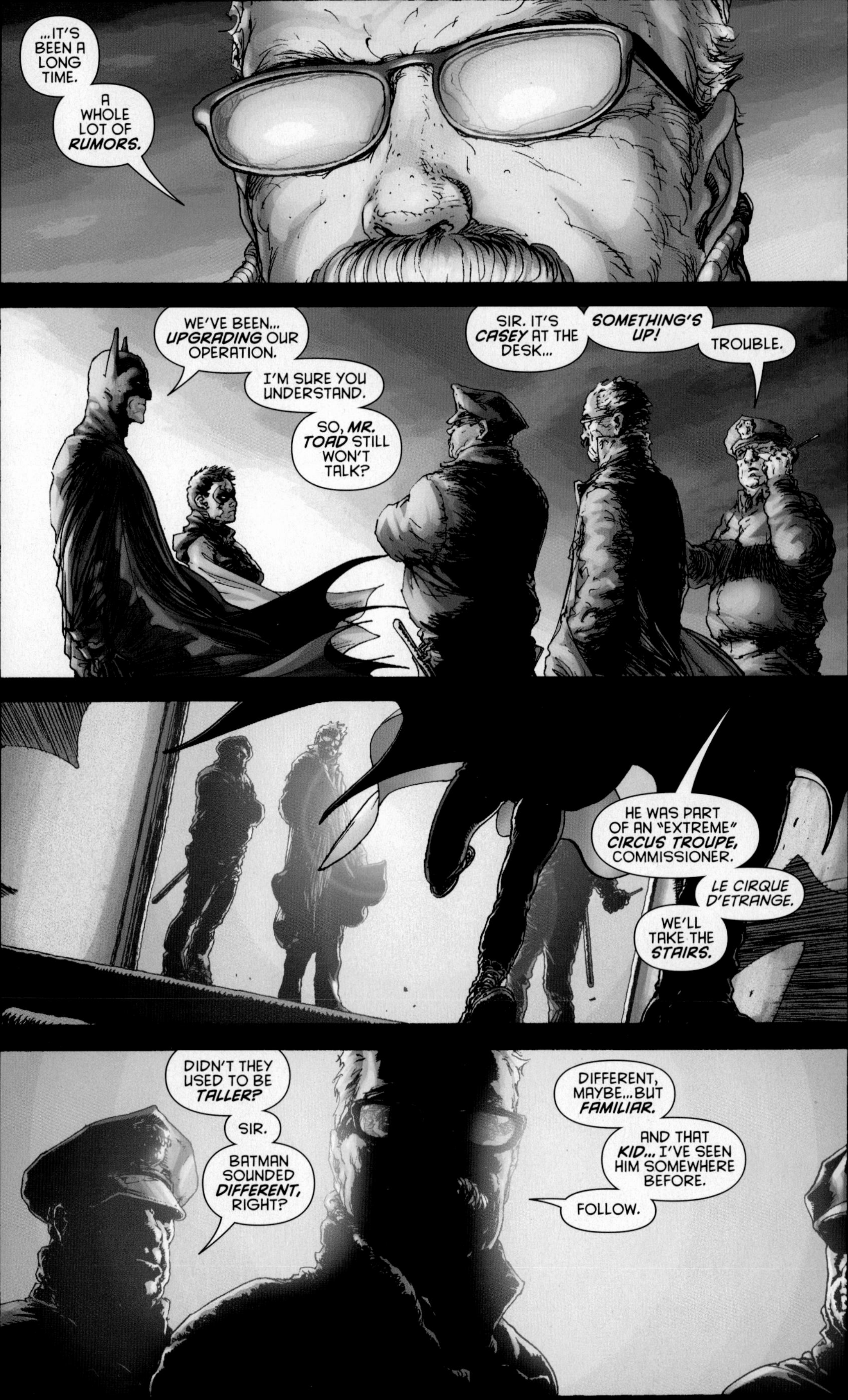
...IT'S BEEN A LONG TIME.
A WHOLE LOT OF RUMORS.
WE'VE BEEN... UPGRADING OUR OPERATION.
I'M SURE YOU UNDERSTAND.
SO, MR. TOAD STILL WON'T TALK?
SIR. IT'S CASEY AT THE DESK...
SOMETHING'S UP!
TROUBLE.
HE WAS PART OF AN "EXTREME" CIRCUS TROUPE, COMMISSIONER.
LE CIRQUE D'ETRANGE.
WE'LL TAKE THE STAIRS.
DIDN'T THEY USED TO BE TALLER?
SIR.
BATMAN SOUNDED DIFFERENT, RIGHT?
DIFFERENT, MAYBE...BUT FAMILIAR.
AND THAT KID... I'VE SEEN HIM SOMEWHERE BEFORE.
FOLLOW.

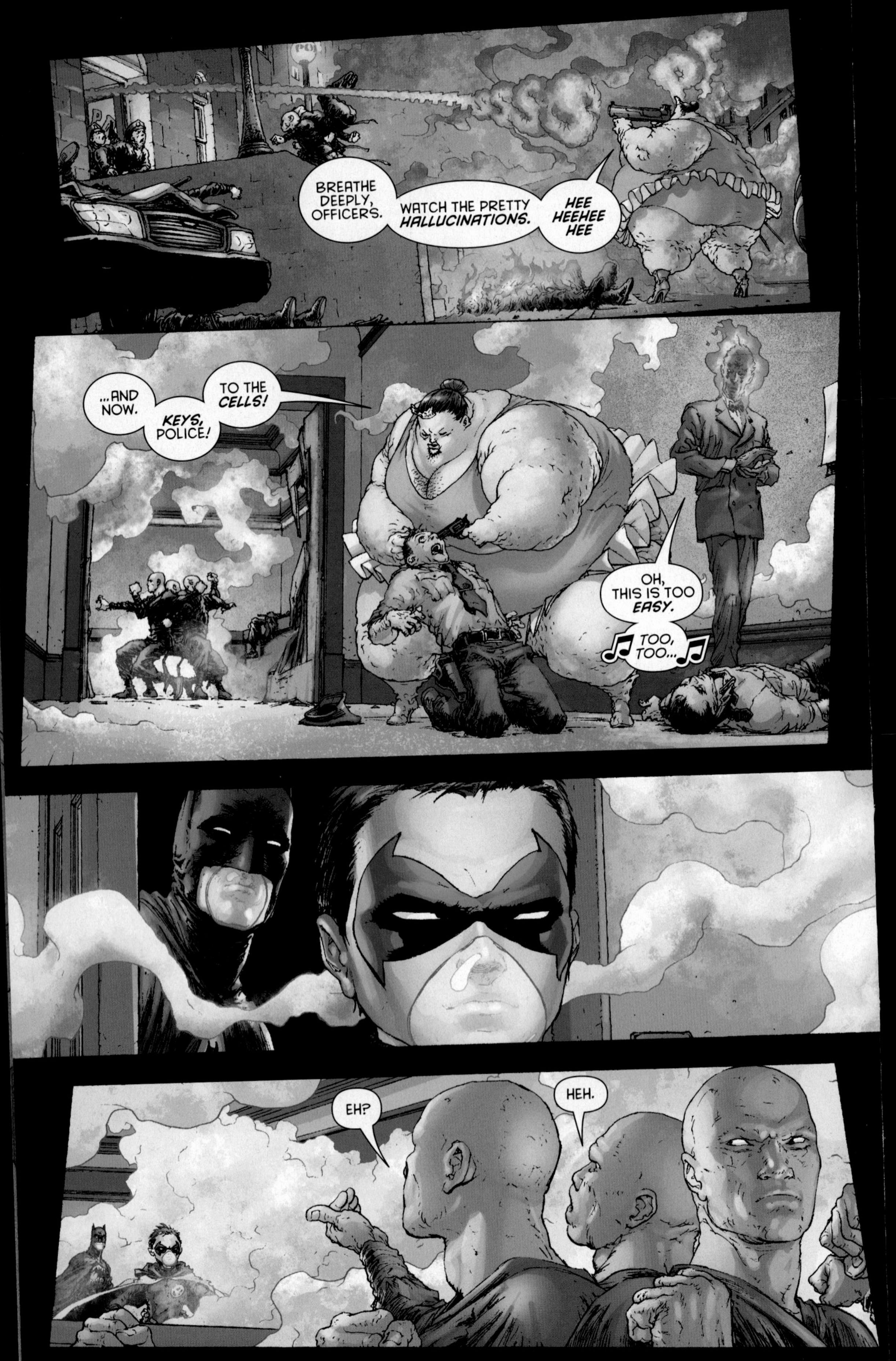
SSSS
POF
BREATHE DEEPLY, OFFICERS.
WATCH THE PRETTY *HALLUCINATIONS.*
HEE HEEHEE HEE
...AND NOW.
KEYS, POLICE!
TO THE ***CELLS!***
OH, THIS IS TOO ***EASY.***
♫ TOO, TOO... ♫
EH?
HEH.

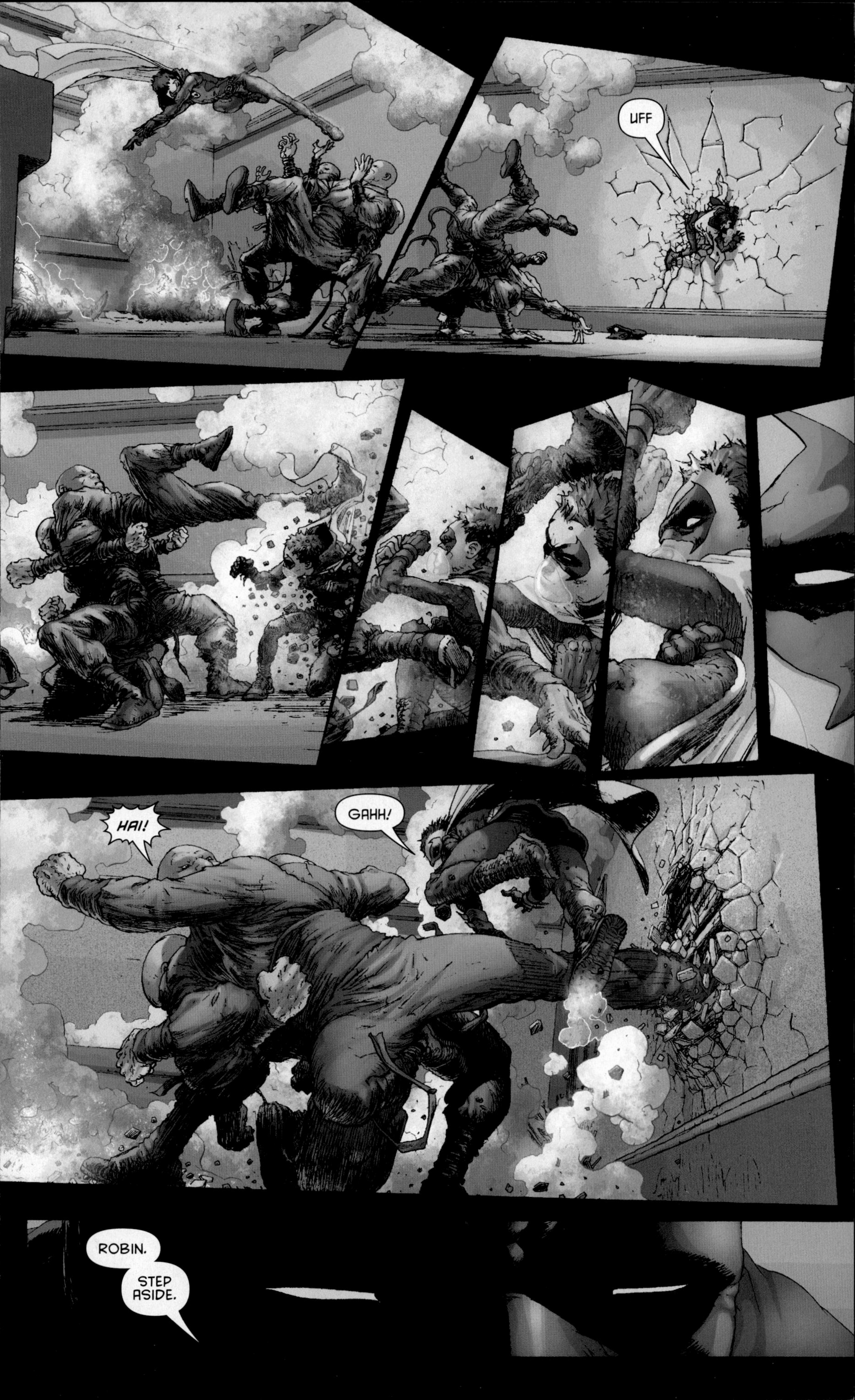
UFF
HAI!
GAHH!
ROBIN.
STEP ASIDE.

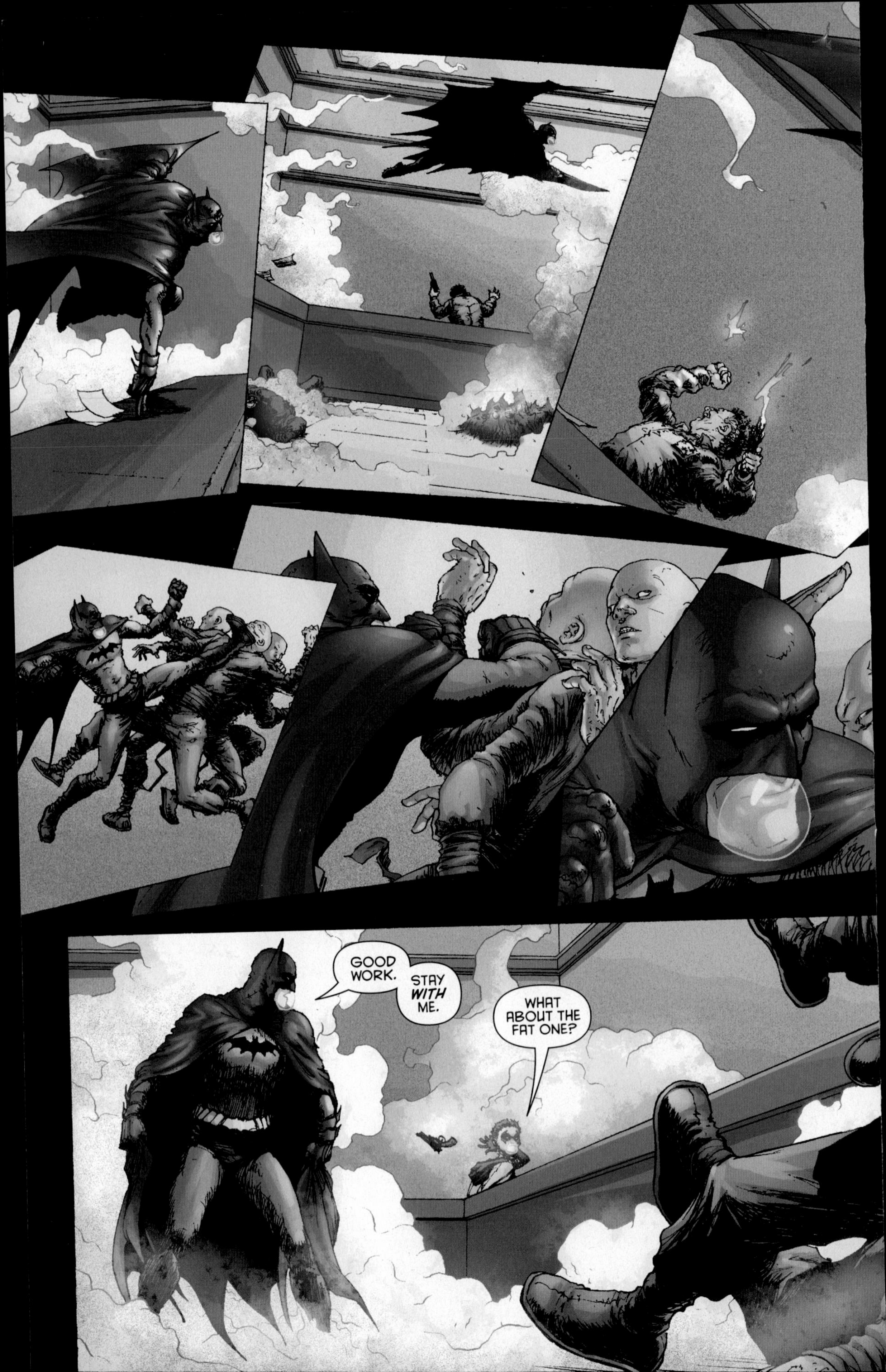
GOOD WORK.
STAY WITH ME.
WHAT ABOUT THE FAT ONE?

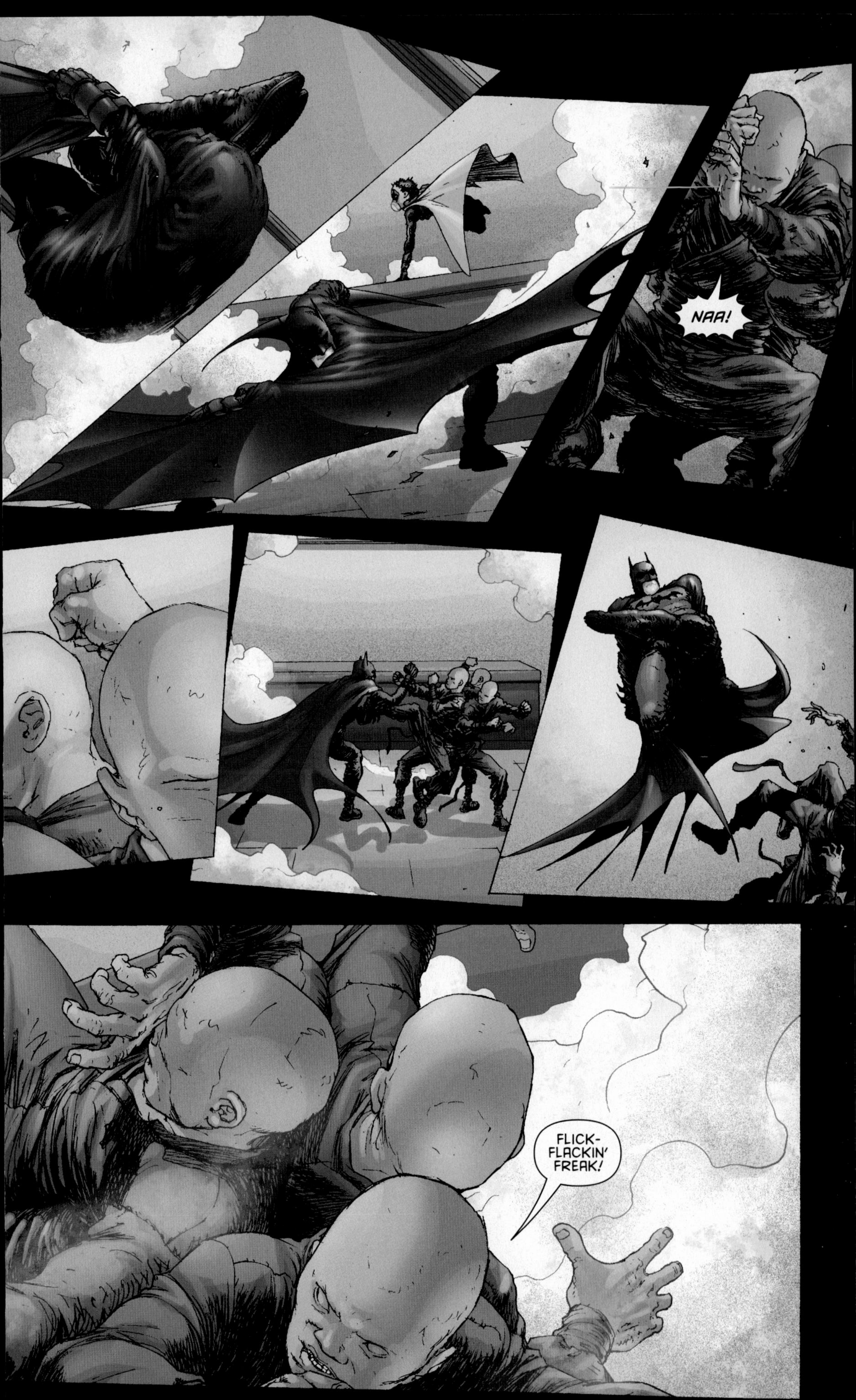
NAA!
FLICK-FLACKIN' FREAK!

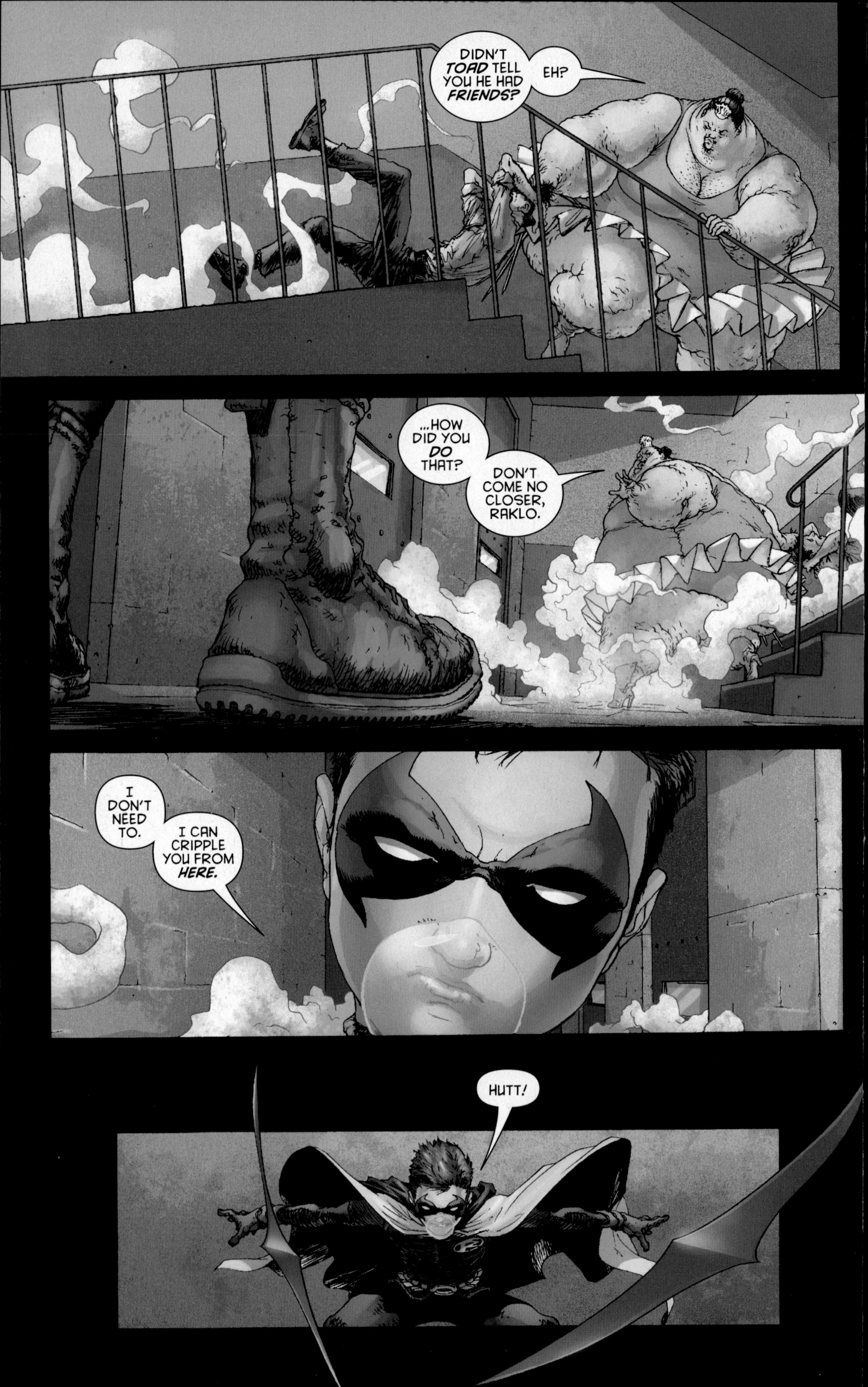
DIDN'T TOAD TELL YOU HE HAD FRIENDS?
EH?
...HOW DID YOU DO THAT?
DON'T COME NO CLOSER, RAKLO.
I DON'T NEED TO.
I CAN CRIPPLE YOU FROM HERE.
HUTT!

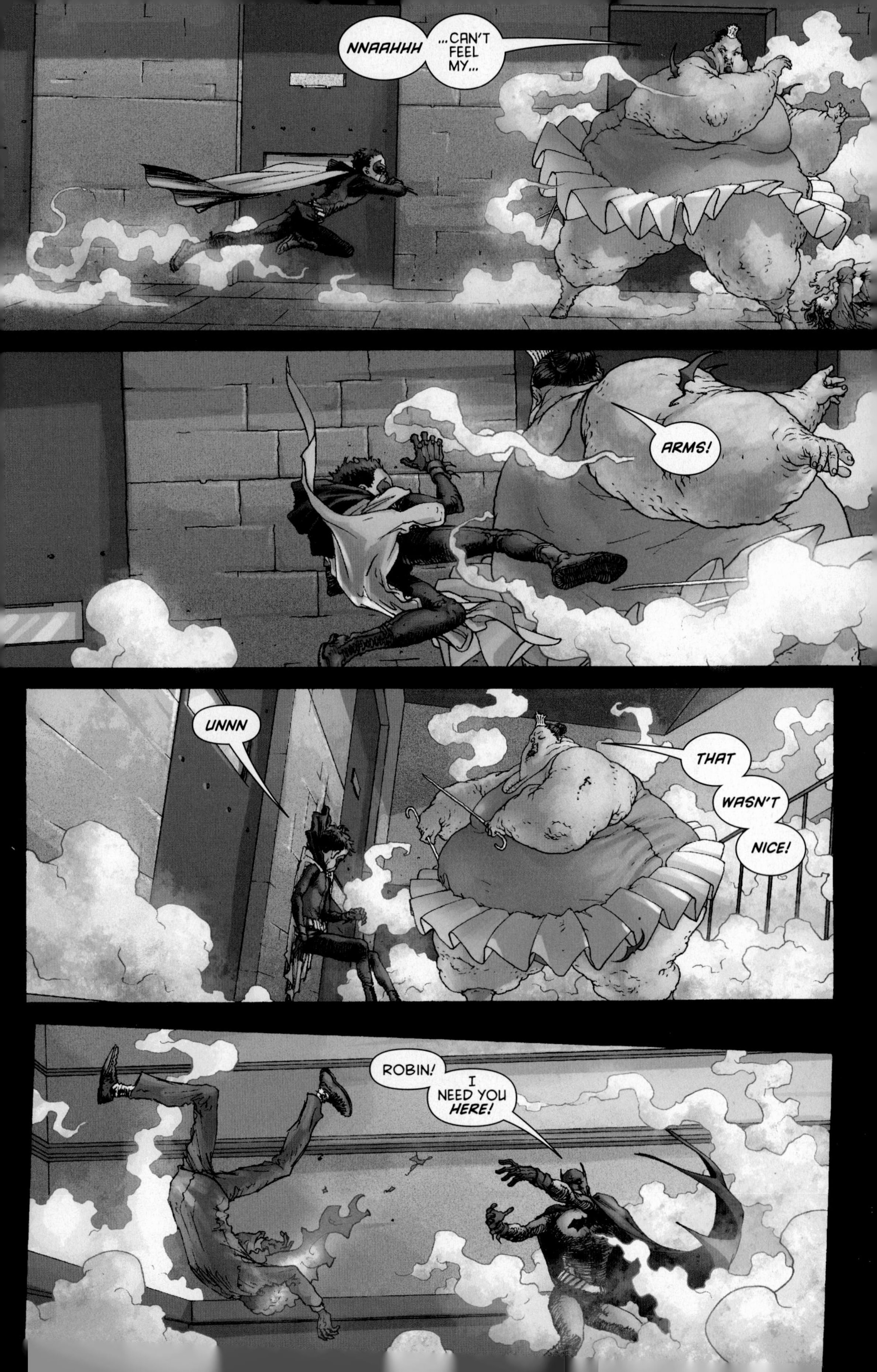
NNAAHHH
...CAN'T FEEL MY...
ARMS!
UNNN
THAT WASN'T NICE!
ROBIN! I NEED YOU HERE!

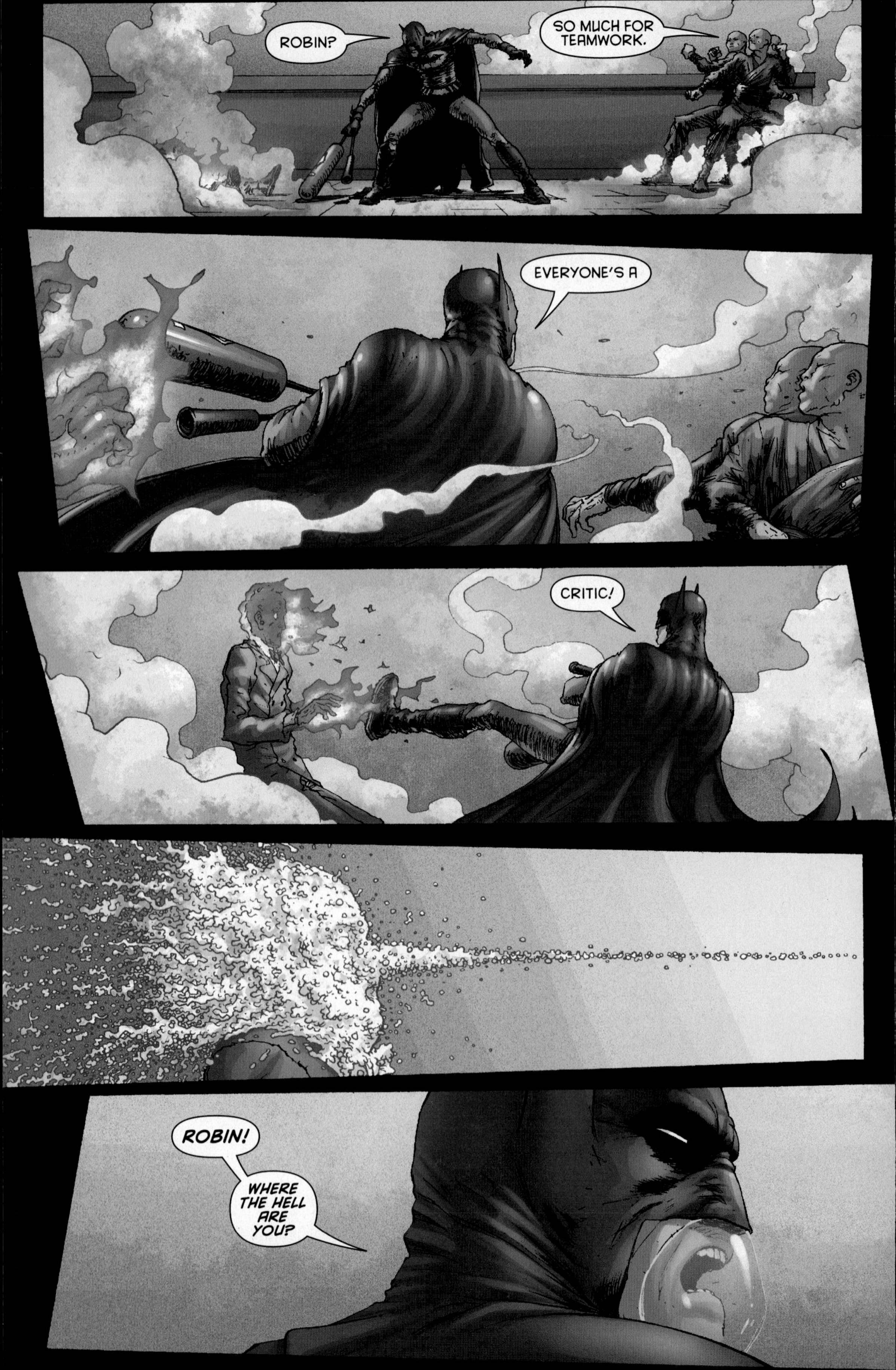
ROBIN?
SO MUCH FOR TEAMWORK.
EVERYONE'S A
CRITIC!
ROBIN!
WHERE THE HELL ARE YOU?

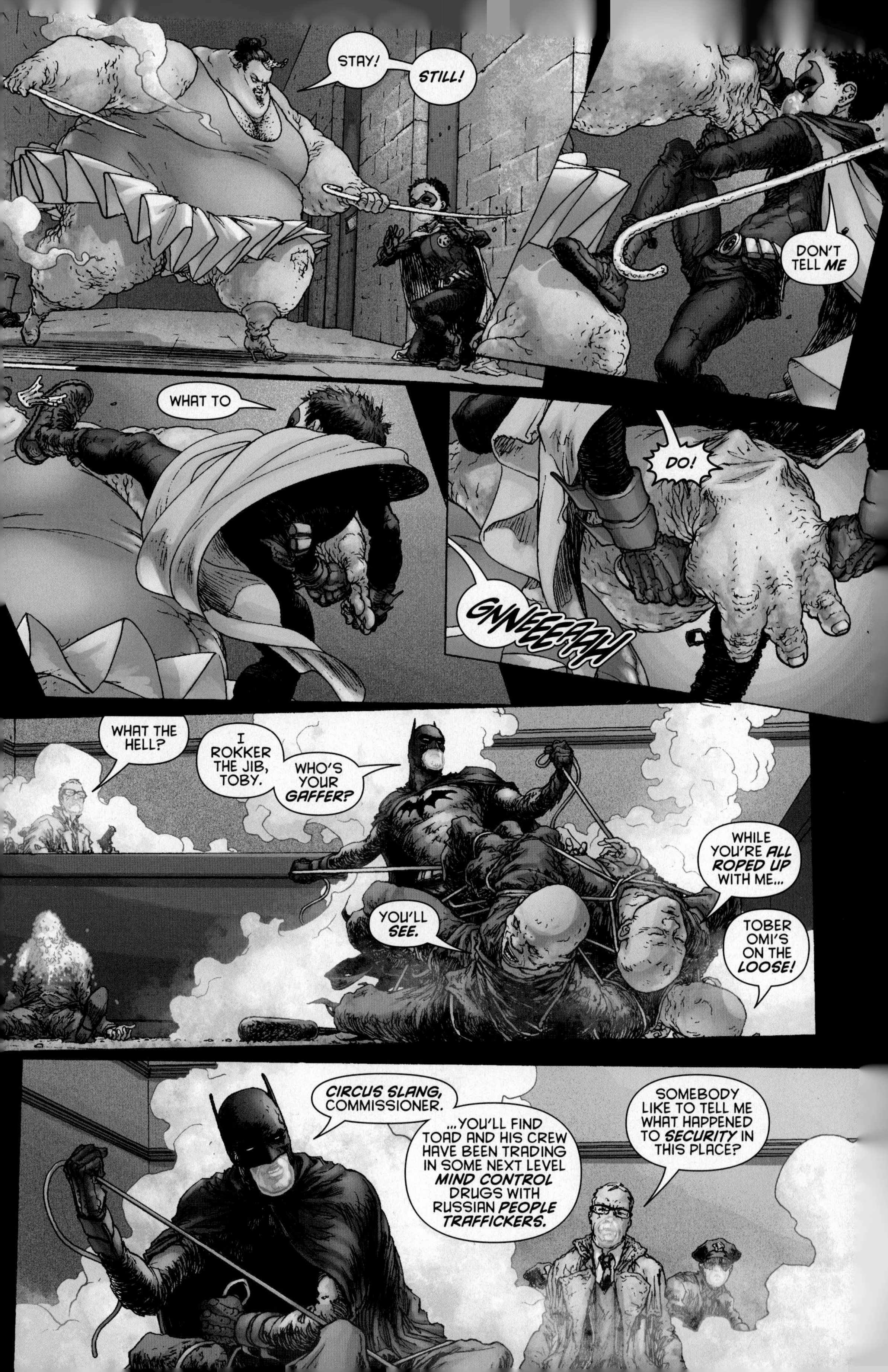
STAY!
STILL!
DON'T TELL *ME*
WHAT TO
DO!
GNNEEEAAH
WHAT THE HELL?
I ROKKER THE JIB, TOBY.
WHO'S YOUR *GAFFER?*
WHILE YOU'RE *ALL ROPED UP* WITH ME...
YOU'LL *SEE.*
TOBER OMI'S ON THE *LOOSE!*
CIRCUS SLANG, COMMISSIONER.
...YOU'LL FIND TOAD AND HIS CREW HAVE BEEN TRADING IN SOME NEXT LEVEL *MIND CONTROL* DRUGS WITH RUSSIAN *PEOPLE TRAFFICKERS.*
SOMEBODY LIKE TO TELL ME WHAT HAPPENED TO *SECURITY* IN THIS PLACE?

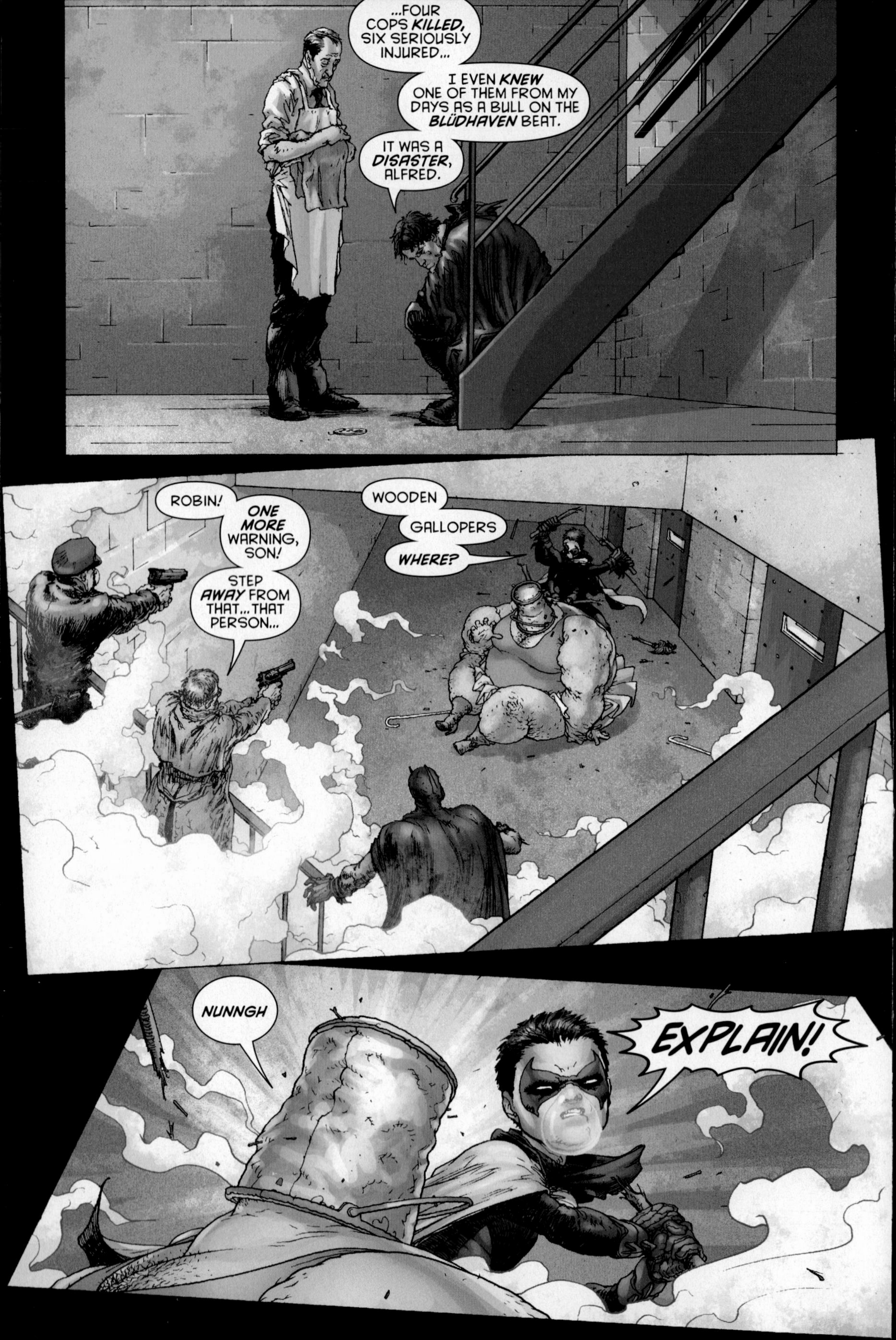
...FOUR COPS KILLED, SIX SERIOUSLY INJURED...
I EVEN KNEW ONE OF THEM FROM MY DAYS AS A BULL ON THE BLÜDHAVEN BEAT.
IT WAS A DISASTER, ALFRED.
ROBIN!
ONE MORE WARNING, SON!
STEP AWAY FROM THAT... THAT PERSON...
WOODEN
GALLOPERS
WHERE?
NUNNGH
EXPLAIN!

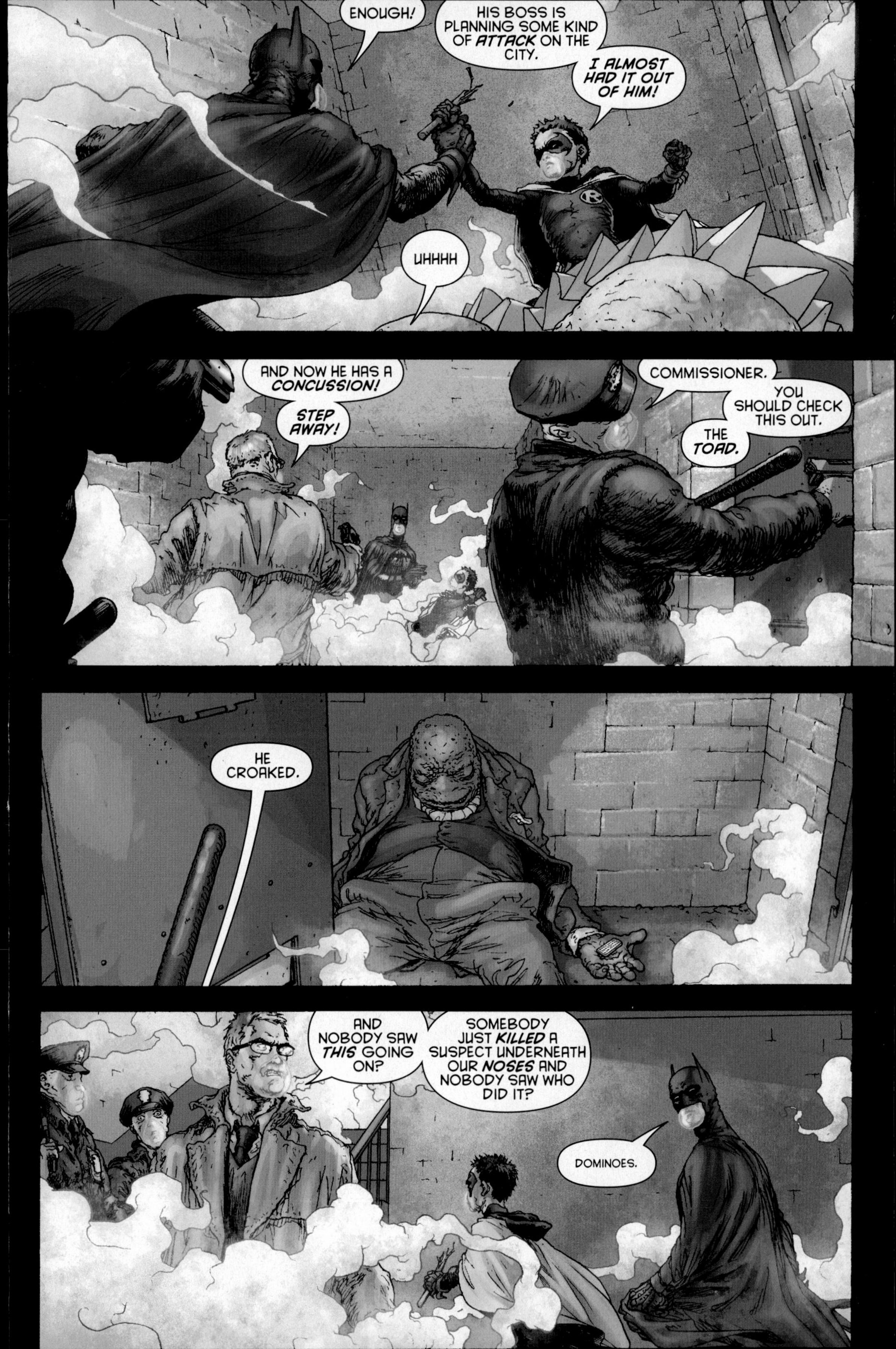

ENOUGH!
HIS BOSS IS PLANNING SOME KIND OF ATTACK ON THE CITY.
I ALMOST HAD IT OUT OF HIM!
UHHHH
AND NOW HE HAS A CONCUSSION!
STEP AWAY!
COMMISSIONER.
YOU SHOULD CHECK THIS OUT.
THE TOAD.
HE CROAKED.
AND NOBODY SAW THIS GOING ON?
SOMEBODY JUST KILLED A SUSPECT UNDERNEATH OUR NOSES AND NOBODY SAW WHO DID IT?
DOMINOES.

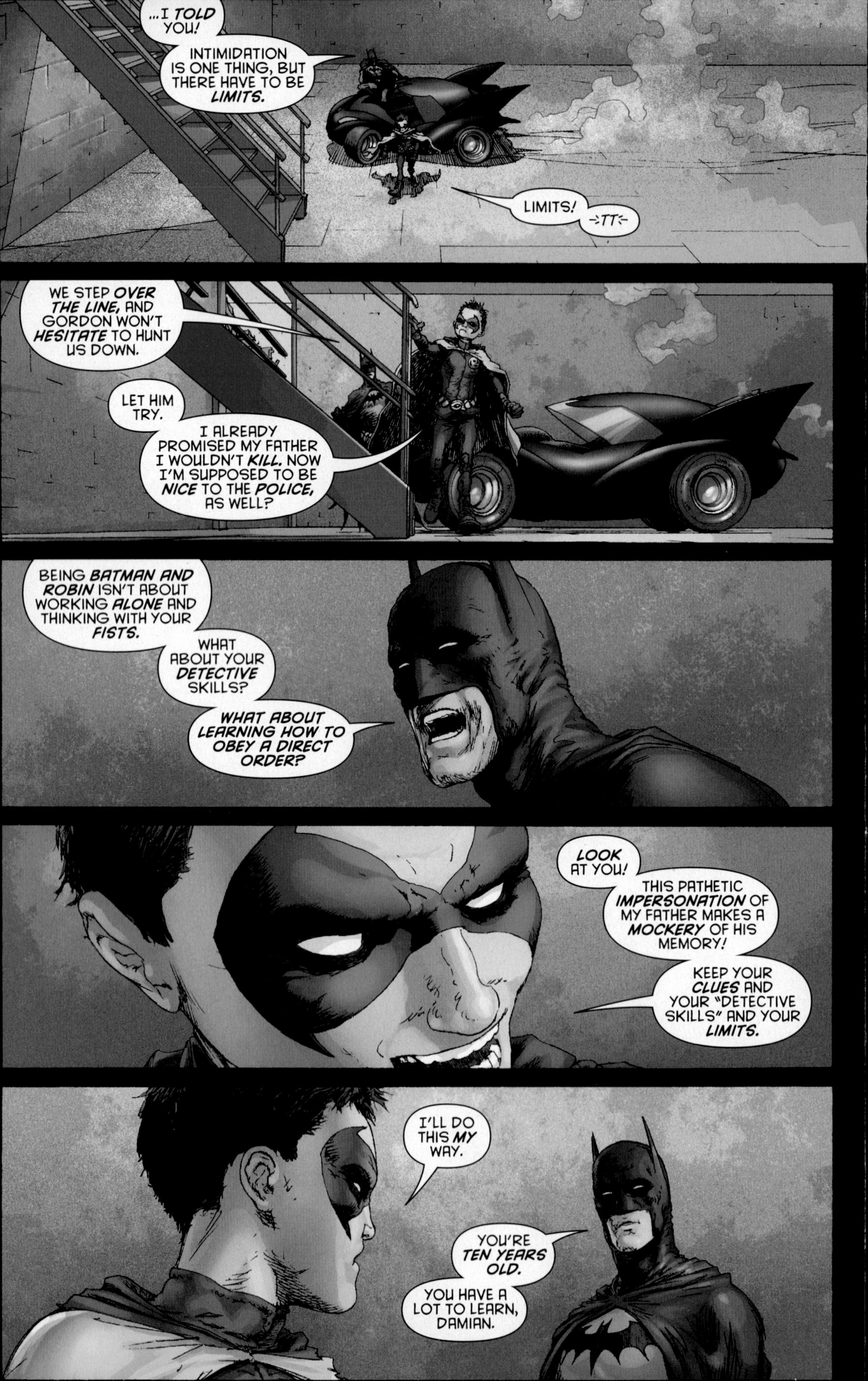

...I TOLD YOU!
INTIMIDATION IS ONE THING, BUT THERE HAVE TO BE LIMITS.
LIMITS! -TT-
WE STEP OVER THE LINE, AND GORDON WON'T HESITATE TO HUNT US DOWN.
LET HIM TRY.
I ALREADY PROMISED MY FATHER I WOULDN'T KILL. NOW I'M SUPPOSED TO BE NICE TO THE POLICE, AS WELL?
BEING BATMAN AND ROBIN ISN'T ABOUT WORKING ALONE AND THINKING WITH YOUR FISTS.
WHAT ABOUT YOUR DETECTIVE SKILLS?
WHAT ABOUT LEARNING HOW TO OBEY A DIRECT ORDER?
LOOK AT YOU!
THIS PATHETIC IMPERSONATION OF MY FATHER MAKES A MOCKERY OF HIS MEMORY!
KEEP YOUR CLUES AND YOUR "DETECTIVE SKILLS" AND YOUR LIMITS.
I'LL DO THIS MY WAY.
YOU'RE TEN YEARS OLD.
YOU HAVE A LOT TO LEARN, DAMIAN.

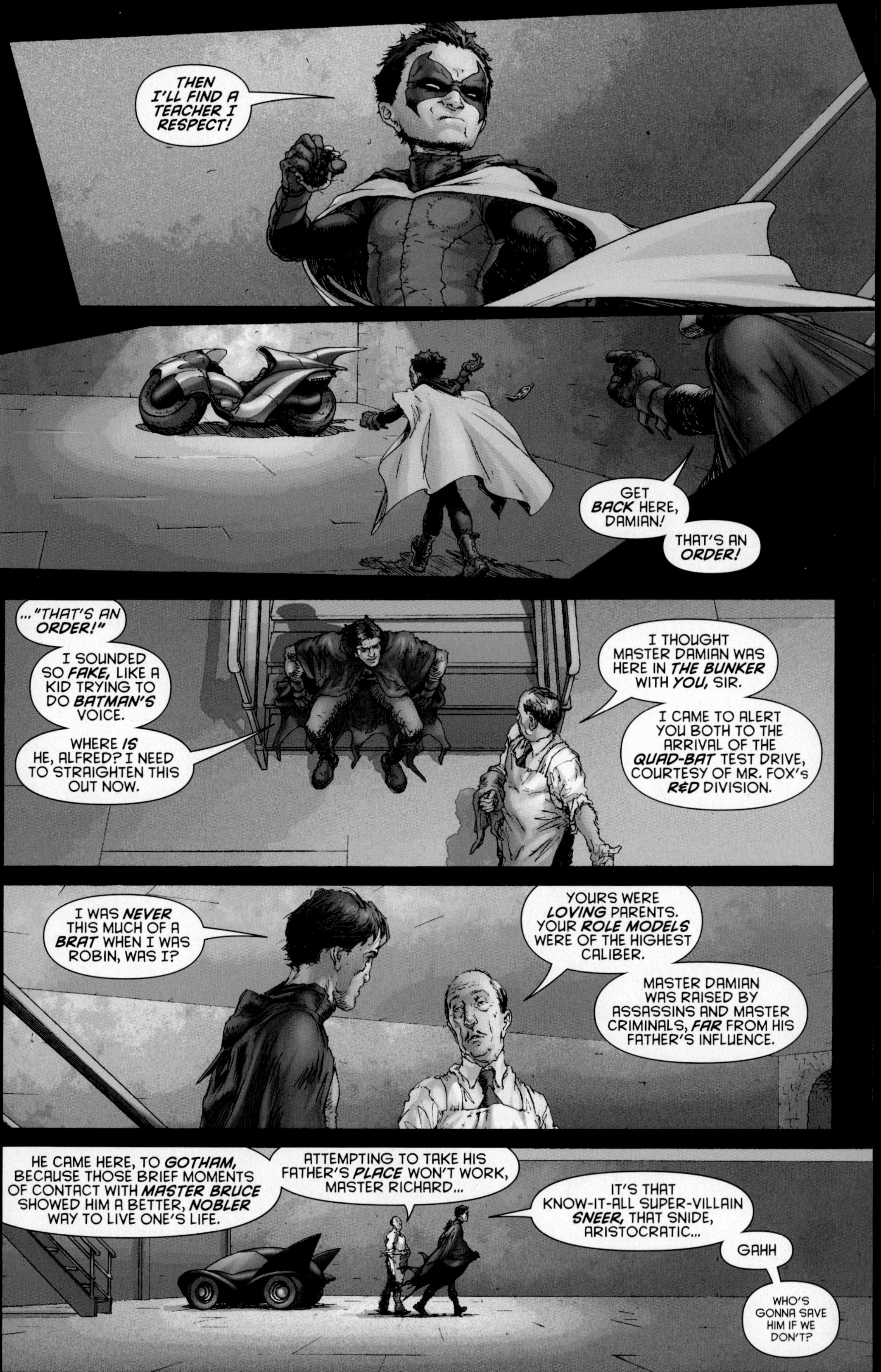
THEN I'LL FIND A TEACHER I RESPECT!
GET BACK HERE, DAMIAN!
THAT'S AN ORDER!
..."THAT'S AN ORDER!"
I SOUNDED SO FAKE, LIKE A KID TRYING TO DO BATMAN'S VOICE.
WHERE IS HE, ALFRED? I NEED TO STRAIGHTEN THIS OUT NOW.
I THOUGHT MASTER DAMIAN WAS HERE IN THE BUNKER WITH YOU, SIR.
I CAME TO ALERT YOU BOTH TO THE ARRIVAL OF THE QUAD-BAT TEST DRIVE, COURTESY OF MR. FOX'S R&D DIVISION.
I WAS NEVER THIS MUCH OF A BRAT WHEN I WAS ROBIN, WAS I?
YOURS WERE LOVING PARENTS. YOUR ROLE MODELS WERE OF THE HIGHEST CALIBER.
MASTER DAMIAN WAS RAISED BY ASSASSINS AND MASTER CRIMINALS, FAR FROM HIS FATHER'S INFLUENCE.
HE CAME HERE, TO GOTHAM, BECAUSE THOSE BRIEF MOMENTS OF CONTACT WITH MASTER BRUCE SHOWED HIM A BETTER, NOBLER WAY TO LIVE ONE'S LIFE.
ATTEMPTING TO TAKE HIS FATHER'S PLACE WON'T WORK, MASTER RICHARD...
IT'S THAT KNOW-IT-ALL SUPER-VILLAIN SNEER, THAT SNIDE, ARISTOCRATIC...
GAHH
WHO'S GONNA SAVE HIM IF WE DON'T?

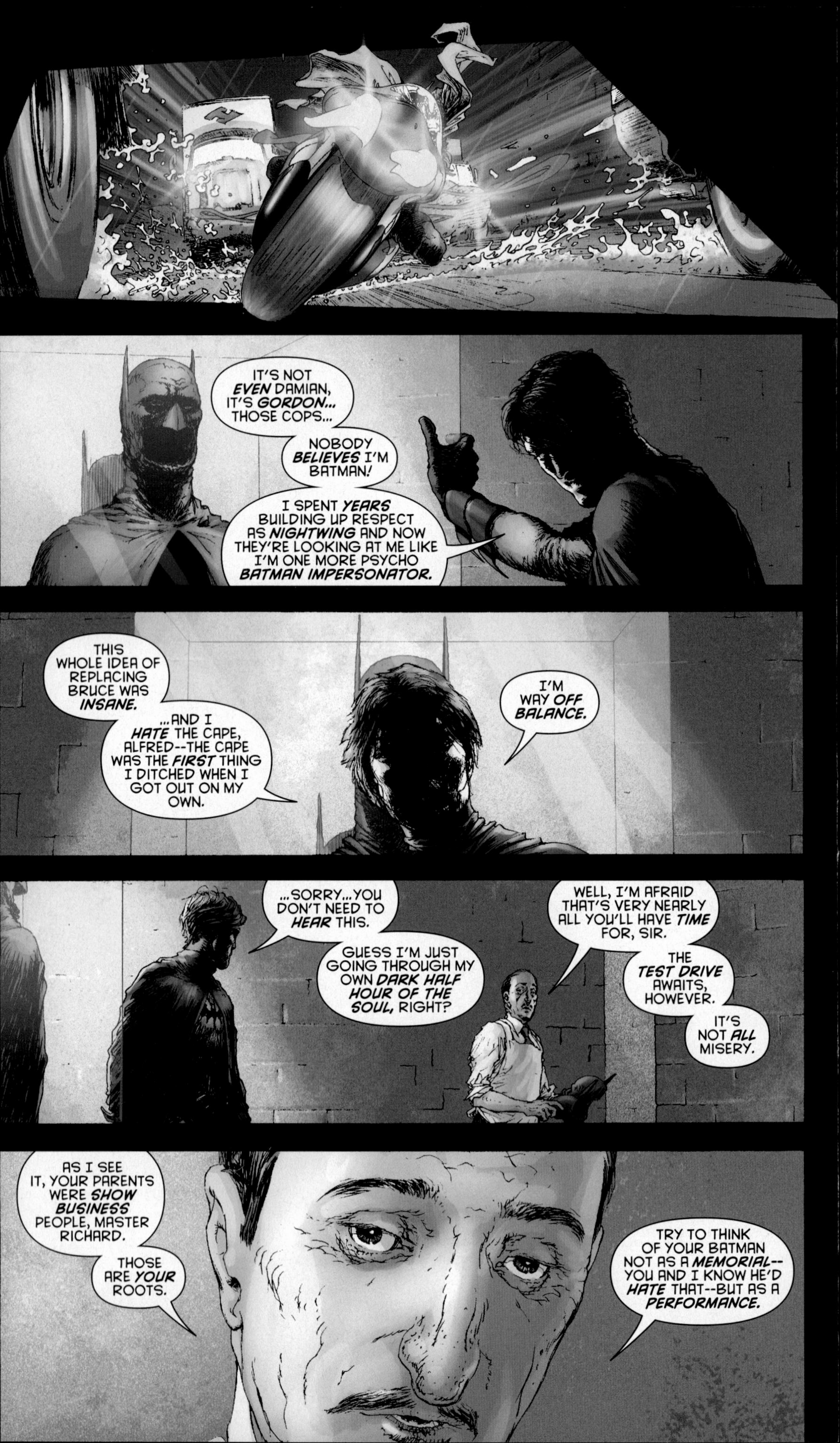
IT'S NOT EVEN DAMIAN, IT'S GORDON... THOSE COPS...
NOBODY BELIEVES I'M BATMAN!
I SPENT YEARS BUILDING UP RESPECT AS NIGHTWING AND NOW THEY'RE LOOKING AT ME LIKE I'M ONE MORE PSYCHO BATMAN IMPERSONATOR.
THIS WHOLE IDEA OF REPLACING BRUCE WAS INSANE.
...AND I HATE THE CAPE, ALFRED--THE CAPE WAS THE FIRST THING I DITCHED WHEN I GOT OUT ON MY OWN.
I'M WAY OFF BALANCE.
...SORRY...YOU DON'T NEED TO HEAR THIS.
GUESS I'M JUST GOING THROUGH MY OWN DARK HALF HOUR OF THE SOUL, RIGHT?
WELL, I'M AFRAID THAT'S VERY NEARLY ALL YOU'LL HAVE TIME FOR, SIR.
THE TEST DRIVE AWAITS, HOWEVER.
IT'S NOT ALL MISERY.
AS I SEE IT, YOUR PARENTS WERE SHOW BUSINESS PEOPLE, MASTER RICHARD.
THOSE ARE YOUR ROOTS.
TRY TO THINK OF YOUR BATMAN NOT AS A MEMORIAL--YOU AND I KNOW HE'D HATE THAT--BUT AS A PERFORMANCE.

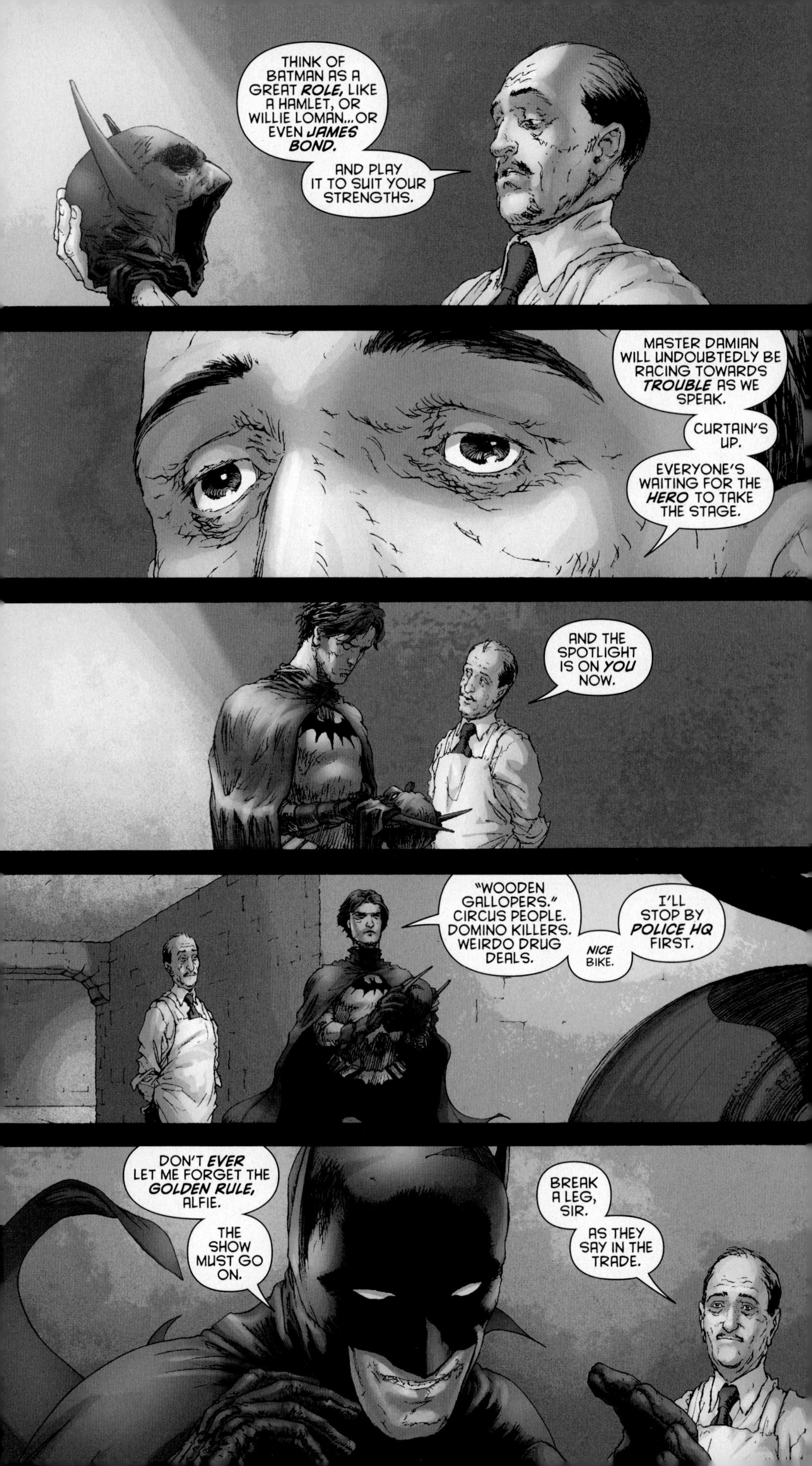
THINK OF BATMAN AS A GREAT ROLE, LIKE A HAMLET, OR WILLIE LOMAN...OR EVEN JAMES BOND.
AND PLAY IT TO SUIT YOUR STRENGTHS.
MASTER DAMIAN WILL UNDOUBTEDLY BE RACING TOWARDS TROUBLE AS WE SPEAK.
CURTAIN'S UP.
EVERYONE'S WAITING FOR THE HERO TO TAKE THE STAGE.
AND THE SPOTLIGHT IS ON YOU NOW.
"WOODEN GALLOPERS." CIRCUS PEOPLE. DOMINO KILLERS. WEIRDO DRUG DEALS.
NICE BIKE.
I'LL STOP BY POLICE HQ FIRST.
DON'T EVER LET ME FORGET THE GOLDEN RULE, ALFIE.
THE SHOW MUST GO ON.
BREAK A LEG, SIR.
AS THEY SAY IN THE TRADE.

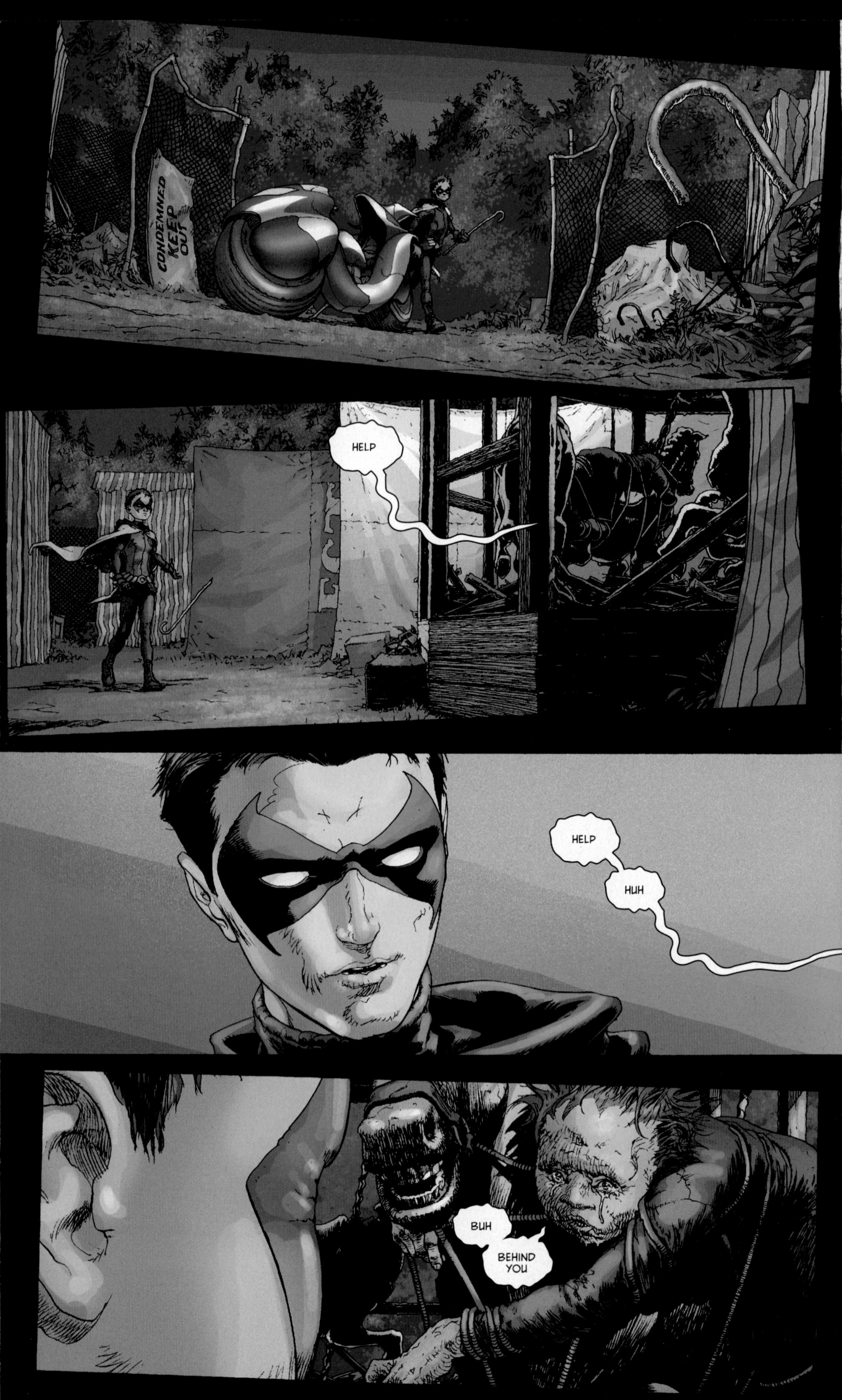
CONDEMNED KEEP OUT
HELP
HELP
HUH
BUH
BEHIND YOU

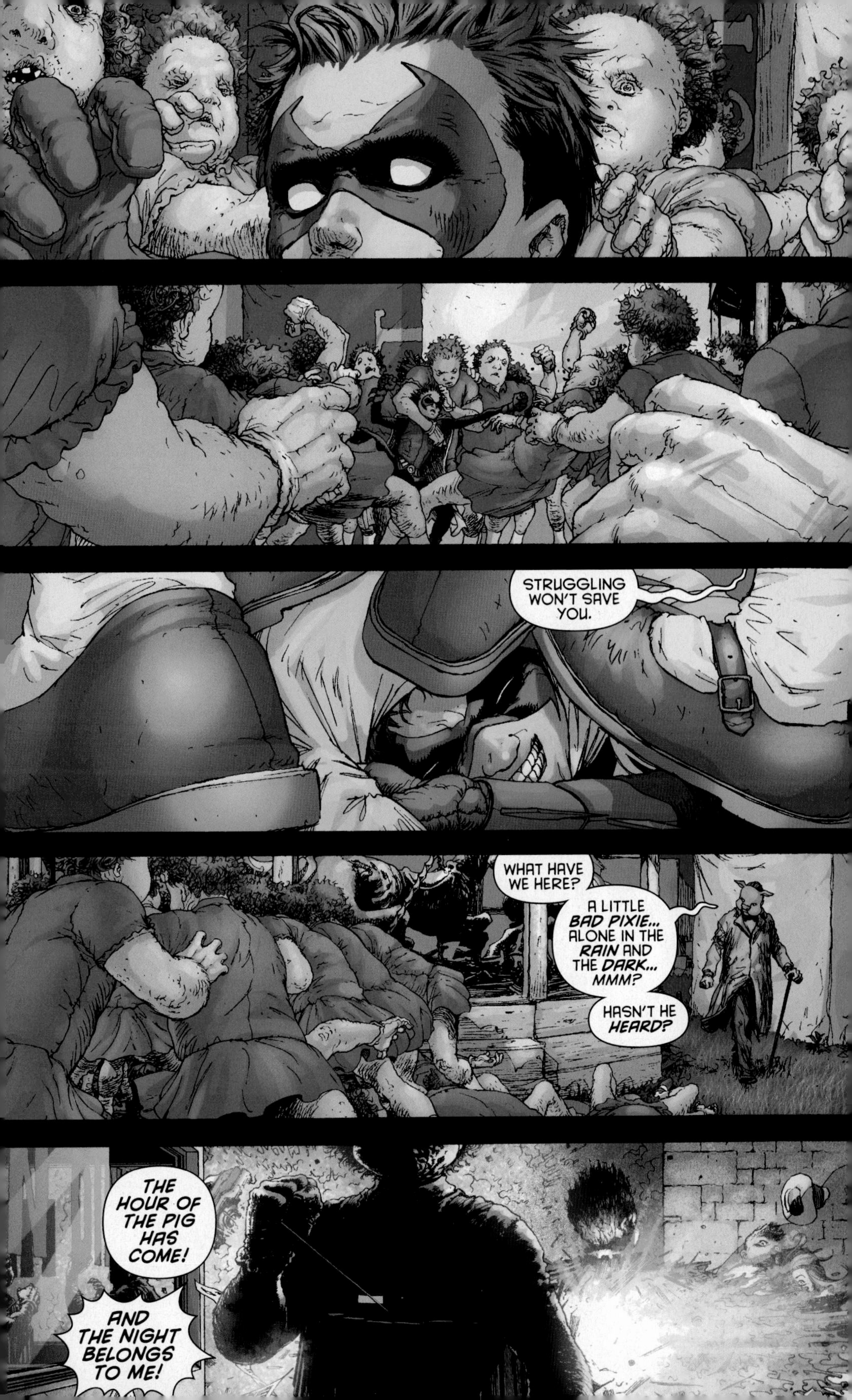
STRUGGLING WON'T SAVE YOU.
WHAT HAVE WE HERE?
A LITTLE *BAD PIXIE*... ALONE IN THE *RAIN* AND THE *DARK*... MMM?
HASN'T HE *HEARD*?
THE HOUR OF THE PIG HAS COME!
AND THE NIGHT BELONGS TO ME!

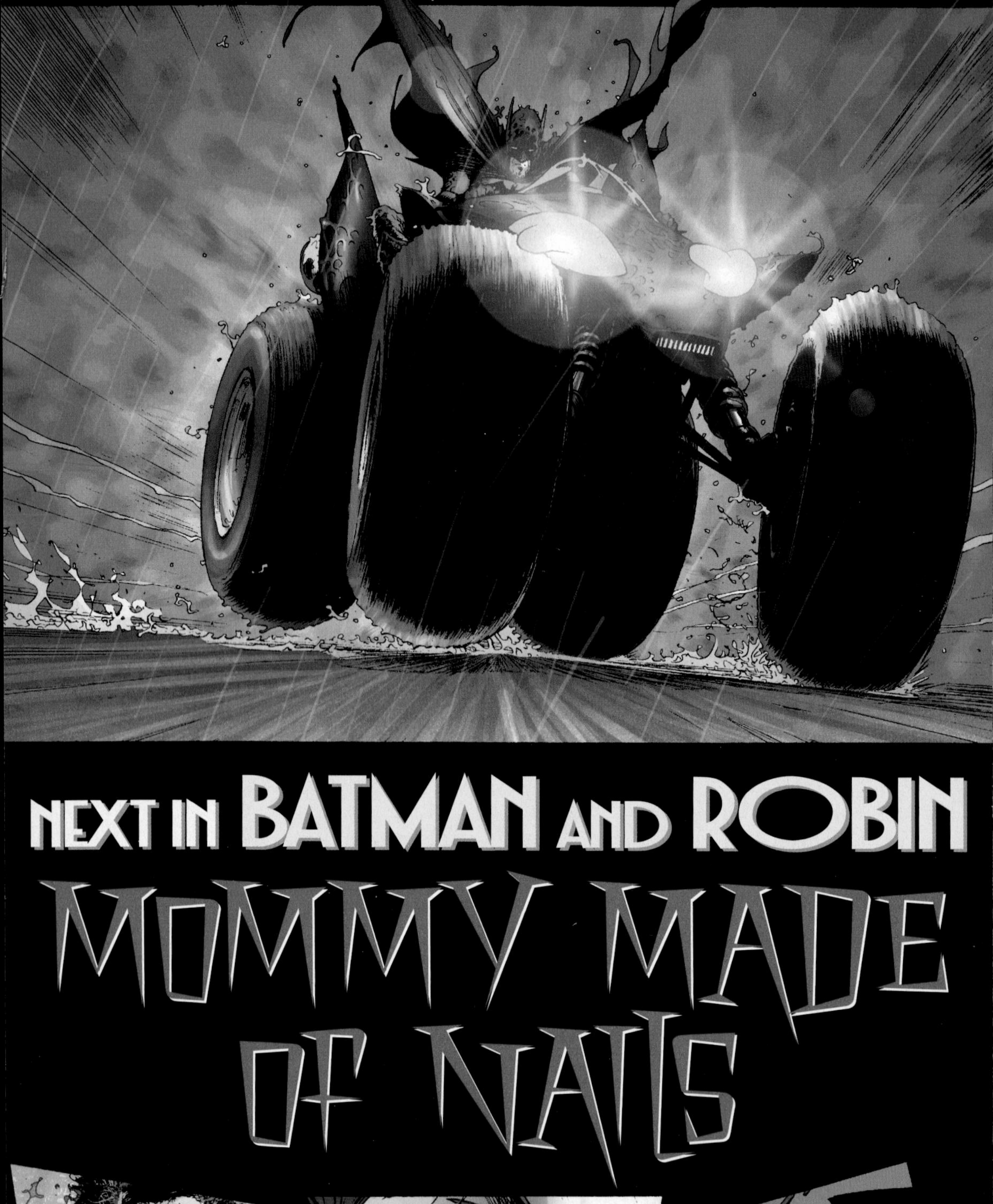

NEXT IN BATMAN AND ROBIN

MOMMY MADE OF NAILS

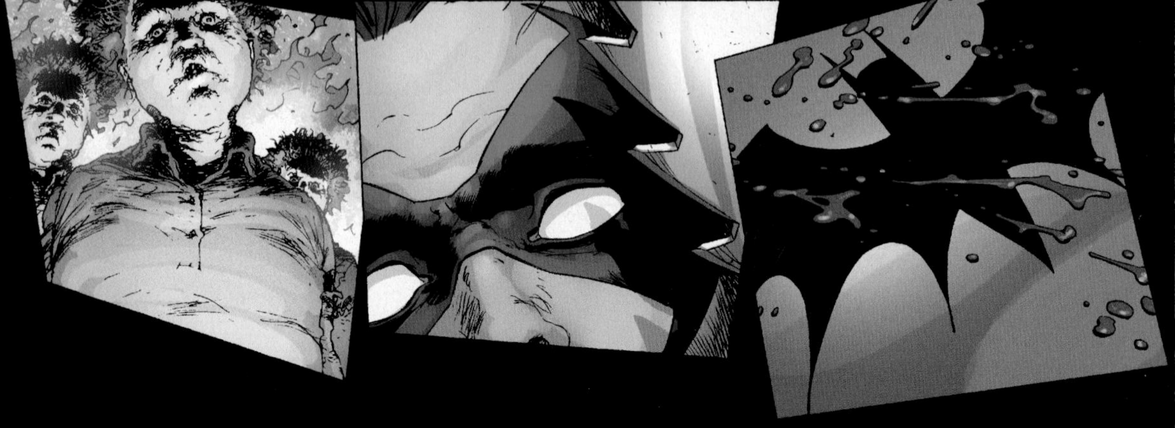

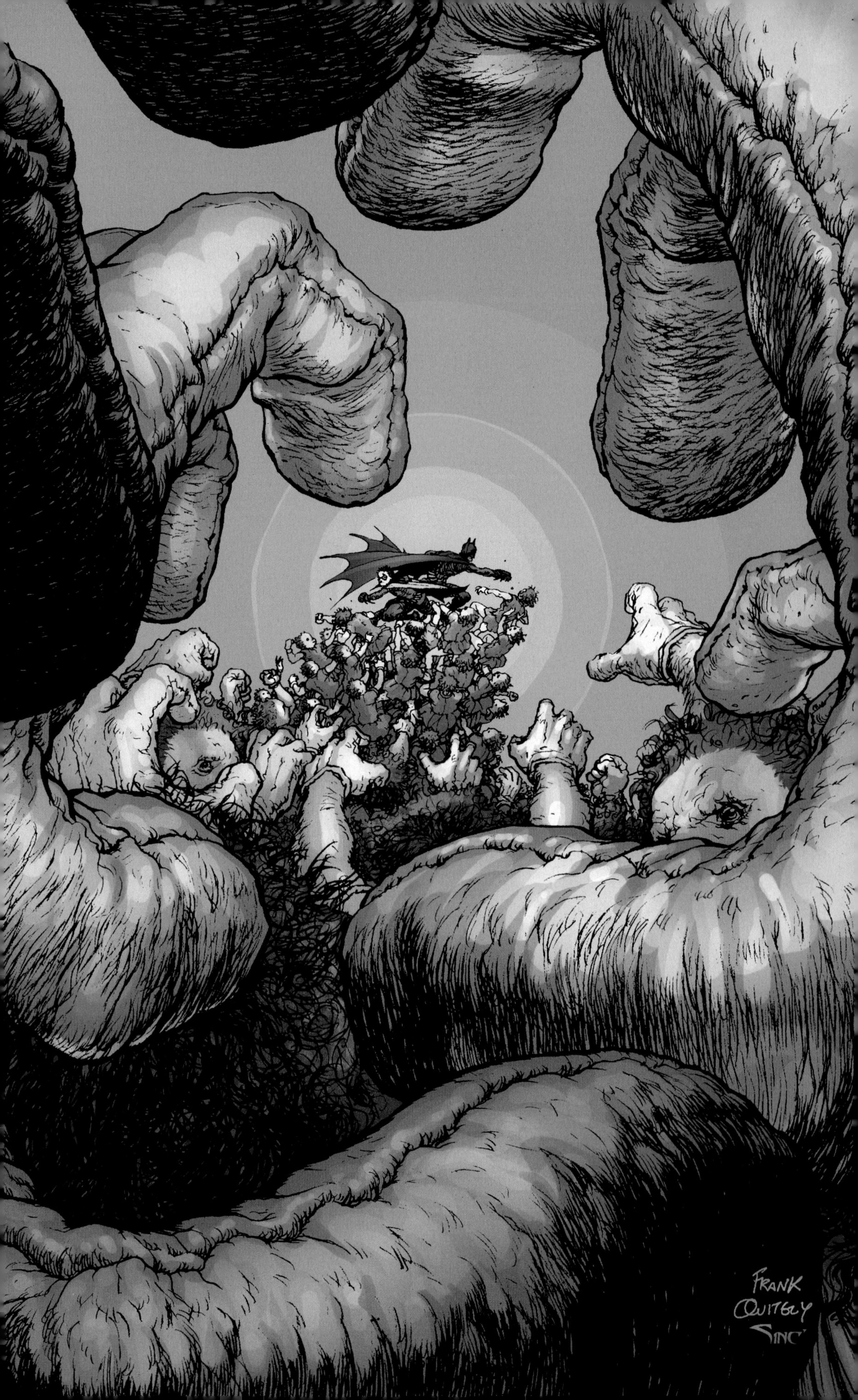
FRANK
QUITELY
SINC

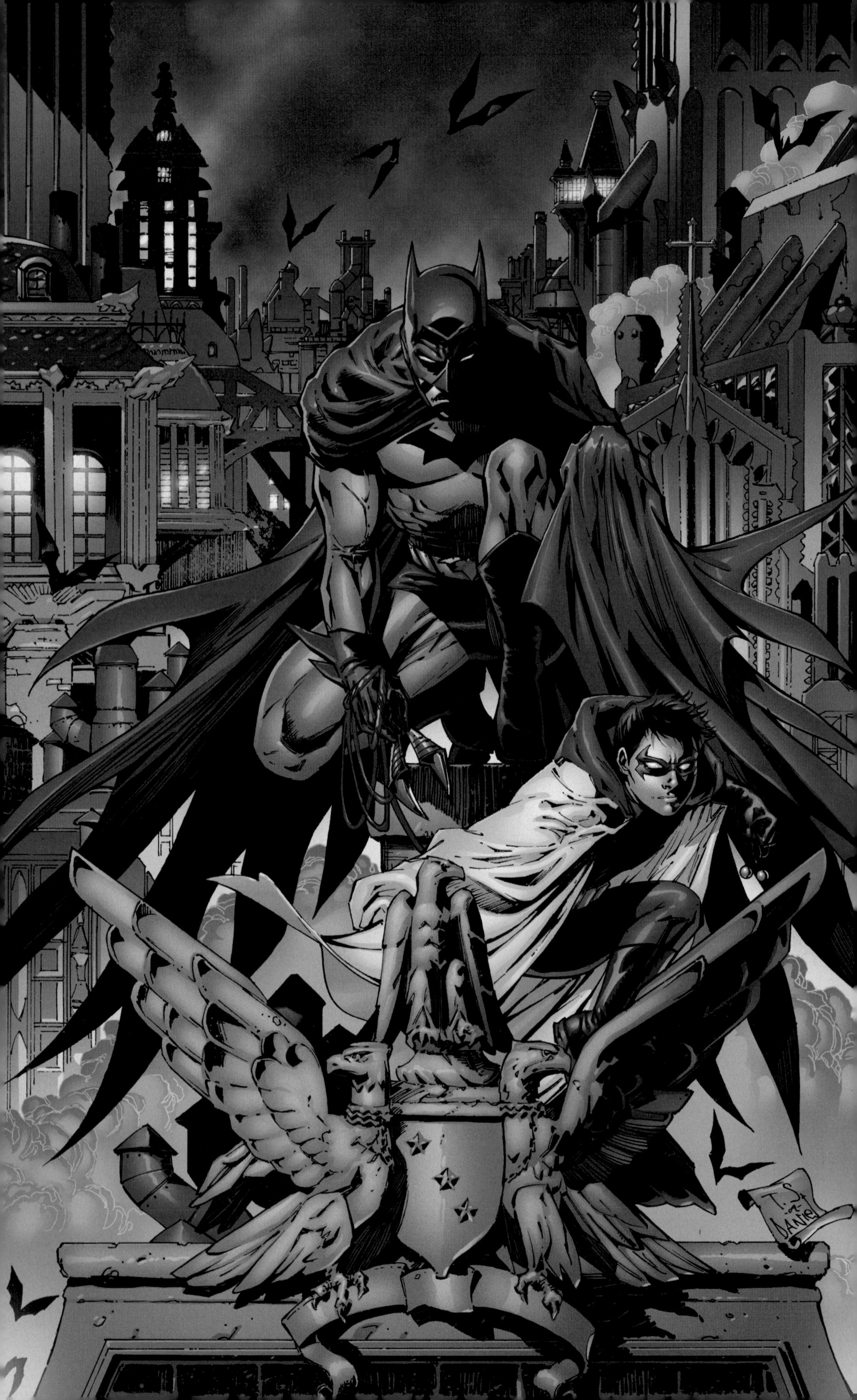
T.S.
DANIEL

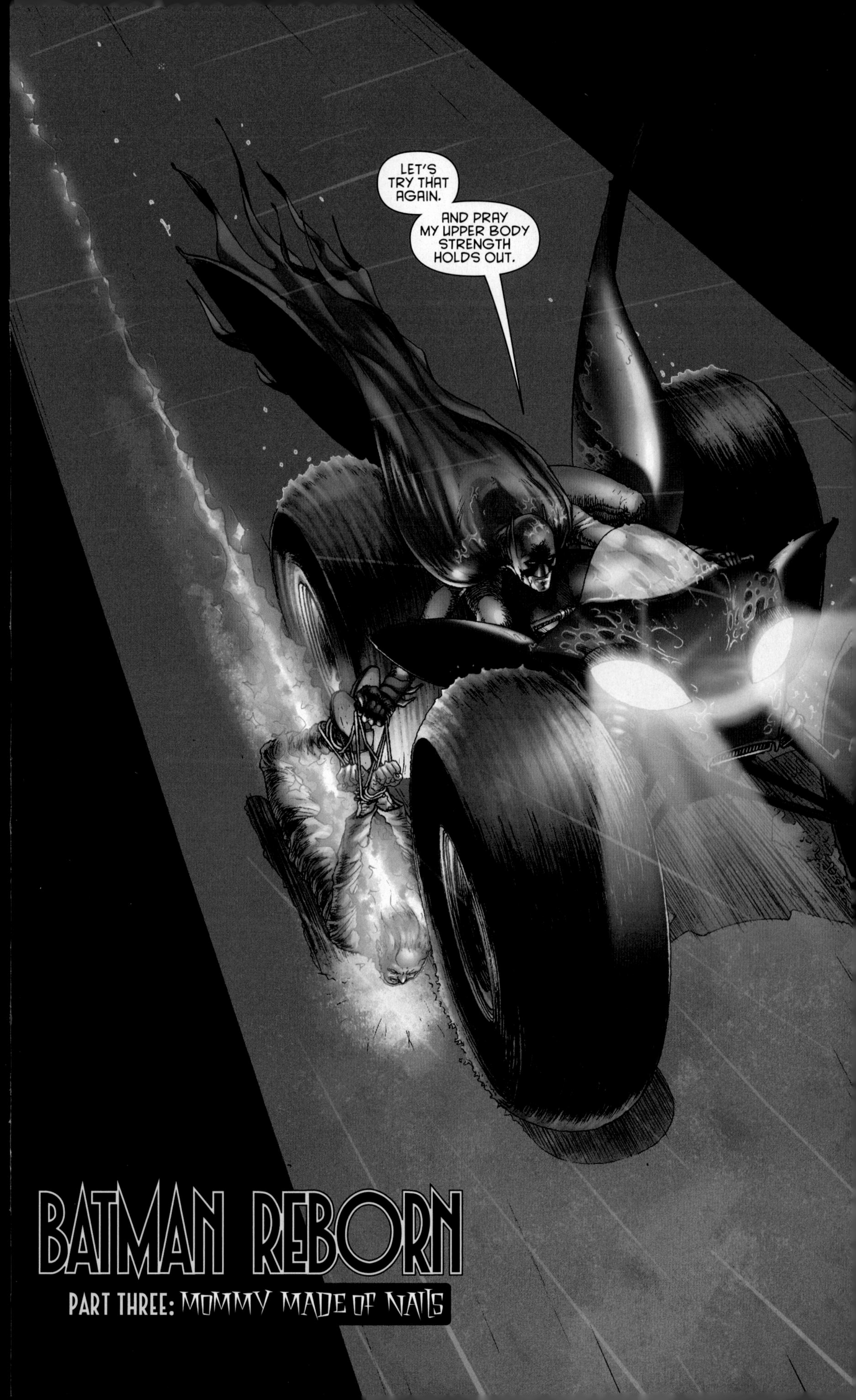
LET'S TRY THAT AGAIN.
AND PRAY MY UPPER BODY STRENGTH HOLDS OUT.
BATMAN REBORN
PART THREE: MOMMY MADE OF NAILS

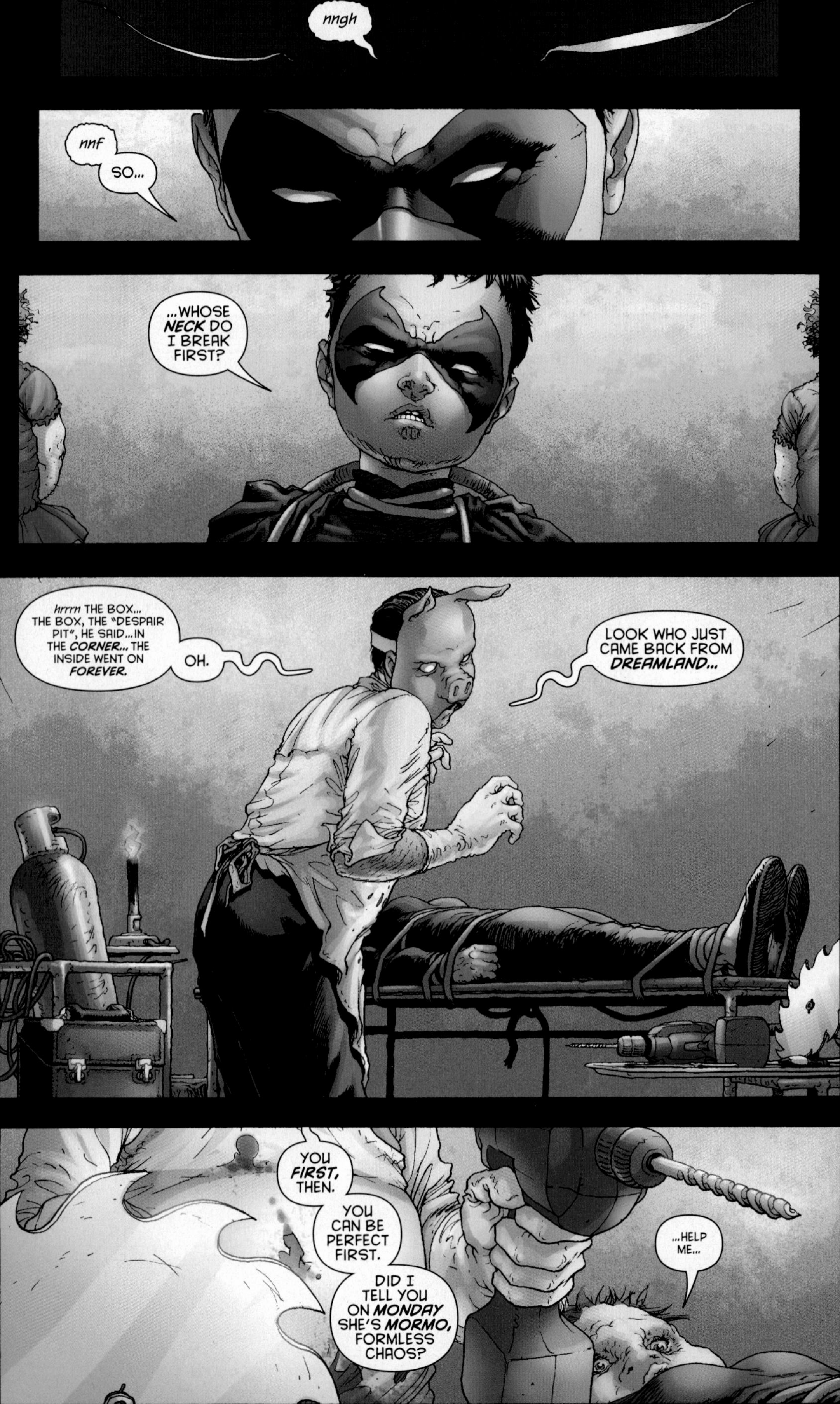
nngh
nnf
SO...
...WHOSE NECK DO I BREAK FIRST?
hrrrn THE BOX... THE BOX, THE "DESPAIR PIT", HE SAID...IN THE CORNER... THE INSIDE WENT ON FOREVER.
OH.
LOOK WHO JUST CAME BACK FROM DREAMLAND...
YOU FIRST, THEN.
YOU CAN BE PERFECT FIRST.
DID I TELL YOU ON MONDAY SHE'S MORMO, FORMLESS CHAOS?
...HELP ME...

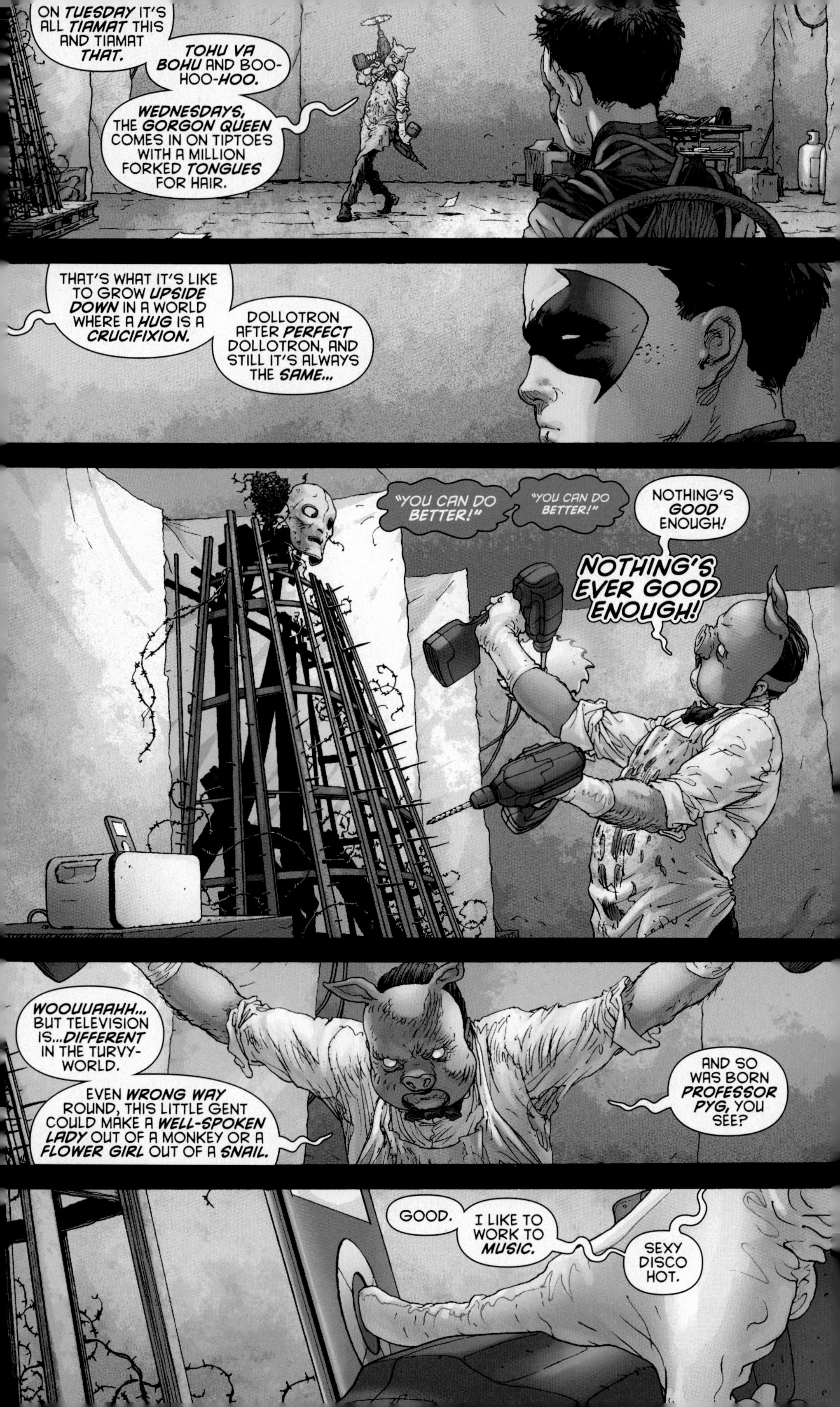
ON TUESDAY IT'S ALL TIAMAT THIS AND TIAMAT THAT.
TOHU VA BOHU AND BOO-HOO-HOO.
WEDNESDAYS, THE GORGON QUEEN COMES IN ON TIPTOES WITH A MILLION FORKED TONGUES FOR HAIR.
THAT'S WHAT IT'S LIKE TO GROW UPSIDE DOWN IN A WORLD WHERE A HUG IS A CRUCIFIXION.
DOLLOTRON AFTER PERFECT DOLLOTRON, AND STILL IT'S ALWAYS THE SAME...
"YOU CAN DO BETTER!"
"YOU CAN DO BETTER!"
NOTHING'S GOOD ENOUGH!
NOTHING'S EVER GOOD ENOUGH!
WOOUUAAHH... BUT TELEVISION IS...DIFFERENT IN THE TURVY-WORLD.
EVEN WRONG WAY ROUND, THIS LITTLE GENT COULD MAKE A WELL-SPOKEN LADY OUT OF A MONKEY OR A FLOWER GIRL OUT OF A SNAIL.
AND SO WAS BORN PROFESSOR PYG, YOU SEE?
GOOD.
I LIKE TO WORK TO MUSIC.
SEXY DISCO HOT.

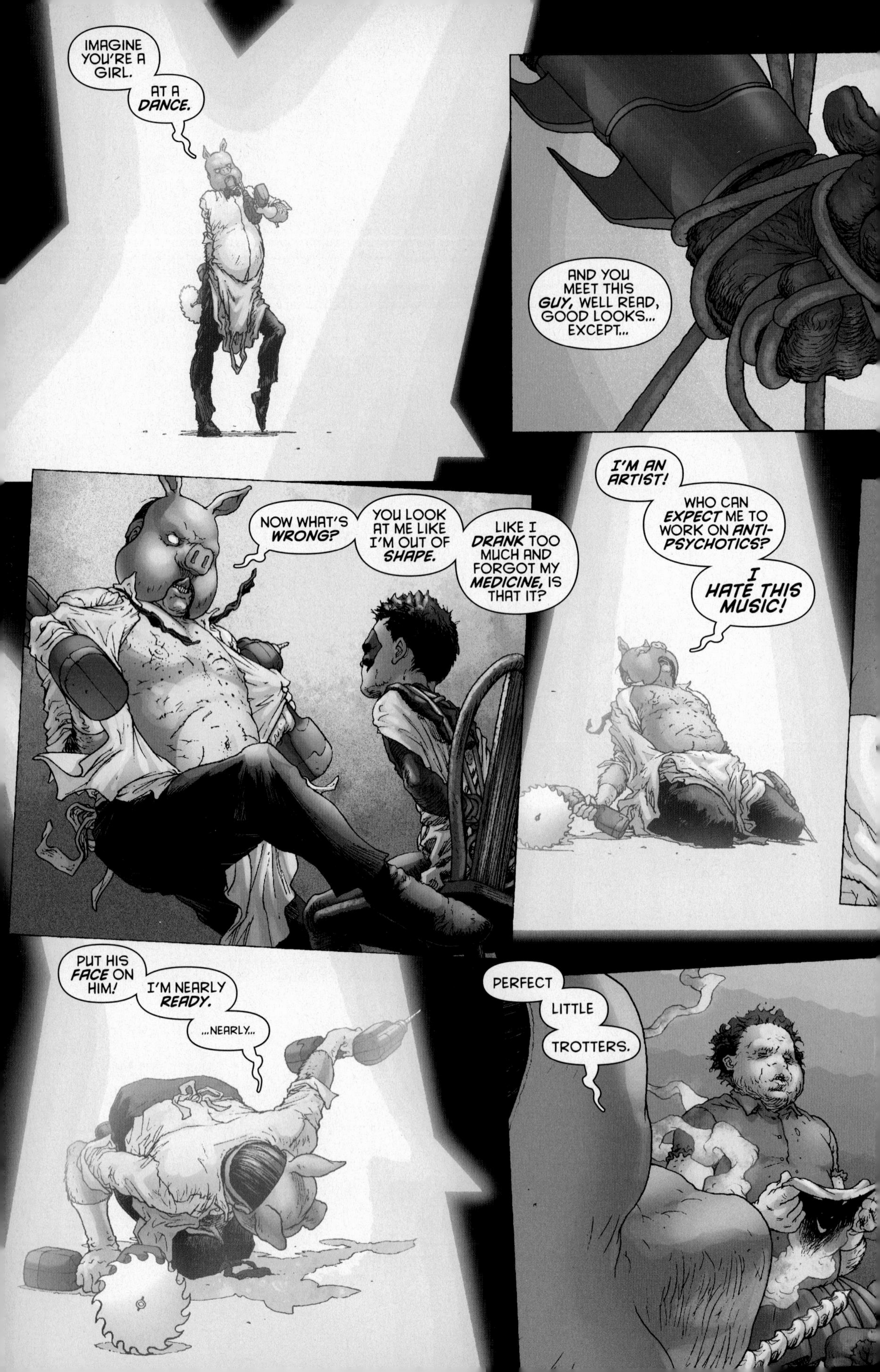
IMAGINE YOU'RE A GIRL.
AT A DANCE.
AND YOU MEET THIS GUY, WELL READ, GOOD LOOKS... EXCEPT...
NOW WHAT'S WRONG?
YOU LOOK AT ME LIKE I'M OUT OF SHAPE.
LIKE I DRANK TOO MUCH AND FORGOT MY MEDICINE, IS THAT IT?
I'M AN ARTIST!
WHO CAN EXPECT ME TO WORK ON ANTI-PSYCHOTICS?
I HATE THIS MUSIC!
PUT HIS FACE ON HIM!
I'M NEARLY READY.
...NEARLY...
PERFECT
LITTLE
TROTTERS.

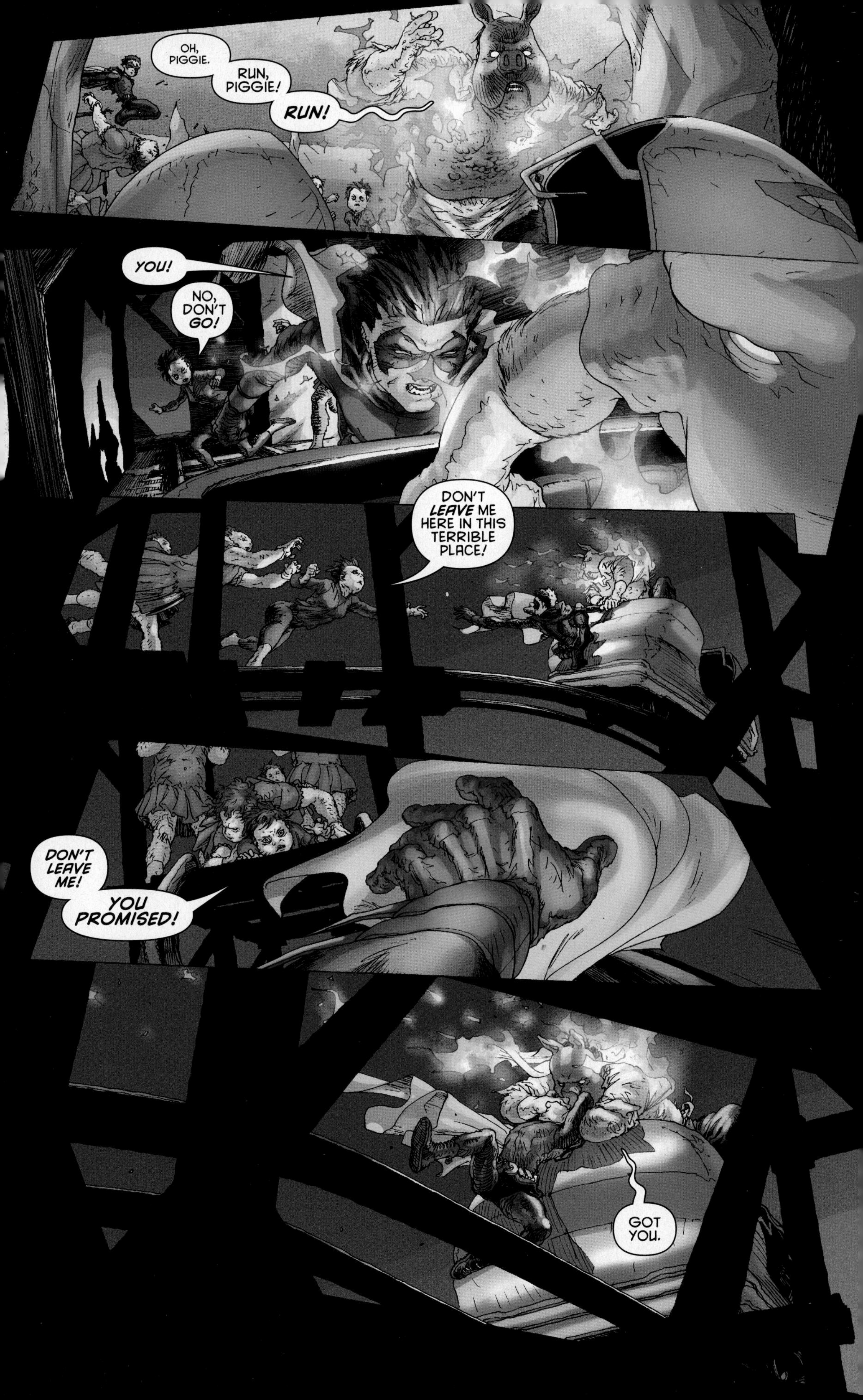
OH, PIGGIE.
RUN, PIGGIE!
RUN!
YOU!
NO, DON'T GO!
DON'T LEAVE ME HERE IN THIS TERRIBLE PLACE!
DON'T LEAVE ME!
YOU PROMISED!
GOT YOU.

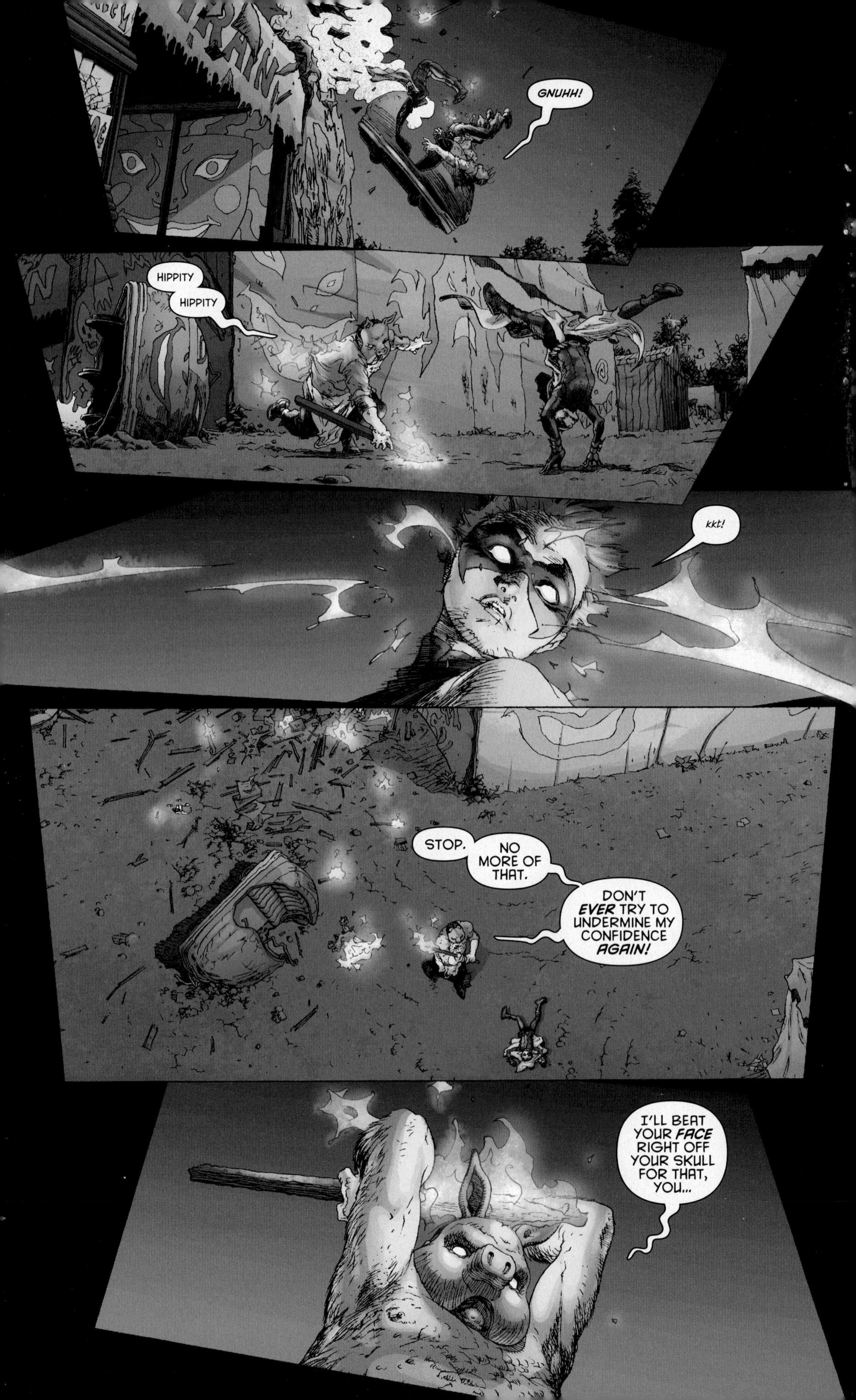
GNUHH!
HIPPITY
HIPPITY
kkt!
STOP.
NO MORE OF THAT.
DON'T EVER TRY TO UNDERMINE MY CONFIDENCE AGAIN!
I'LL BEAT YOUR FACE RIGHT OFF YOUR SKULL FOR THAT, YOU...

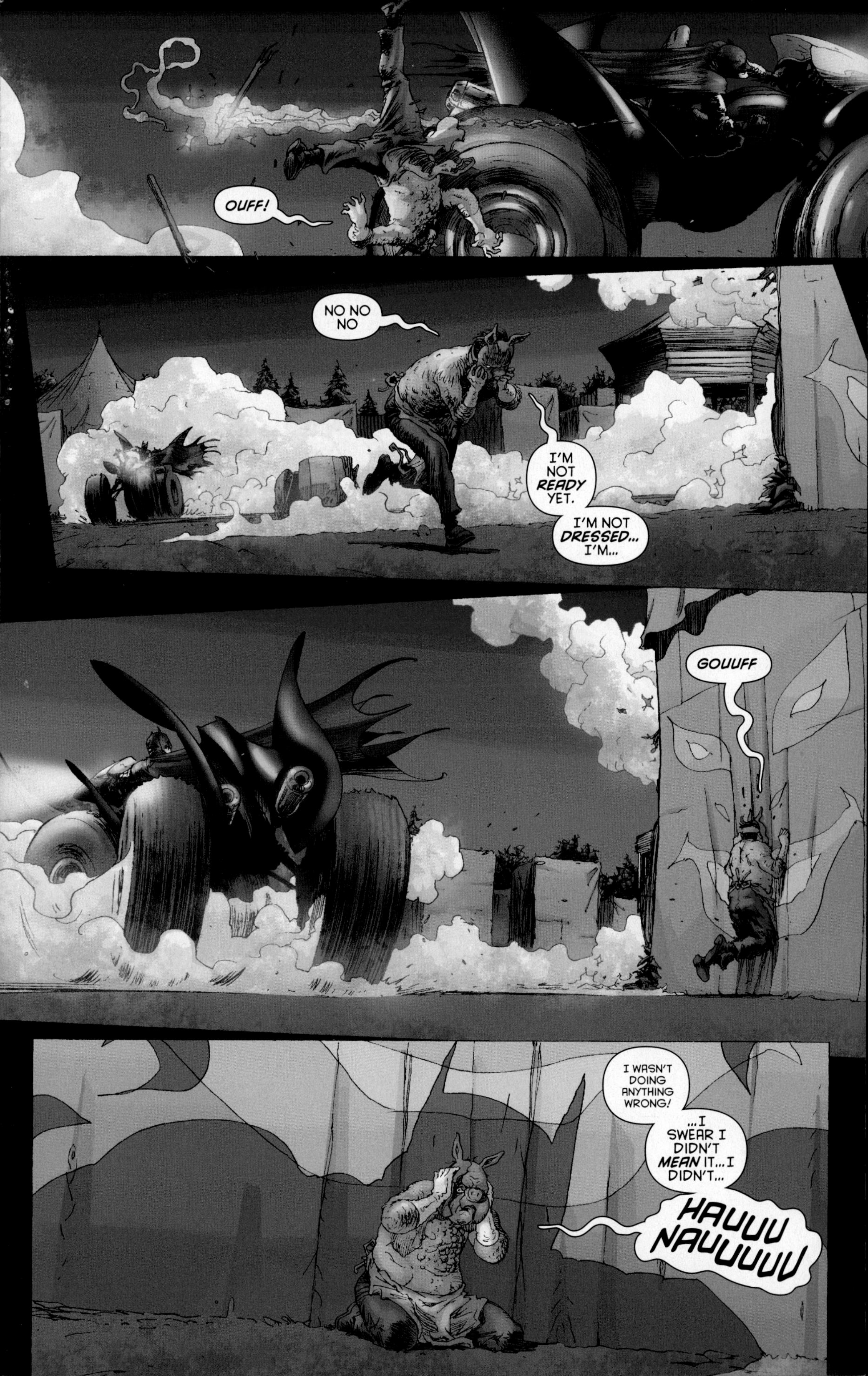
OUFF!
NO NO NO
I'M NOT *READY* YET.
I'M NOT *DRESSED...* I'M...
GOUUFF
I WASN'T DOING ANYTHING WRONG!
...I SWEAR I DIDN'T *MEAN* IT...I DIDN'T...
HAUUU NAUUUUU

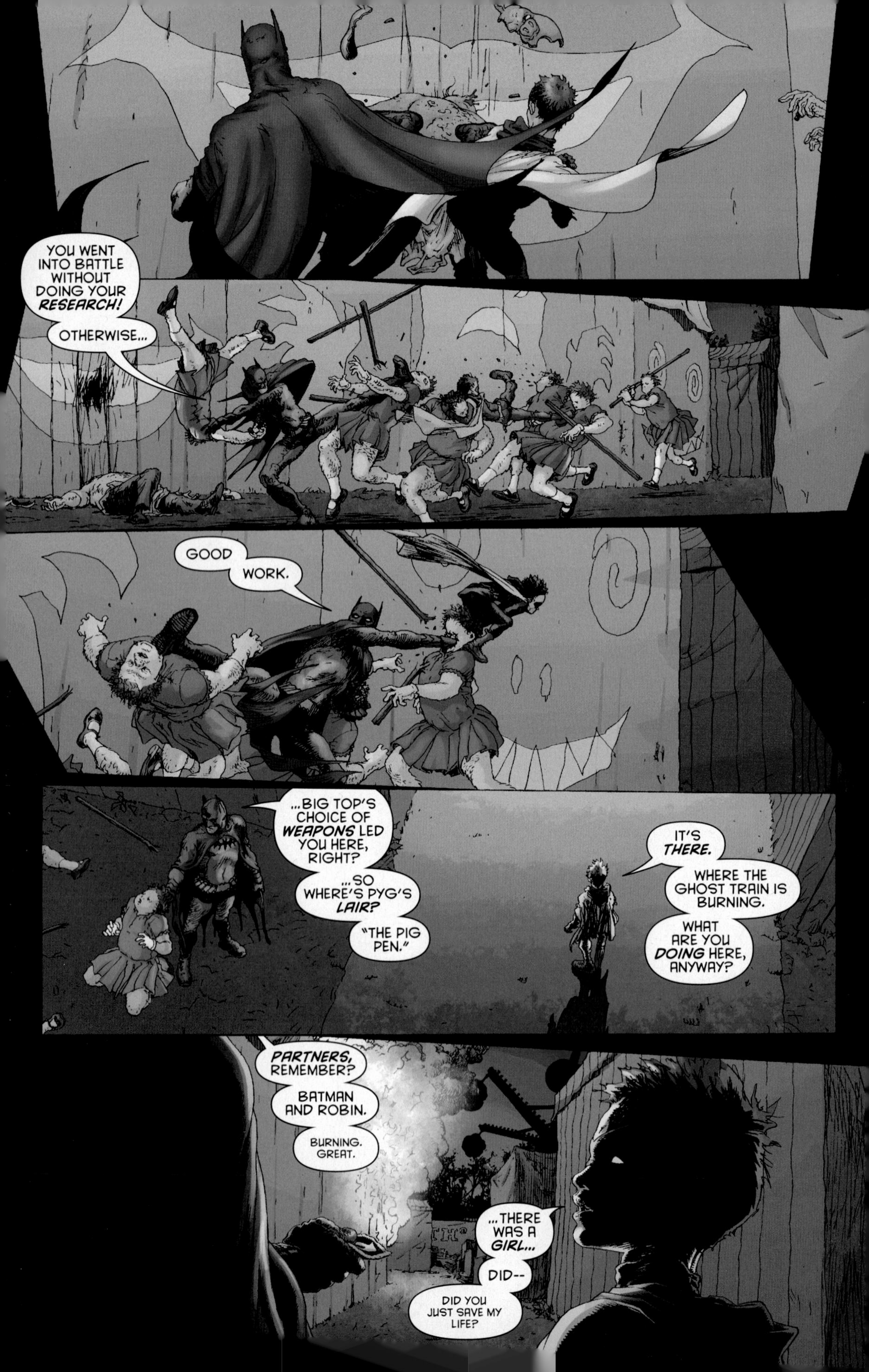
YOU WENT INTO BATTLE WITHOUT DOING YOUR RESEARCH!
OTHERWISE...
GOOD
WORK.
...BIG TOP'S CHOICE OF WEAPONS LED YOU HERE, RIGHT?
...SO WHERE'S PYG'S LAIR?
"THE PIG PEN."
IT'S THERE.
WHERE THE GHOST TRAIN IS BURNING.
WHAT ARE YOU DOING HERE, ANYWAY?
PARTNERS, REMEMBER?
BATMAN AND ROBIN.
BURNING. GREAT.
...THERE WAS A GIRL...
DID--
DID YOU JUST SAVE MY LIFE?

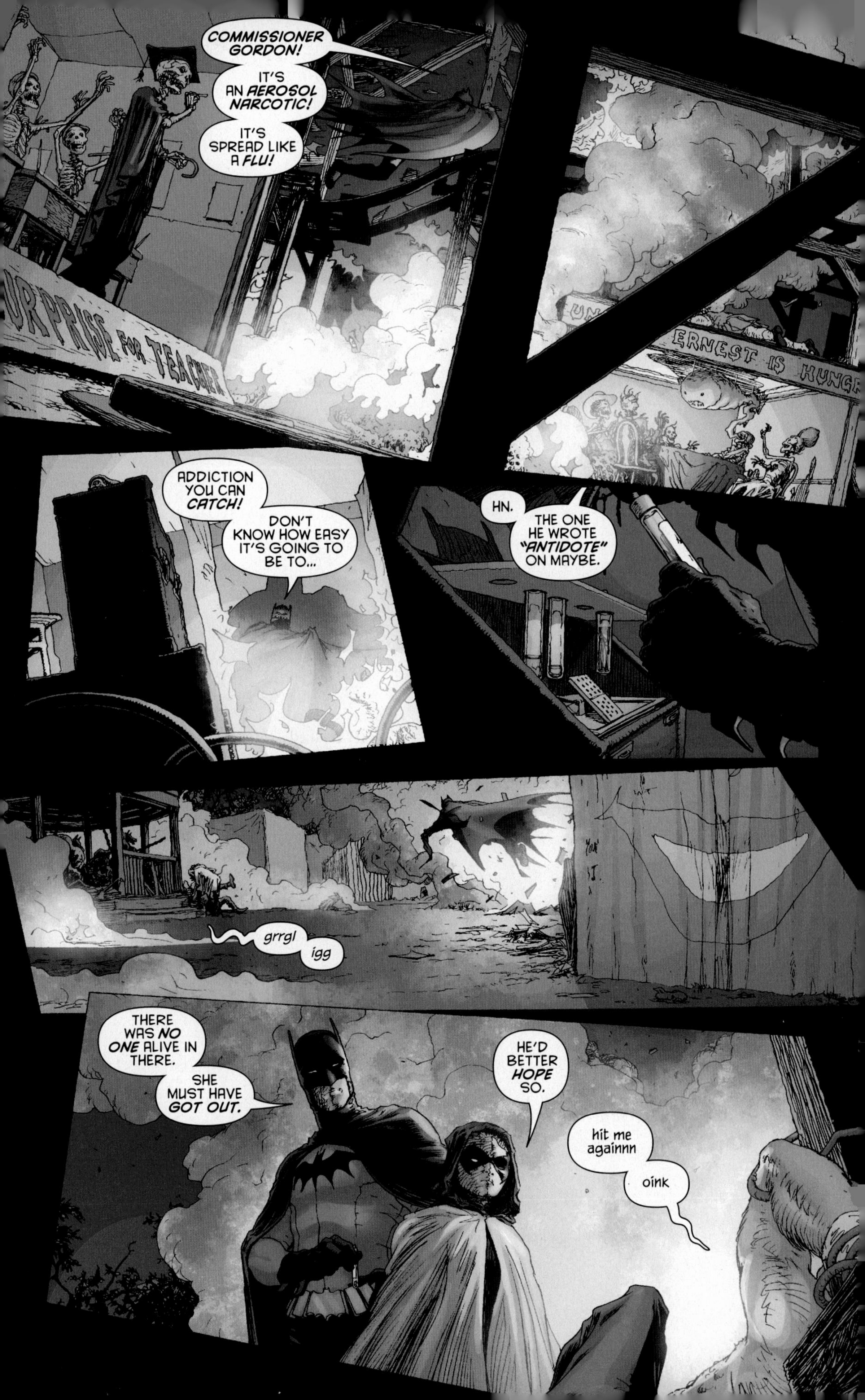

COMMISSIONER GORDON!
IT'S AN AEROSOL NARCOTIC!
IT'S SPREAD LIKE A FLU!
URPRISE FOR TEACHER
ERNEST IS HUNG
ADDICTION YOU CAN CATCH!
DON'T KNOW HOW EASY IT'S GOING TO BE TO...
HN.
THE ONE HE WROTE "ANTIDOTE" ON MAYBE.
grrgl
igg
THERE WAS NO ONE ALIVE IN THERE.
SHE MUST HAVE GOT OUT.
HE'D BETTER HOPE SO.
hit me againnn
oink

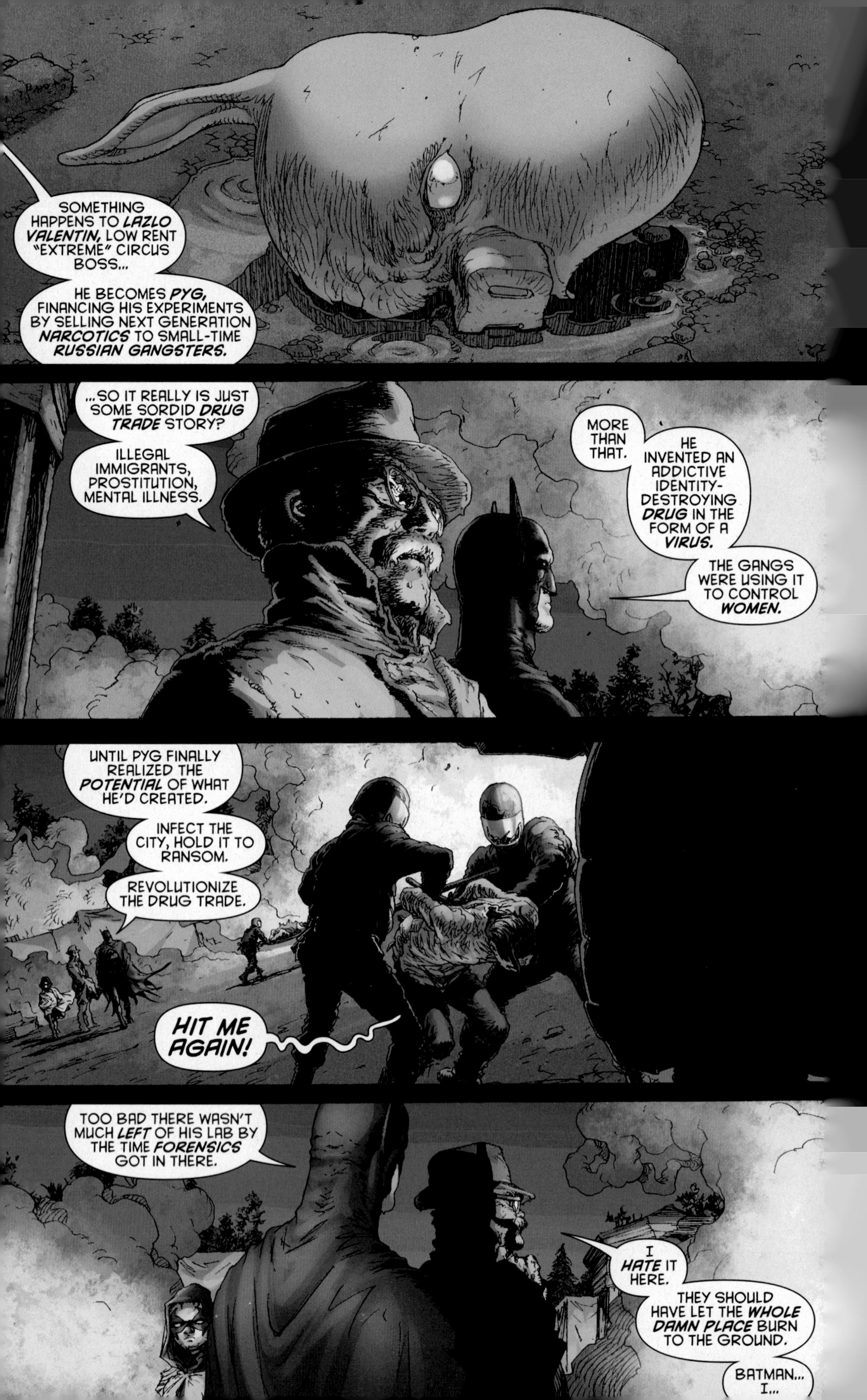
SOMETHING HAPPENS TO LAZLO VALENTIN, LOW RENT "EXTREME" CIRCUS BOSS...
HE BECOMES PYG, FINANCING HIS EXPERIMENTS BY SELLING NEXT GENERATION NARCOTICS TO SMALL-TIME RUSSIAN GANGSTERS.
...SO IT REALLY IS JUST SOME SORDID DRUG TRADE STORY?
ILLEGAL IMMIGRANTS, PROSTITUTION, MENTAL ILLNESS.
MORE THAN THAT.
HE INVENTED AN ADDICTIVE IDENTITY-DESTROYING DRUG IN THE FORM OF A VIRUS.
THE GANGS WERE USING IT TO CONTROL WOMEN.
UNTIL PYG FINALLY REALIZED THE POTENTIAL OF WHAT HE'D CREATED.
INFECT THE CITY, HOLD IT TO RANSOM.
REVOLUTIONIZE THE DRUG TRADE.
HIT ME AGAIN!
TOO BAD THERE WASN'T MUCH LEFT OF HIS LAB BY THE TIME FORENSICS GOT IN THERE.
I HATE IT HERE.
THEY SHOULD HAVE LET THE WHOLE DAMN PLACE BURN TO THE GROUND.
BATMAN... I...

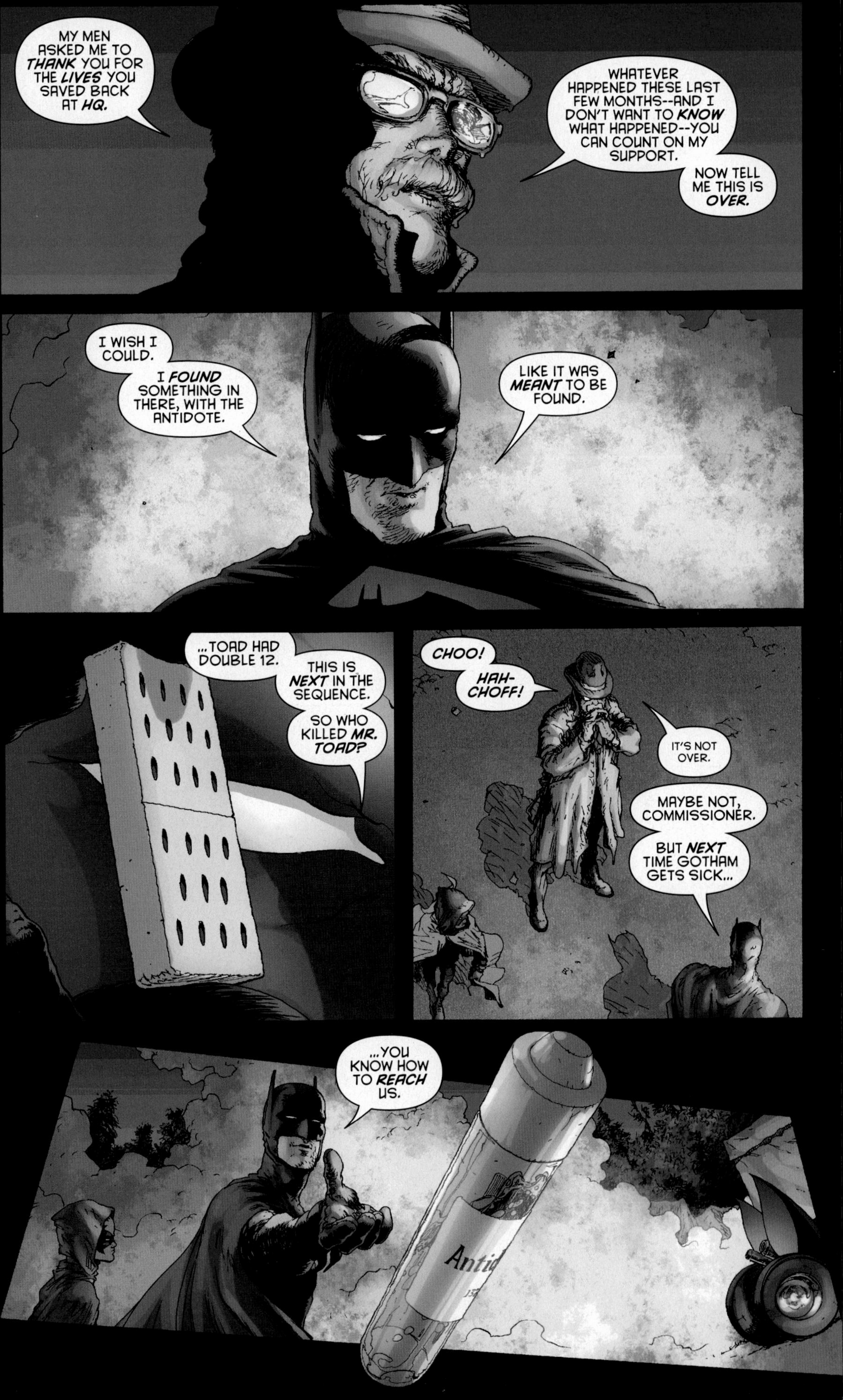
MY MEN ASKED ME TO THANK YOU FOR THE LIVES YOU SAVED BACK AT HQ.
WHATEVER HAPPENED THESE LAST FEW MONTHS--AND I DON'T WANT TO KNOW WHAT HAPPENED--YOU CAN COUNT ON MY SUPPORT.
NOW TELL ME THIS IS OVER.
I WISH I COULD.
I FOUND SOMETHING IN THERE, WITH THE ANTIDOTE.
LIKE IT WAS MEANT TO BE FOUND.
...TOAD HAD DOUBLE 12.
THIS IS NEXT IN THE SEQUENCE.
SO WHO KILLED MR. TOAD?
CHOO!
HAH-CHOFF!
IT'S NOT OVER.
MAYBE NOT, COMMISSIONER.
BUT NEXT TIME GOTHAM GETS SICK...
...YOU KNOW HOW TO REACH US.
Antid

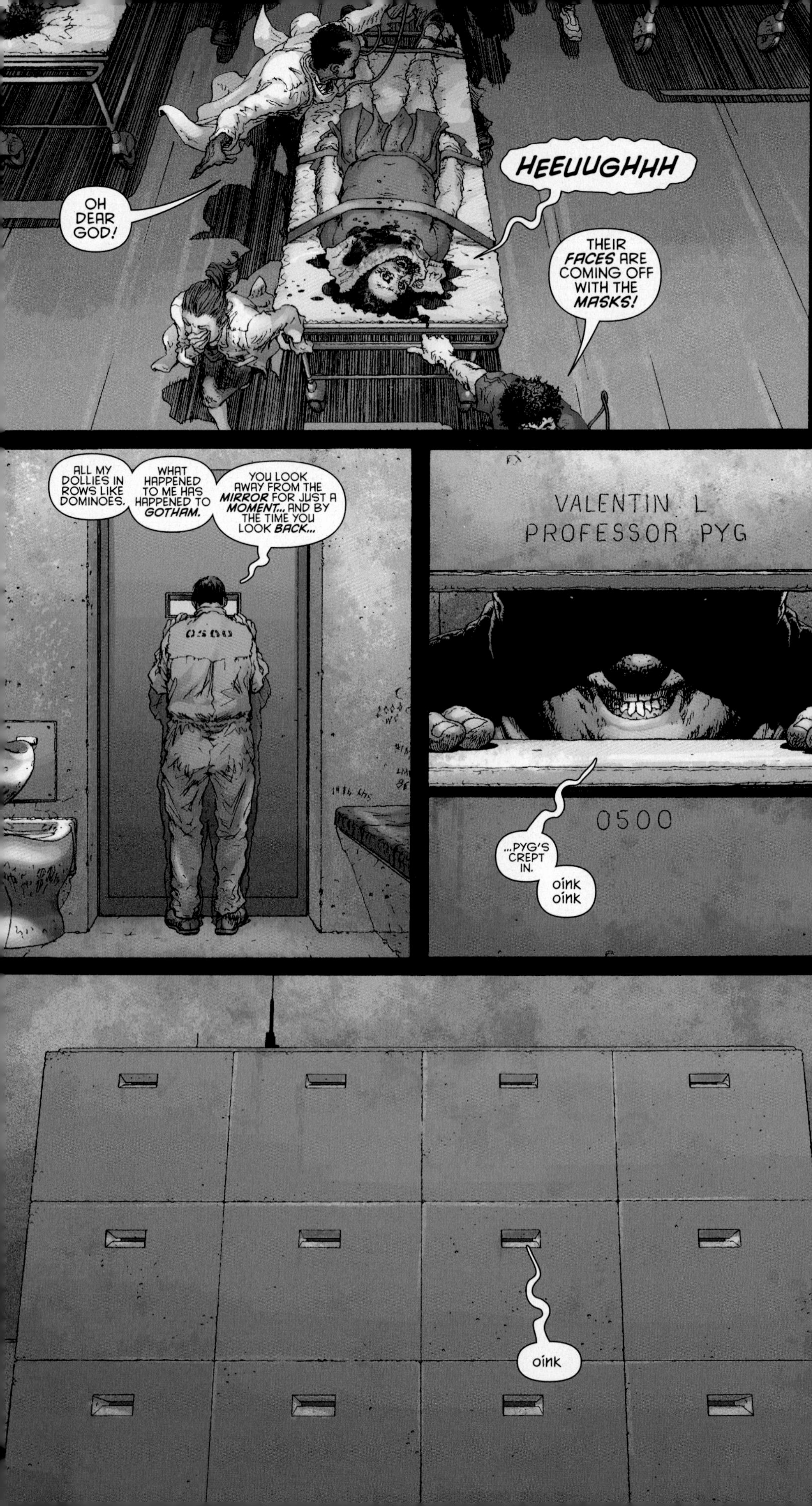
OH DEAR GOD!
HEEUUGHHH
THEIR FACES ARE COMING OFF WITH THE MASKS!
ALL MY DOLLIES IN ROWS LIKE DOMINOES.
WHAT HAPPENED TO ME HAS HAPPENED TO GOTHAM.
YOU LOOK AWAY FROM THE MIRROR FOR JUST A MOMENT... AND BY THE TIME YOU LOOK BACK...
0500
VALENTIN L
PROFESSOR PYG
0500
...PYG'S CREPT IN.
oink oink
oink

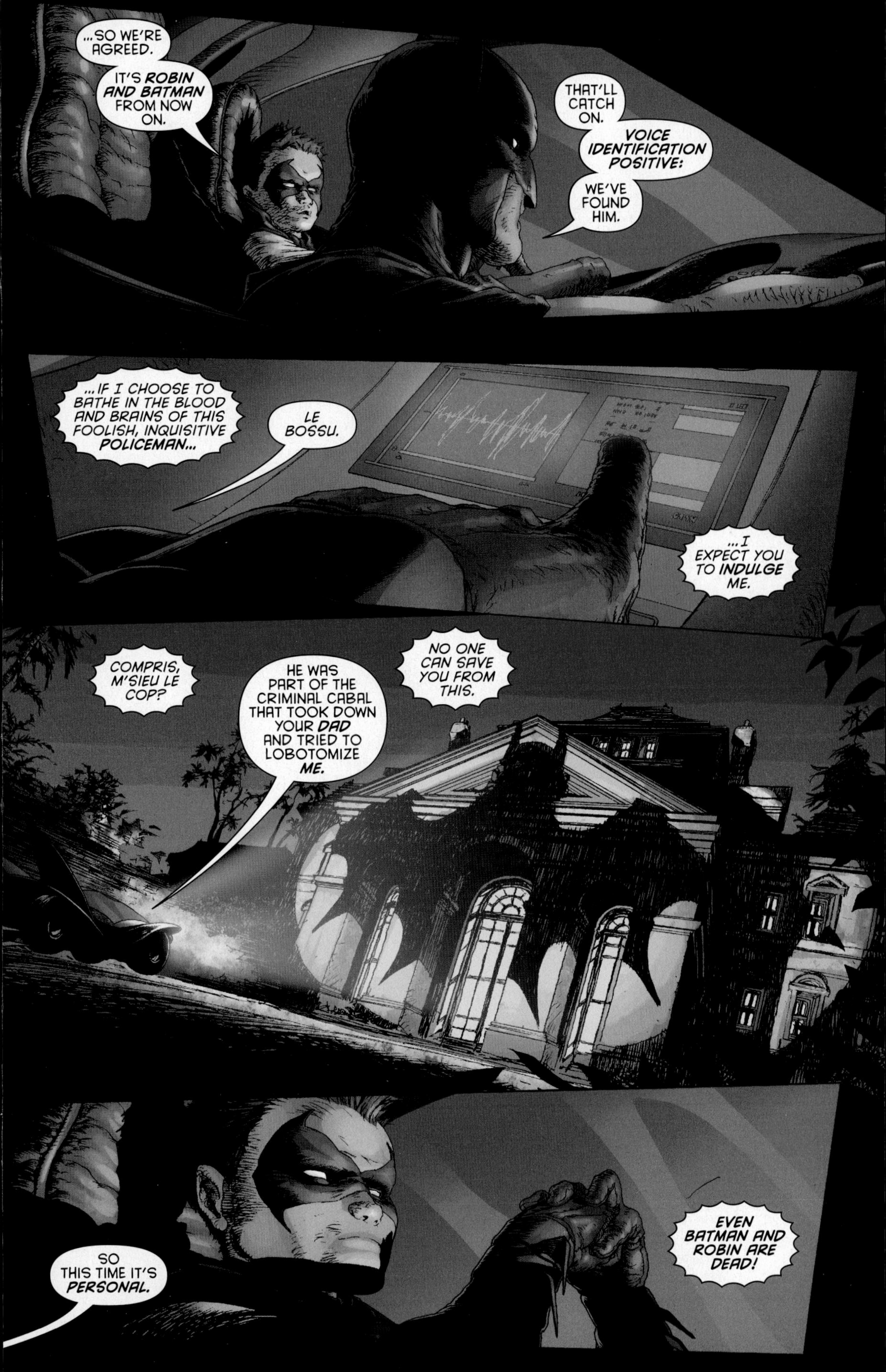

...SO WE'RE AGREED.
IT'S ROBIN AND BATMAN FROM NOW ON.
THAT'LL CATCH ON.
VOICE IDENTIFICATION POSITIVE:
WE'VE FOUND HIM.
...IF I CHOOSE TO BATHE IN THE BLOOD AND BRAINS OF THIS FOOLISH, INQUISITIVE POLICEMAN...
LE BOSSU.
...I EXPECT YOU TO INDULGE ME.
COMPRIS, M'SIEU LE COP?
HE WAS PART OF THE CRIMINAL CABAL THAT TOOK DOWN YOUR DAD AND TRIED TO LOBOTOMIZE ME.
NO ONE CAN SAVE YOU FROM THIS.
SO THIS TIME IT'S PERSONAL.
EVEN BATMAN AND ROBIN ARE DEAD!

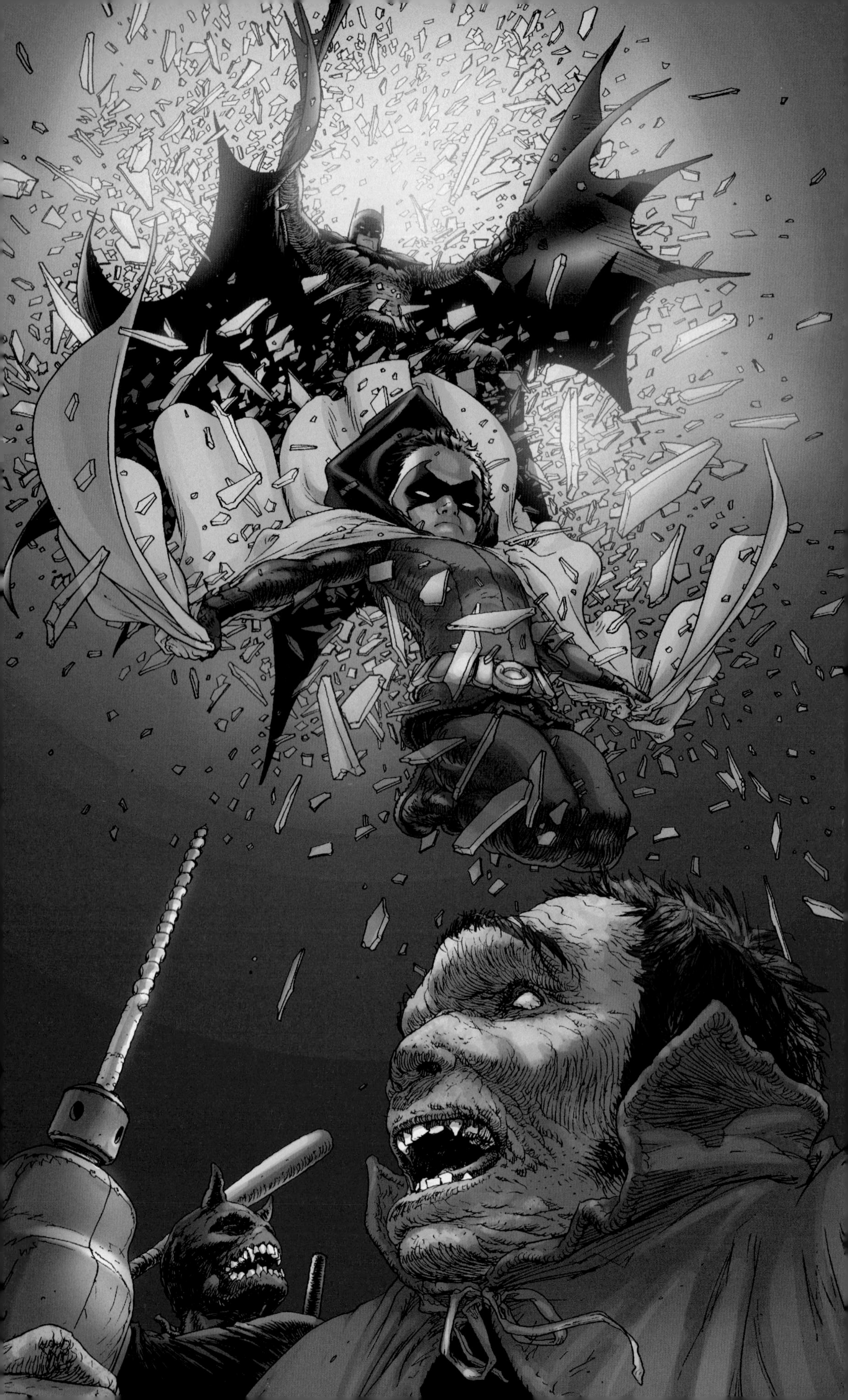

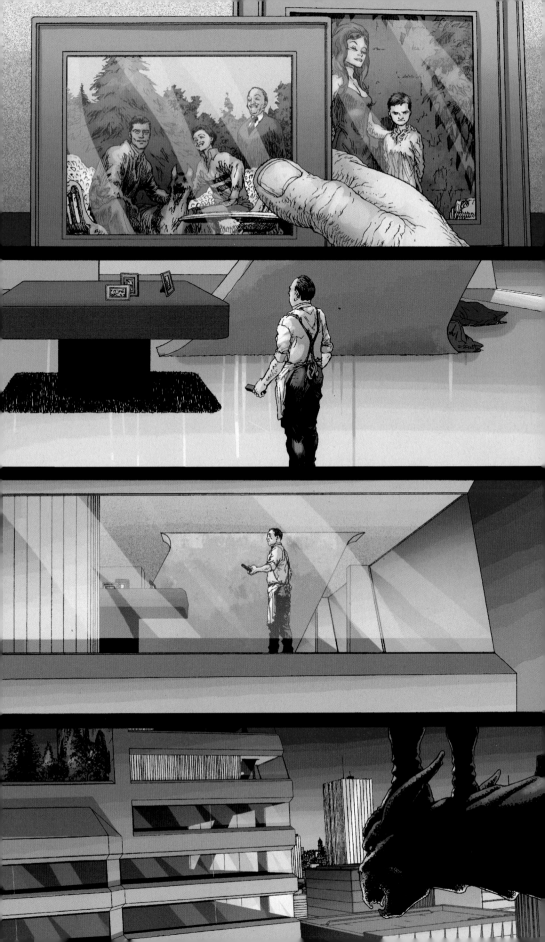

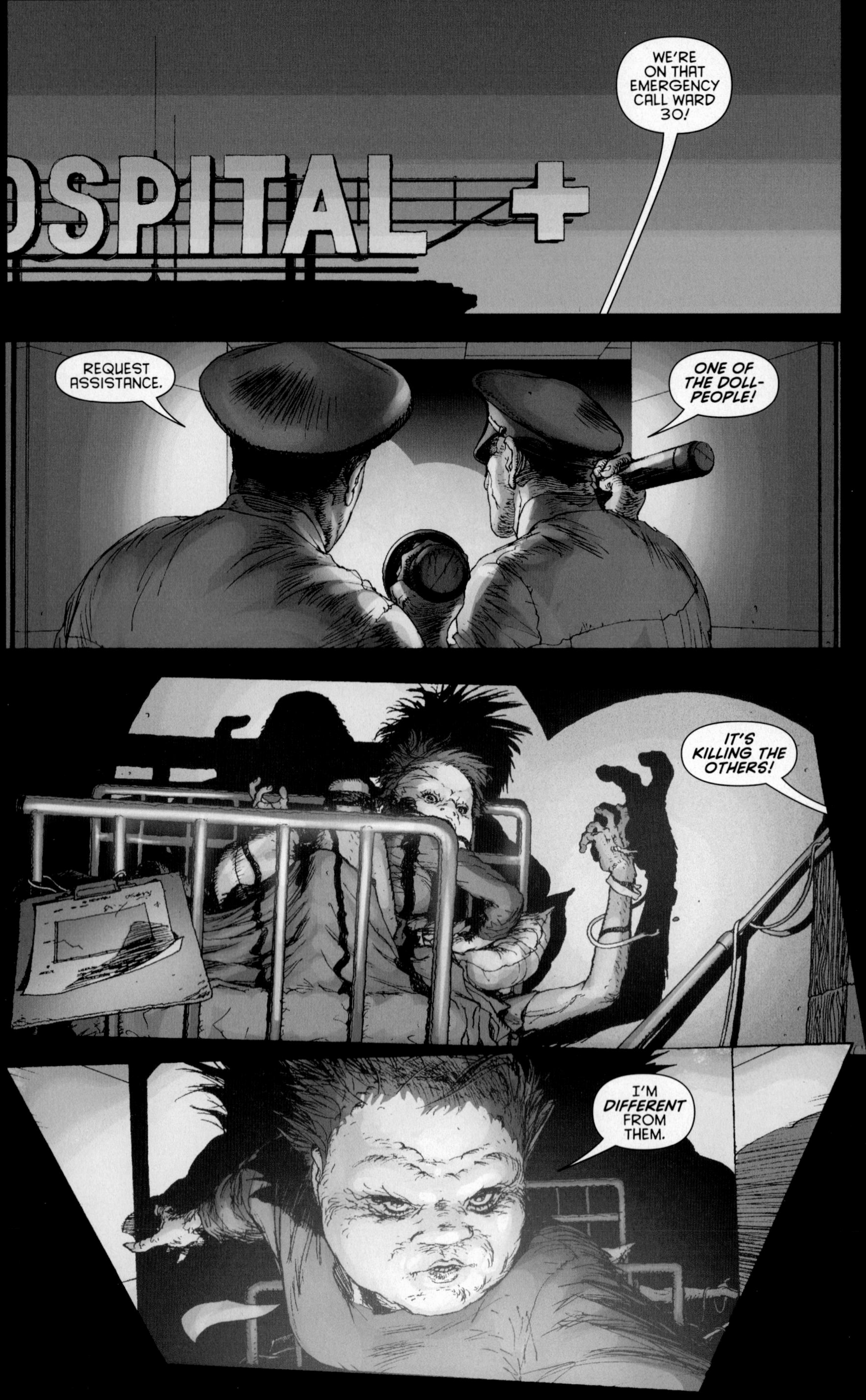
OSPITAL
WE'RE ON THAT EMERGENCY CALL WARD 30!
REQUEST ASSISTANCE.
ONE OF THE DOLL-PEOPLE!
IT'S KILLING THE OTHERS!
I'M DIFFERENT FROM THEM.

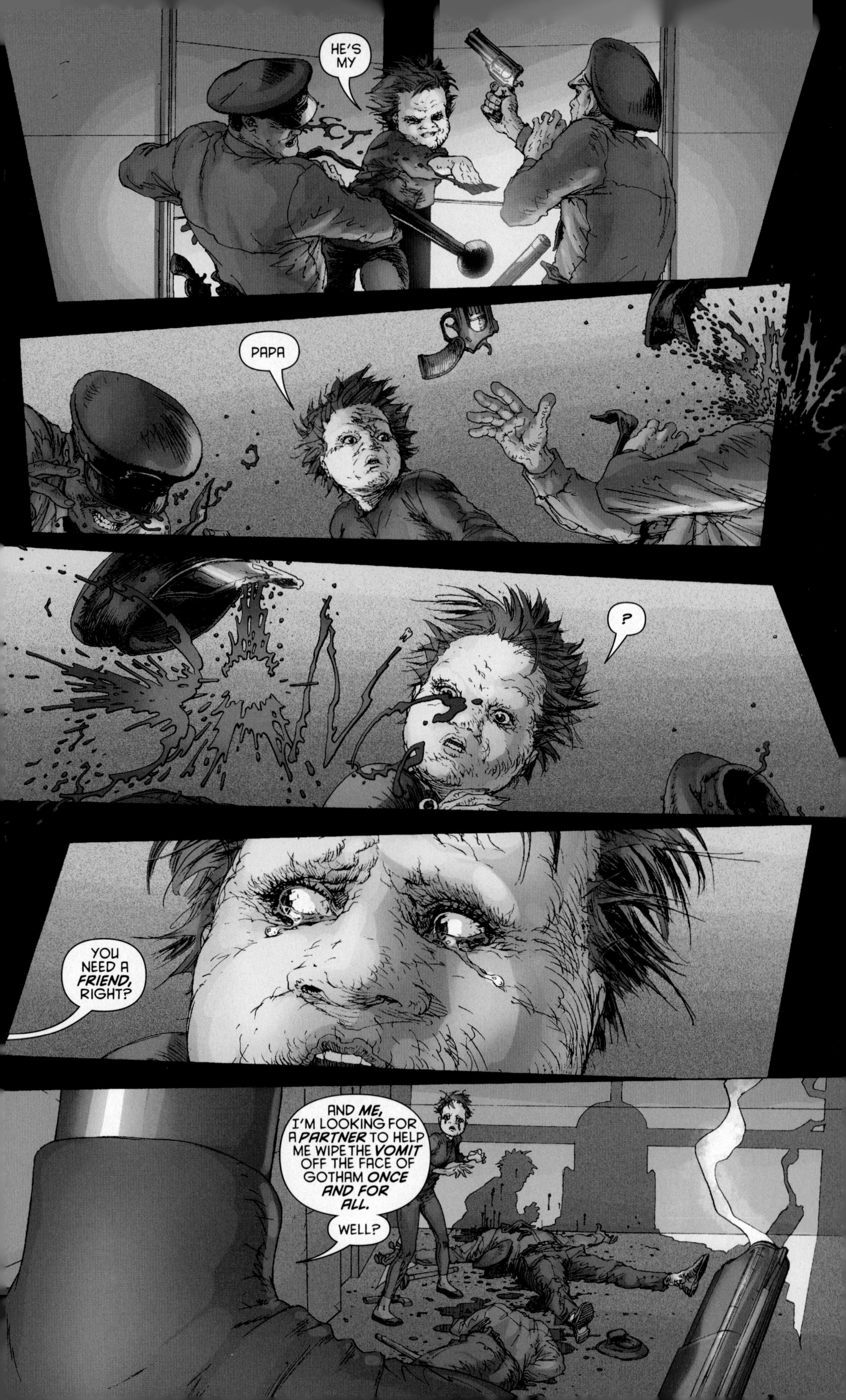
HE'S MY
PAPA
?
YOU NEED A *FRIEND,* RIGHT?
AND *ME,* I'M LOOKING FOR A *PARTNER* TO HELP ME WIPE THE *VOMIT* OFF THE FACE OF GOTHAM *ONCE AND FOR ALL.*
WELL?

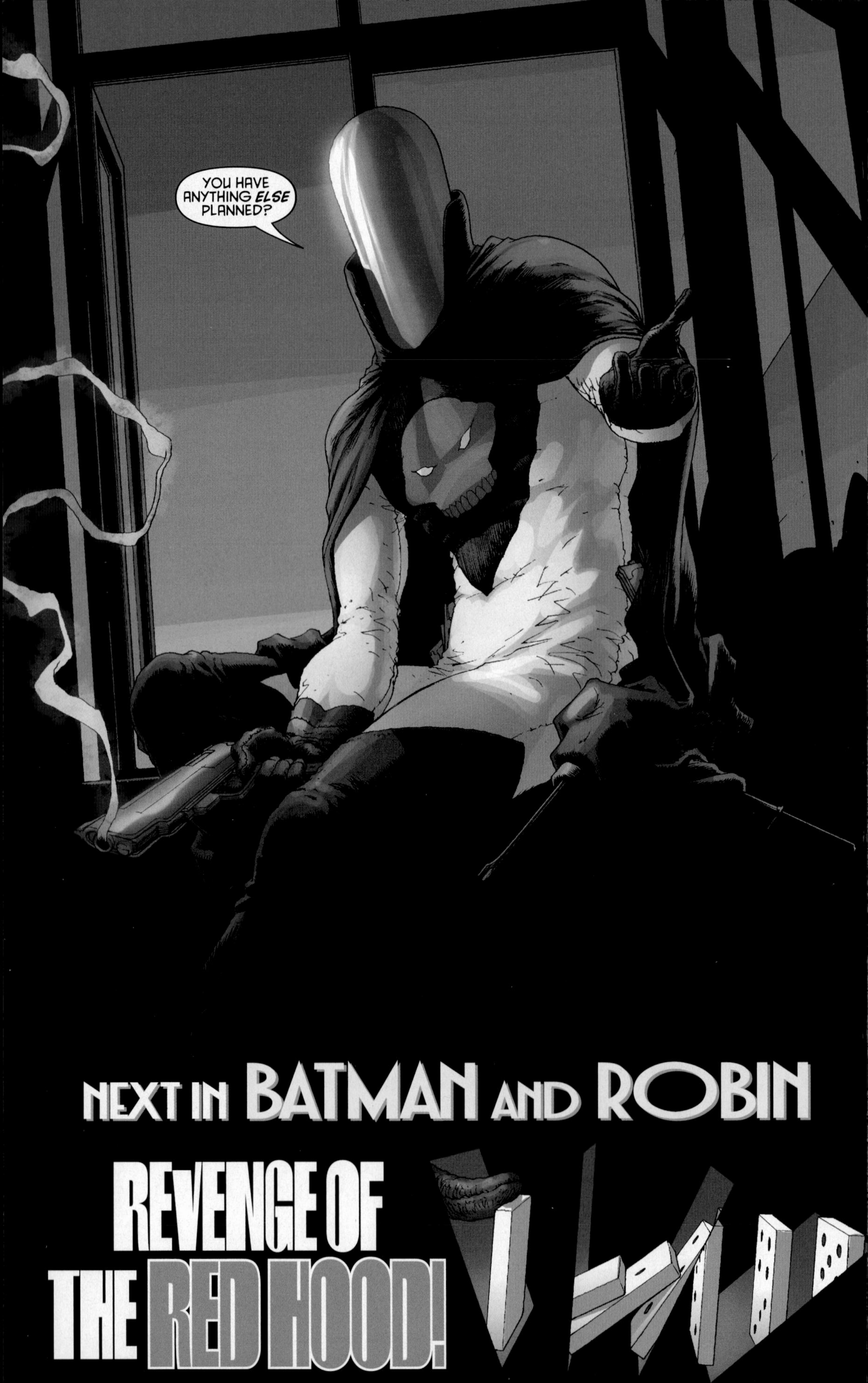

YOU HAVE ANYTHING ELSE PLANNED?
NEXT IN BATMAN AND ROBIN
REVENGE OF THE RED HOOD!

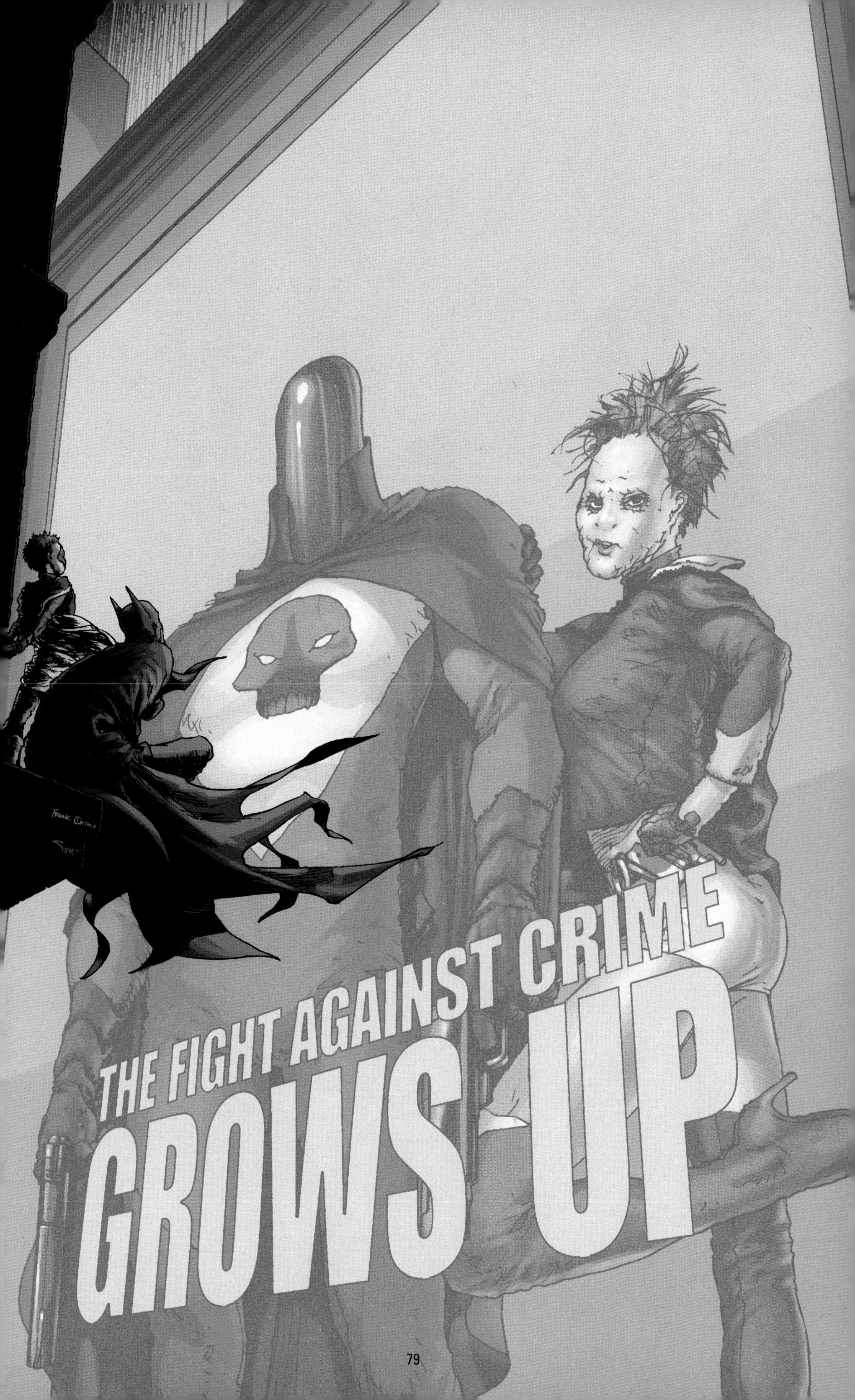
THE FIGHT AGAINST CRIME
GROWS UP

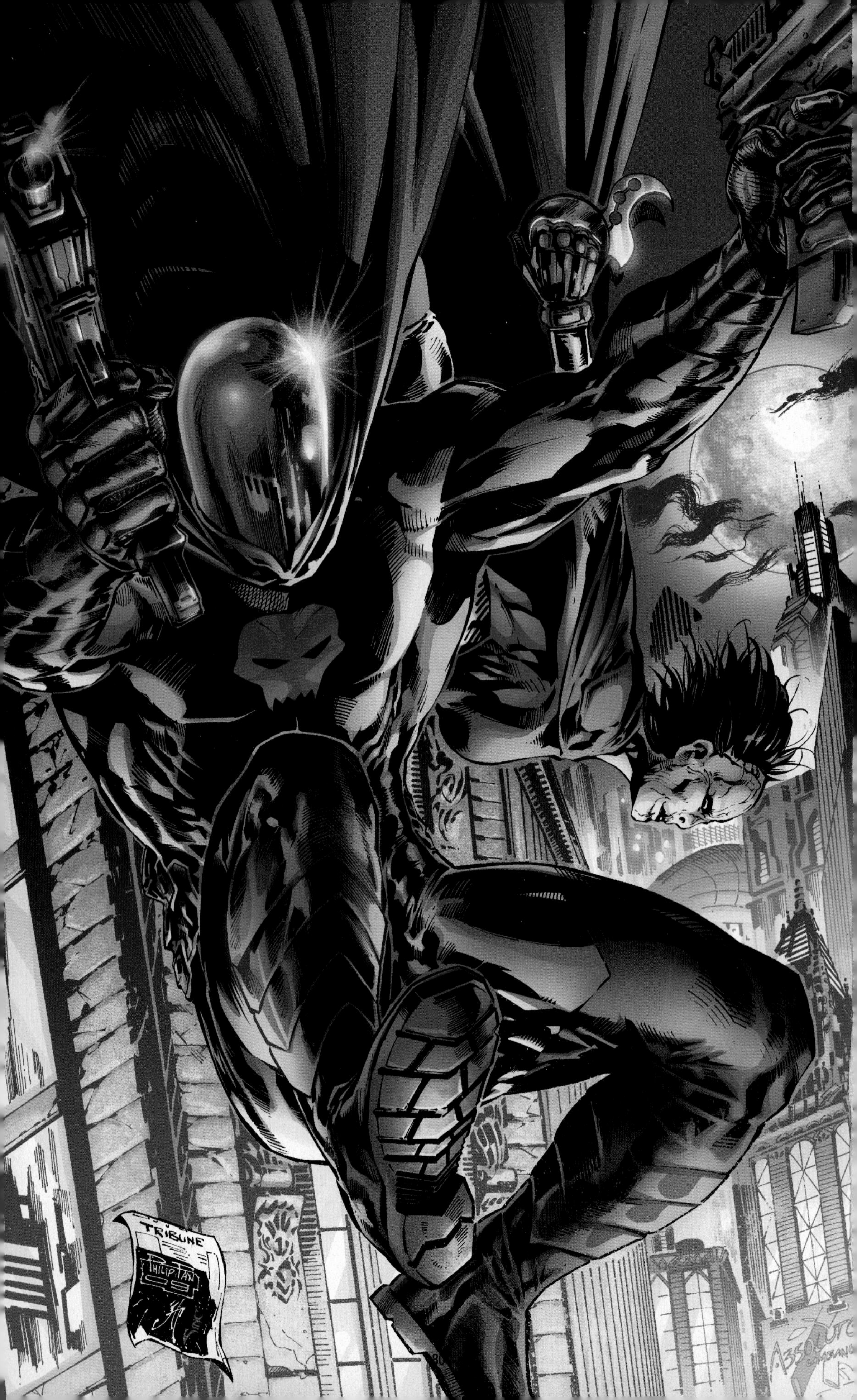
TRIBUNE
PHILIP TAN

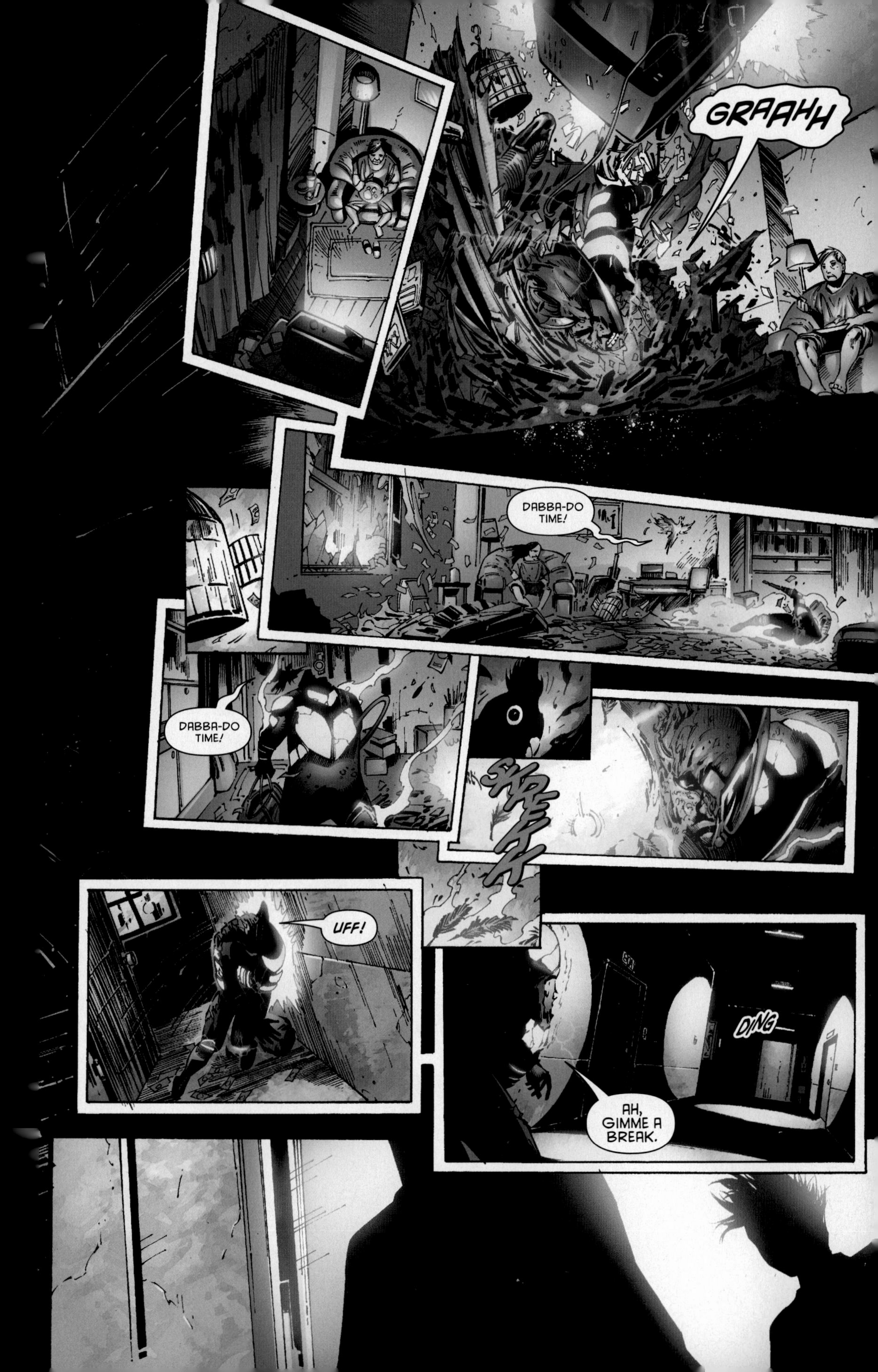
GRAAHH
DABBA-DO TIME!
DABBA-DO TIME!
SKREEK
UFF!
DING
AH, GIMME A BREAK.

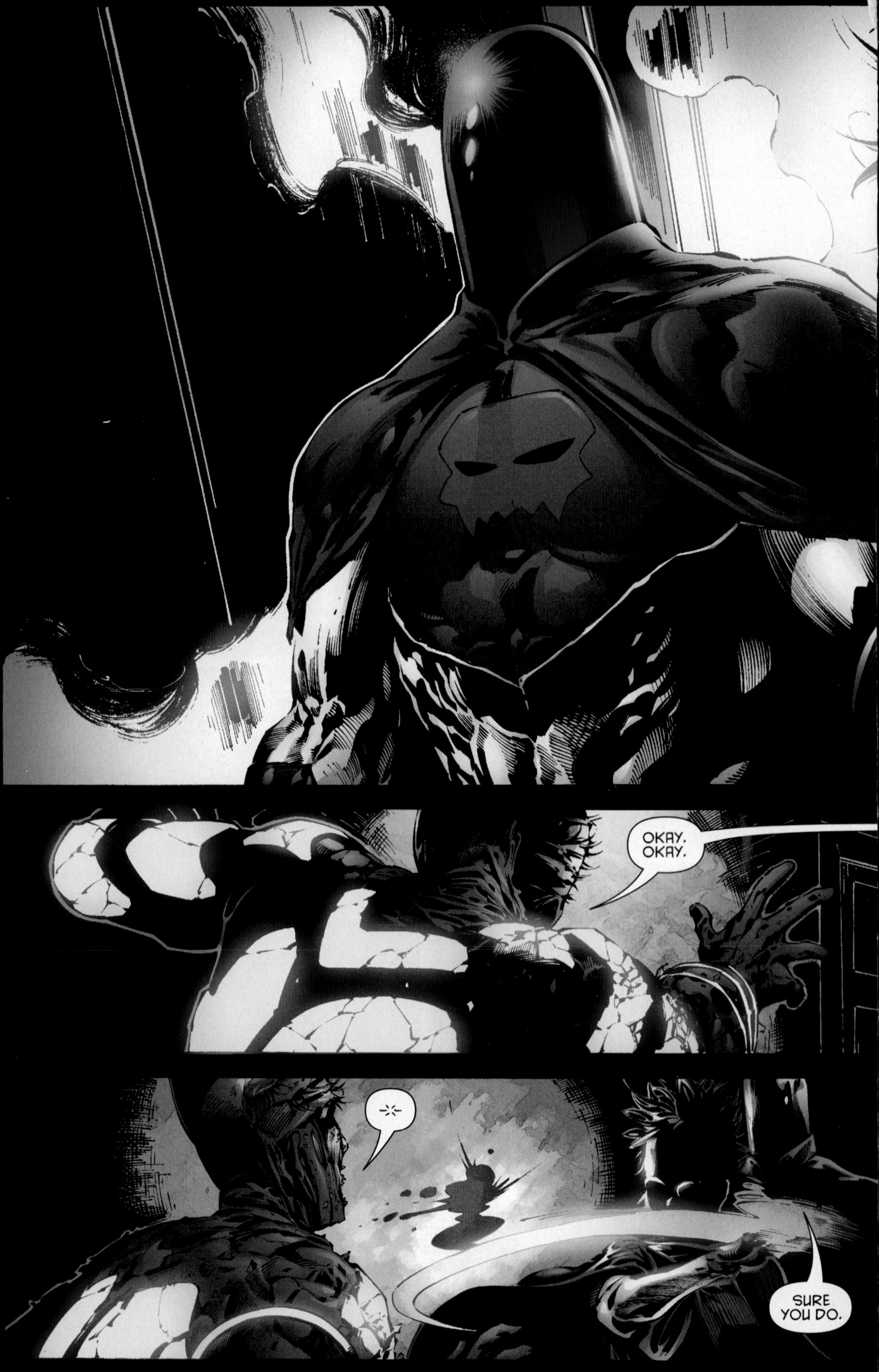
OKAY. OKAY.
...!
SURE YOU DO.

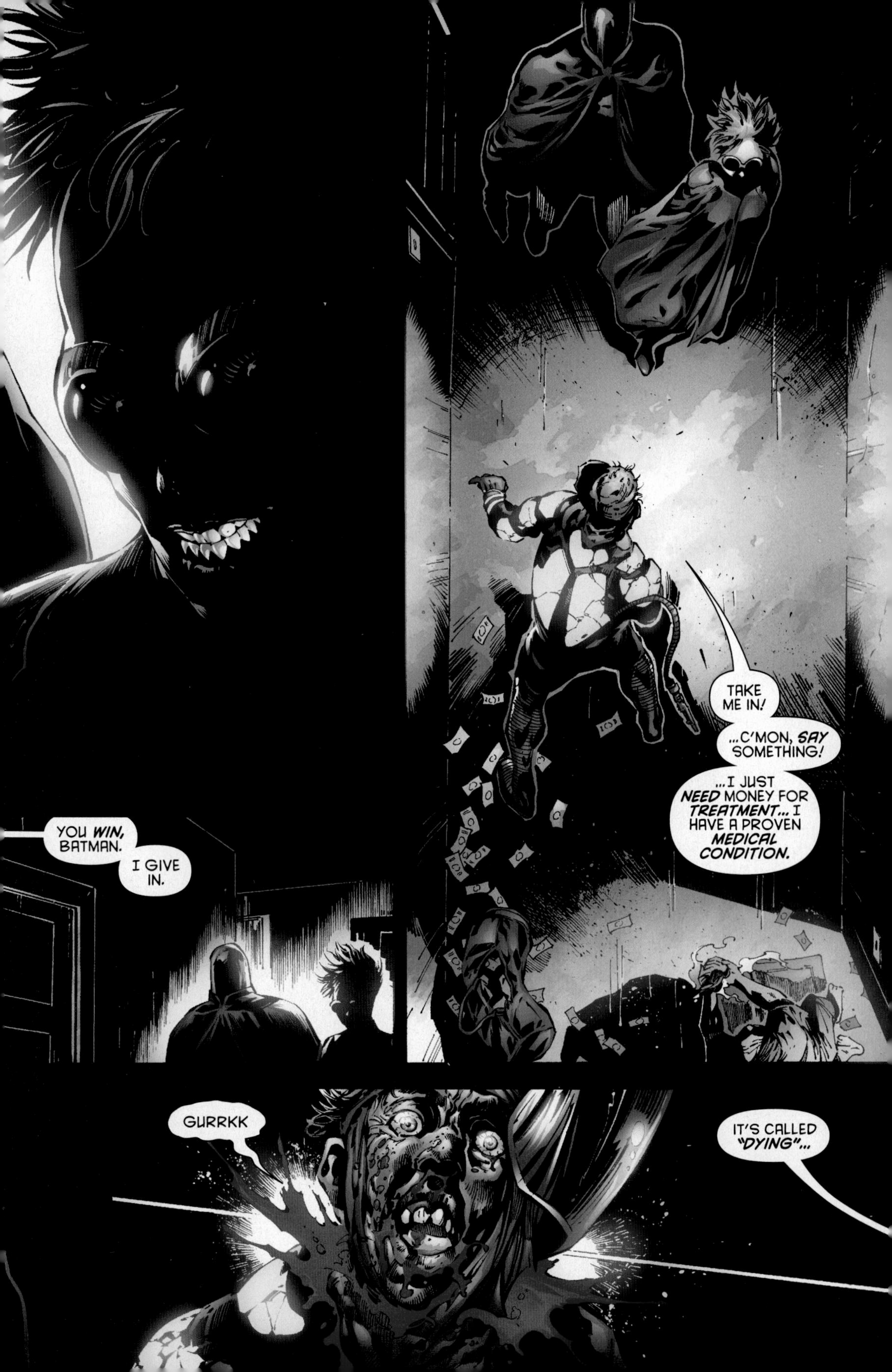
TAKE ME IN!
...C'MON, SAY SOMETHING!
...I JUST NEED MONEY FOR TREATMENT... I HAVE A PROVEN MEDICAL CONDITION.
YOU WIN, BATMAN.
I GIVE IN.
GURRKK
IT'S CALLED "DYING"...

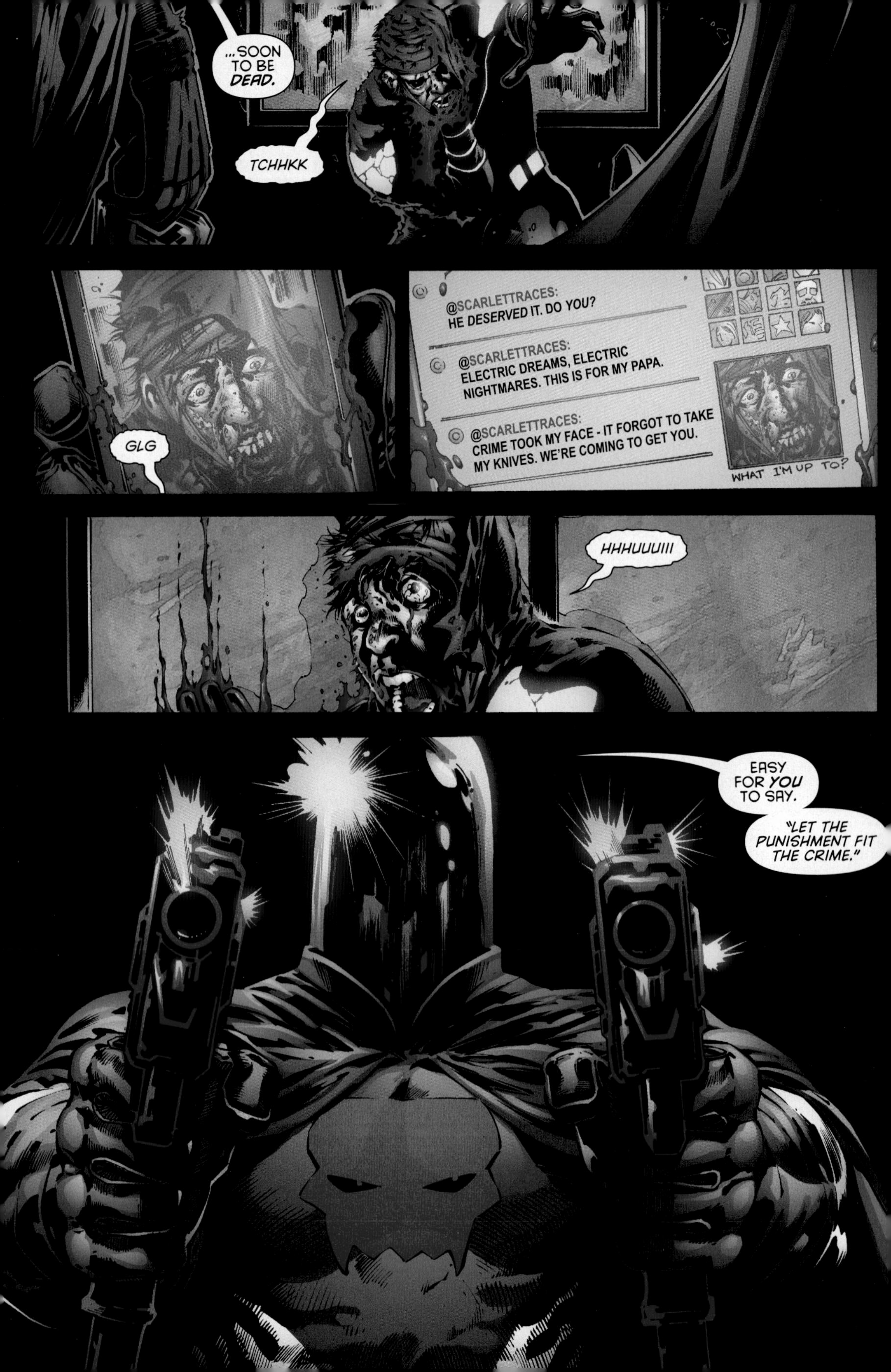

...SOON TO BE DEAD.
TCHHKK
GLG
@SCARLETTRACES: HE DESERVED IT. DO YOU?
@SCARLETTRACES: ELECTRIC DREAMS, ELECTRIC NIGHTMARES. THIS IS FOR MY PAPA.
@SCARLETTRACES: CRIME TOOK MY FACE - IT FORGOT TO TAKE MY KNIVES. WE'RE COMING TO GET YOU.
WHAT I'M UP TO?
HHHUUUIII
EASY FOR YOU TO SAY.
"LET THE PUNISHMENT FIT THE CRIME."

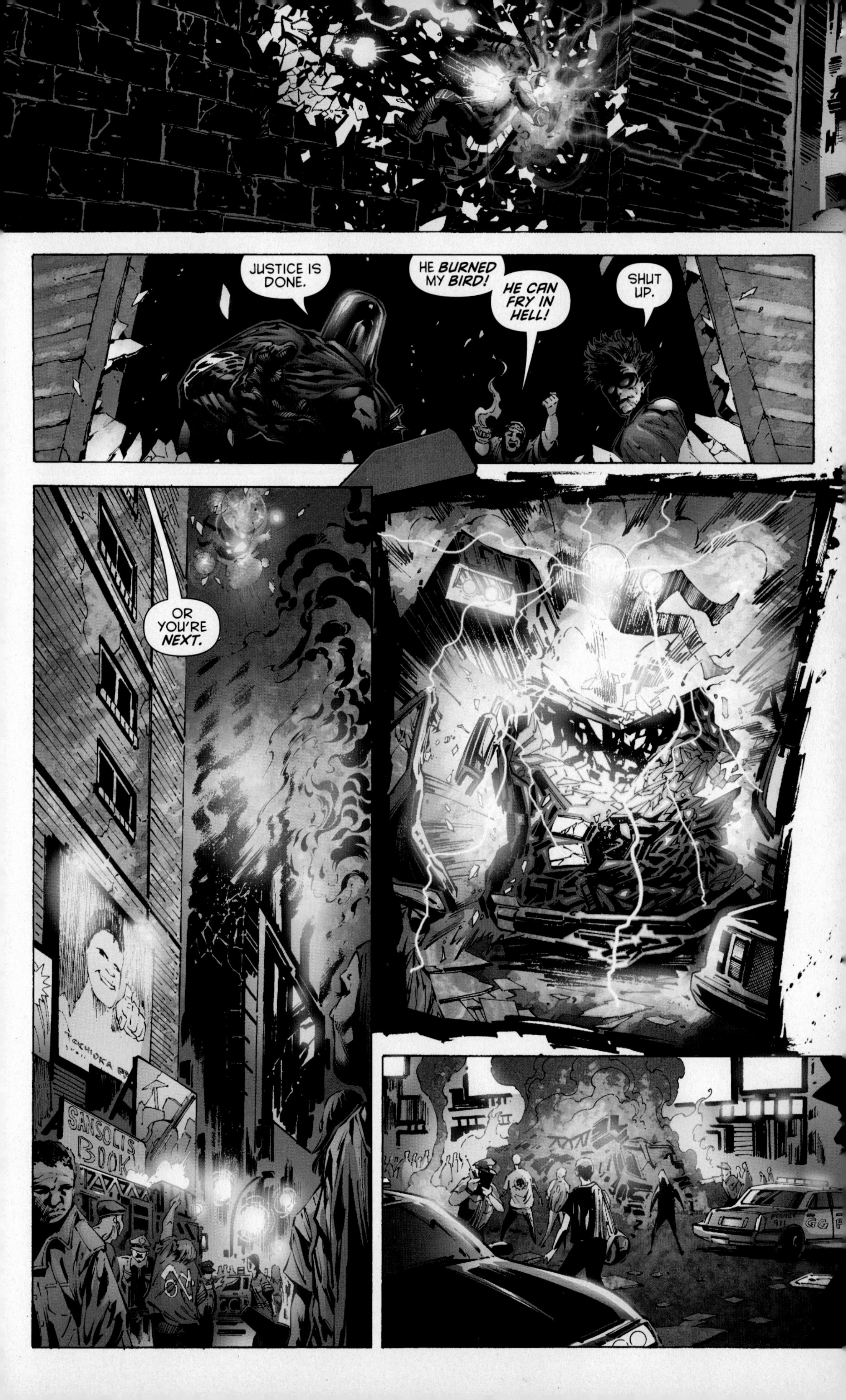
JUSTICE IS DONE.
HE BURNED MY BIRD!
HE CAN FRY IN HELL!
SHUT UP.
OR YOU'RE NEXT.
SANSOLIS BOOK

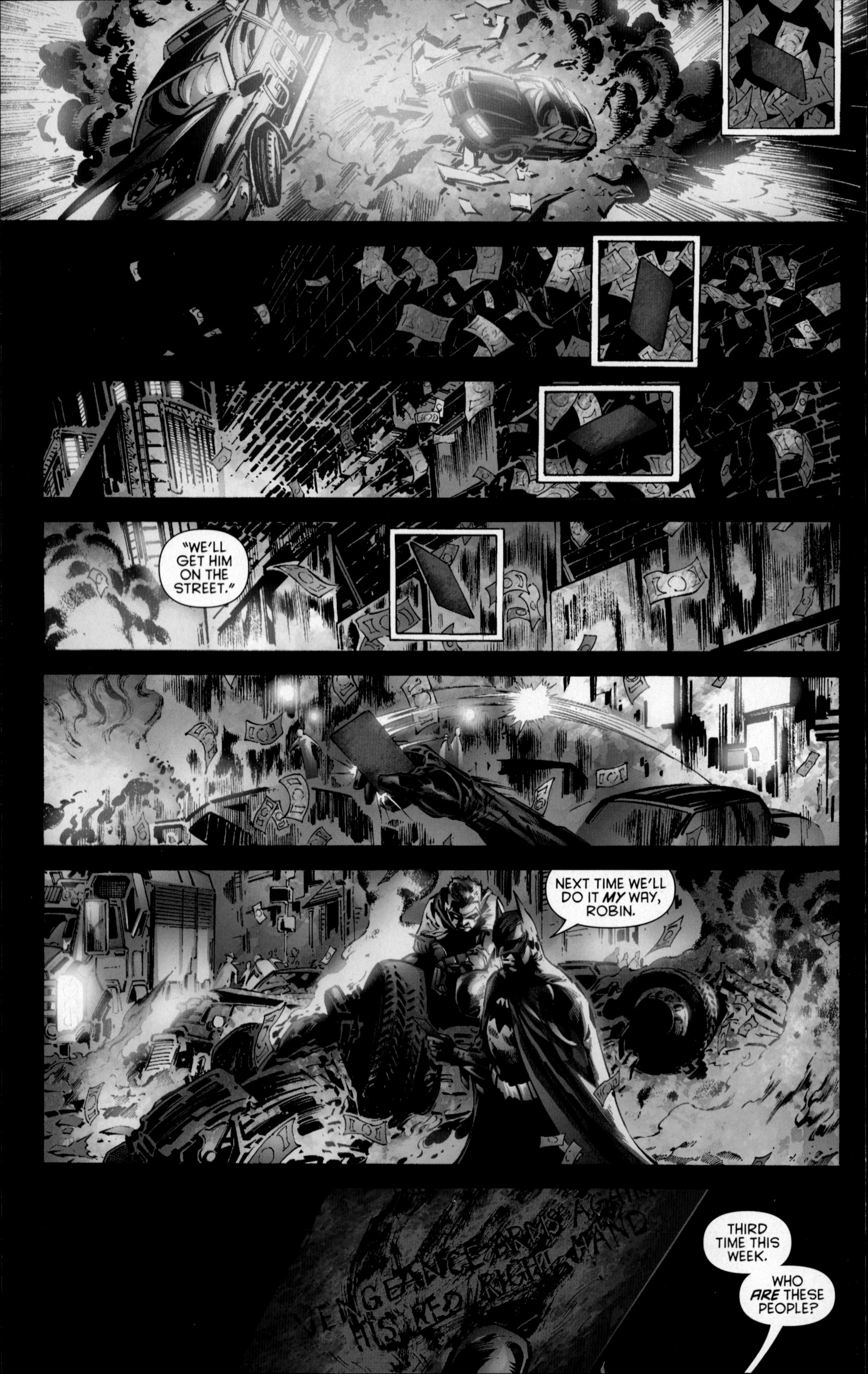
"WE'LL GET HIM ON THE STREET."
NEXT TIME WE'LL DO IT *MY* WAY, ROBIN.
THIRD TIME THIS WEEK.
WHO *ARE* THESE PEOPLE?

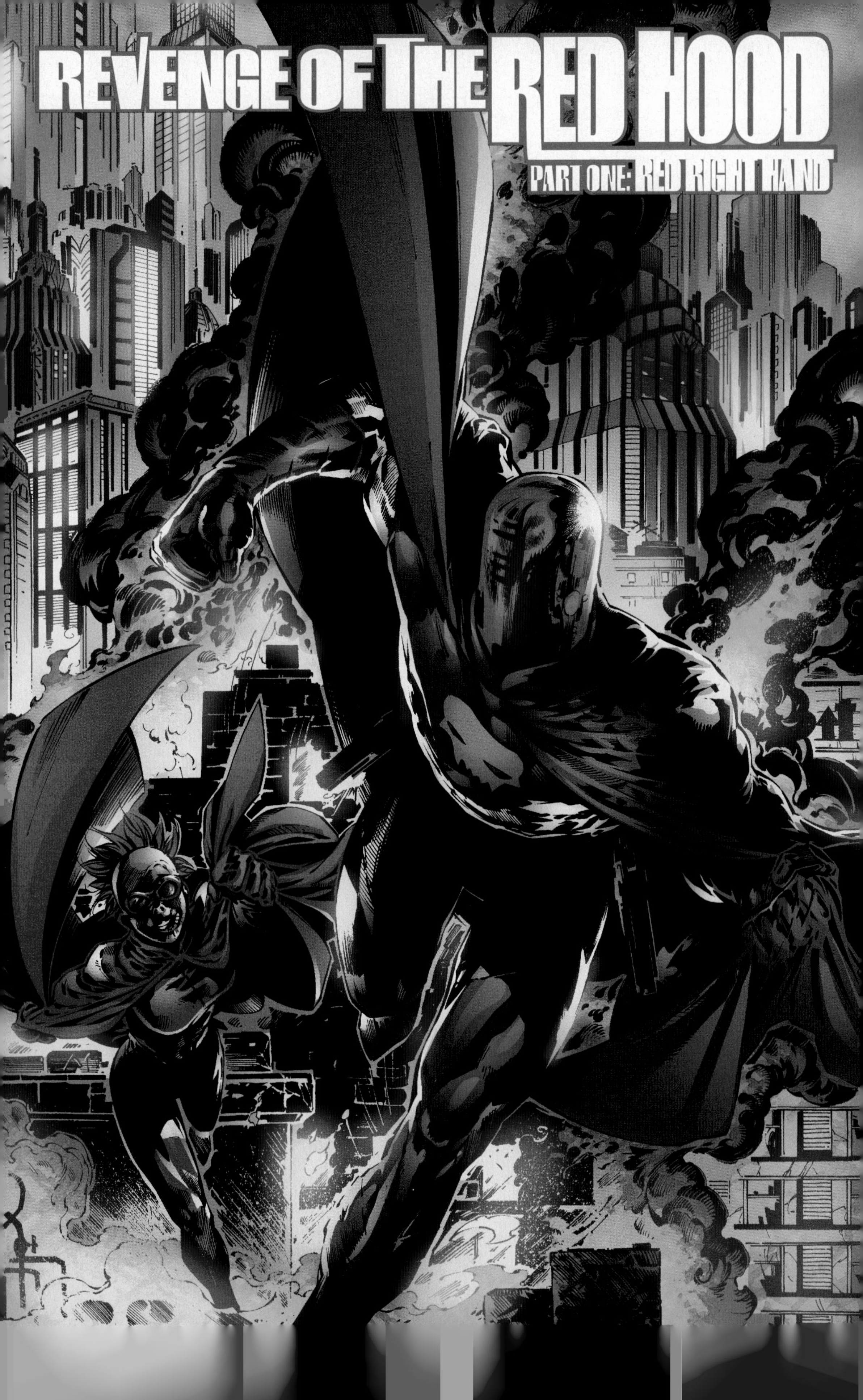
REVENGE OF THE RED HOOD
PART ONE: RED RIGHT HAND

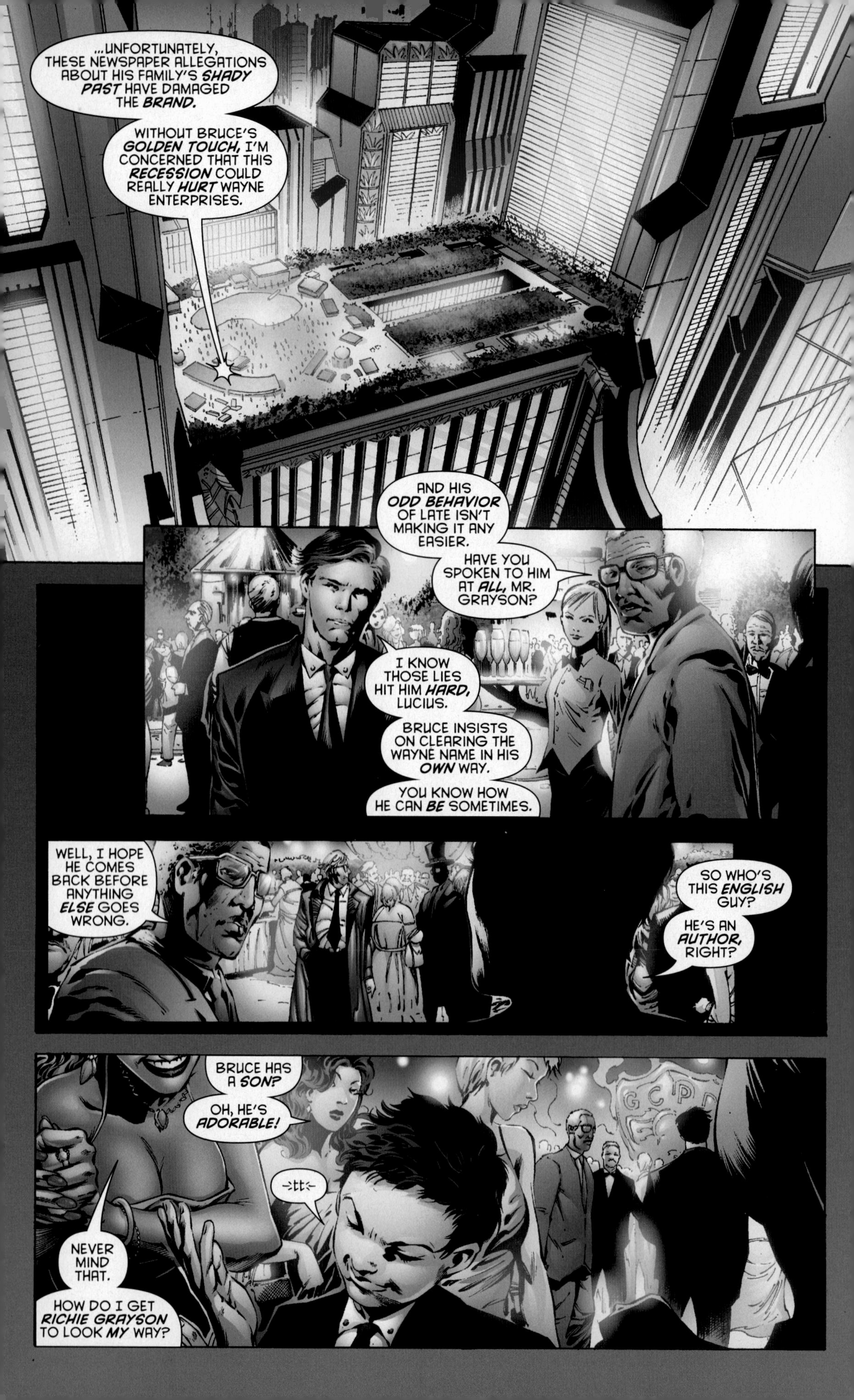
...UNFORTUNATELY, THESE NEWSPAPER ALLEGATIONS ABOUT HIS FAMILY'S SHADY PAST HAVE DAMAGED THE BRAND.
WITHOUT BRUCE'S GOLDEN TOUCH, I'M CONCERNED THAT THIS RECESSION COULD REALLY HURT WAYNE ENTERPRISES.
AND HIS ODD BEHAVIOR OF LATE ISN'T MAKING IT ANY EASIER.
HAVE YOU SPOKEN TO HIM AT ALL, MR. GRAYSON?
I KNOW THOSE LIES HIT HIM HARD, LUCIUS.
BRUCE INSISTS ON CLEARING THE WAYNE NAME IN HIS OWN WAY.
YOU KNOW HOW HE CAN BE SOMETIMES.
WELL, I HOPE HE COMES BACK BEFORE ANYTHING ELSE GOES WRONG.
SO WHO'S THIS ENGLISH GUY?
HE'S AN AUTHOR, RIGHT?
BRUCE HAS A SON?
OH, HE'S ADORABLE!
-tt-
NEVER MIND THAT.
HOW DO I GET RICHIE GRAYSON TO LOOK MY WAY?
GCPD

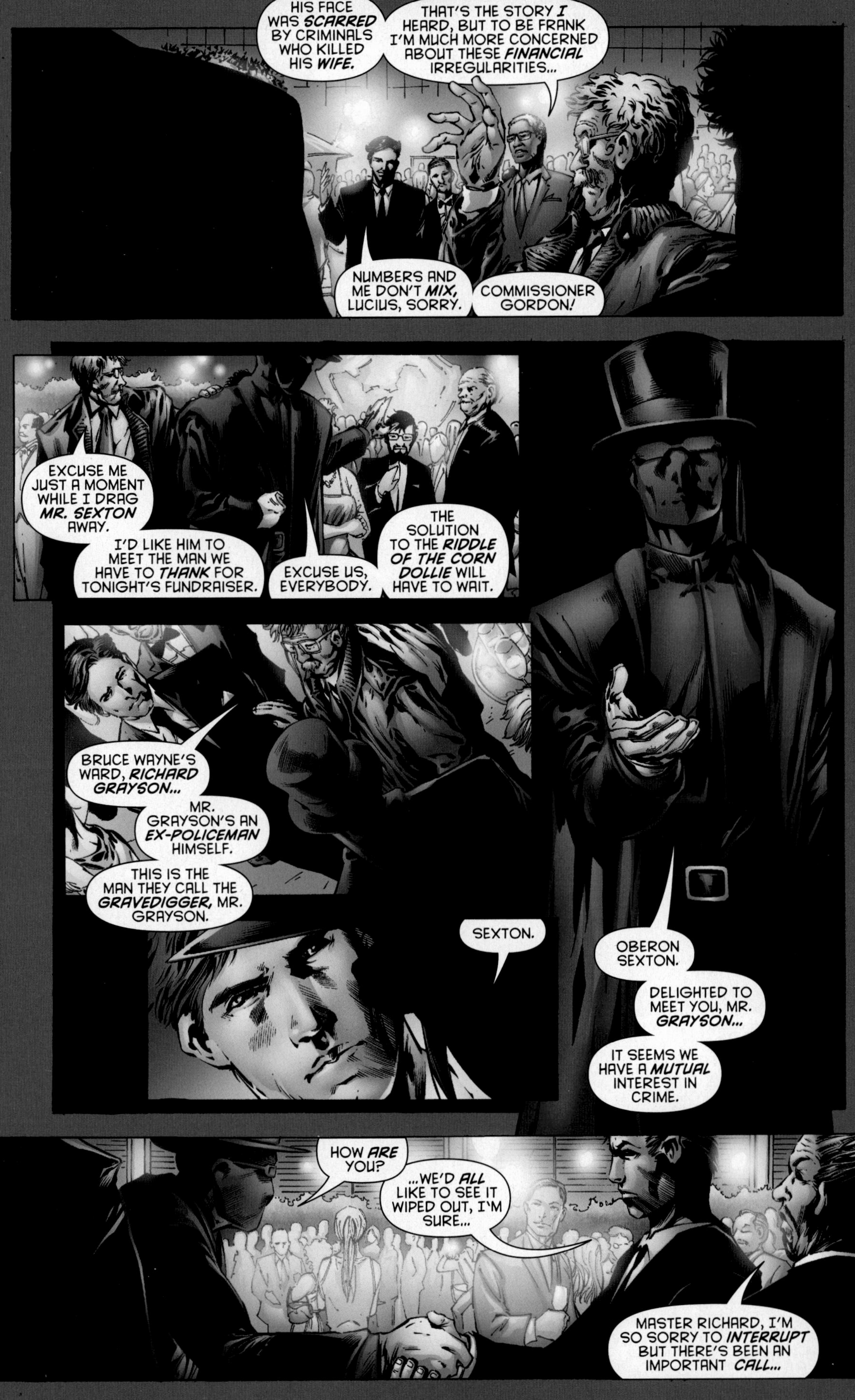

HIS FACE WAS SCARRED BY CRIMINALS WHO KILLED HIS WIFE.
THAT'S THE STORY I HEARD, BUT TO BE FRANK I'M MUCH MORE CONCERNED ABOUT THESE FINANCIAL IRREGULARITIES...
NUMBERS AND ME DON'T MIX, LUCIUS, SORRY.
COMMISSIONER GORDON!
EXCUSE ME JUST A MOMENT WHILE I DRAG MR. SEXTON AWAY.
I'D LIKE HIM TO MEET THE MAN WE HAVE TO THANK FOR TONIGHT'S FUNDRAISER.
EXCUSE US, EVERYBODY.
THE SOLUTION TO THE RIDDLE OF THE CORN DOLLIE WILL HAVE TO WAIT.
BRUCE WAYNE'S WARD, RICHARD GRAYSON...
MR. GRAYSON'S AN EX-POLICEMAN HIMSELF.
THIS IS THE MAN THEY CALL THE GRAVEDIGGER, MR. GRAYSON.
SEXTON.
OBERON SEXTON.
DELIGHTED TO MEET YOU, MR. GRAYSON...
IT SEEMS WE HAVE A MUTUAL INTEREST IN CRIME.
HOW ARE YOU?
...WE'D ALL LIKE TO SEE IT WIPED OUT, I'M SURE...
MASTER RICHARD, I'M SO SORRY TO INTERRUPT BUT THERE'S BEEN AN IMPORTANT CALL...

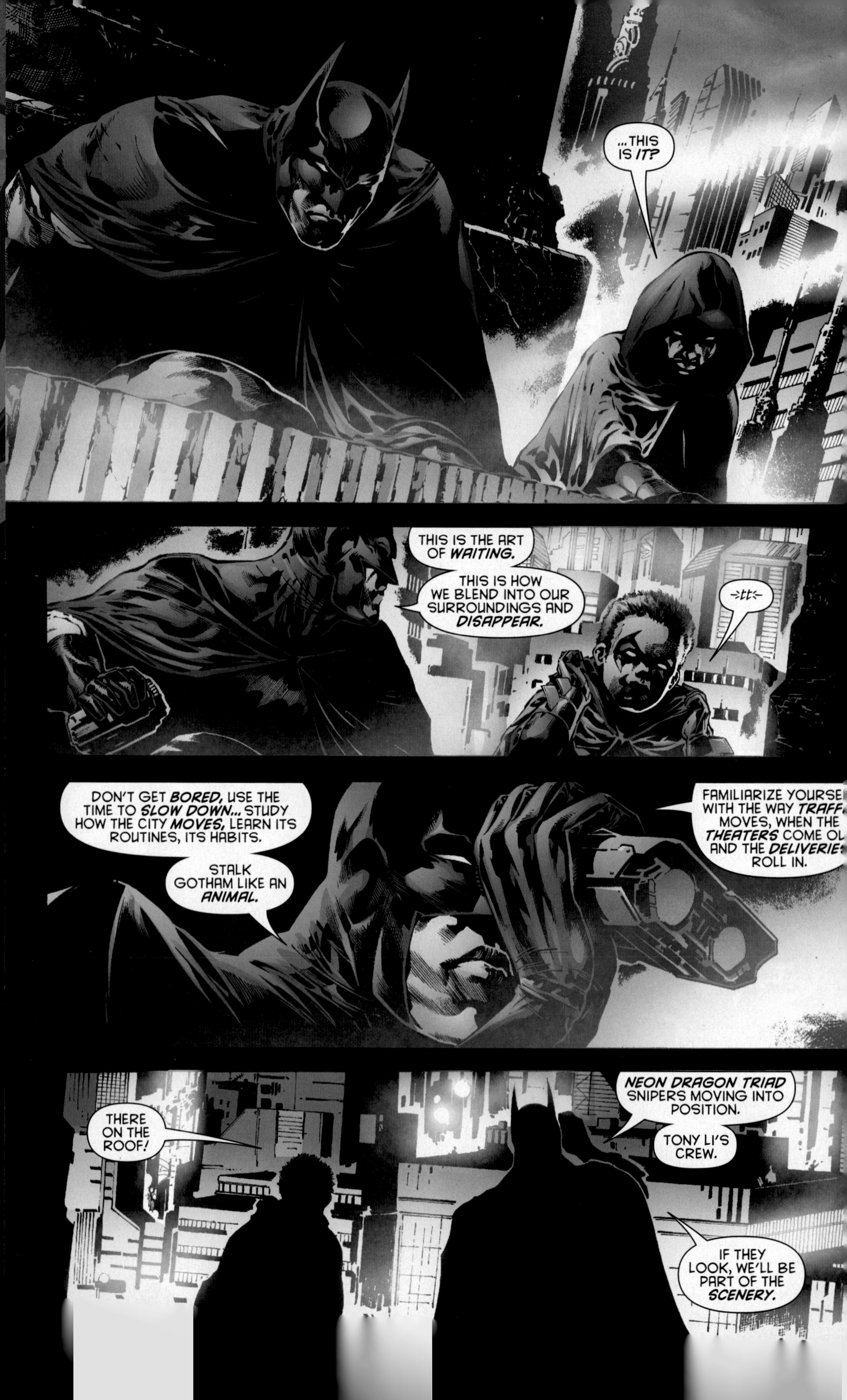
...THIS IS IT?
THIS IS THE ART OF WAITING.
THIS IS HOW WE BLEND INTO OUR SURROUNDINGS AND DISAPPEAR.
-TT-
DON'T GET BORED, USE THE TIME TO SLOW DOWN... STUDY HOW THE CITY MOVES, LEARN ITS ROUTINES, ITS HABITS.
STALK GOTHAM LIKE AN ANIMAL.
FAMILIARIZE YOURSE WITH THE WAY TRAFF MOVES, WHEN THE THEATERS COME OU AND THE DELIVERIE ROLL IN.
THERE ON THE ROOF!
NEON DRAGON TRIAD SNIPERS MOVING INTO POSITION.
TONY LI'S CREW.
IF THEY LOOK, WE'LL BE PART OF THE SCENERY.

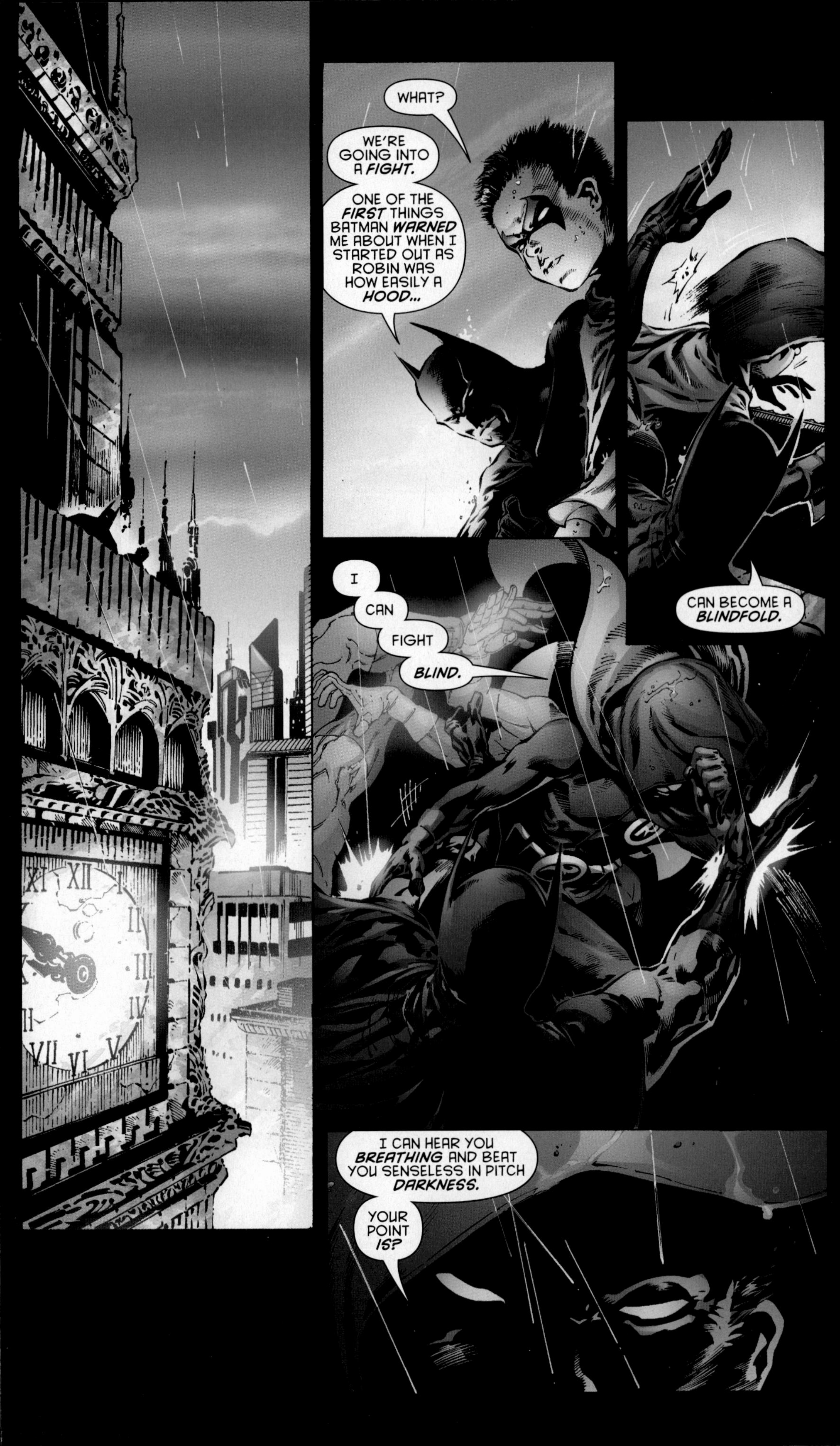
WHAT?
WE'RE GOING INTO A FIGHT.
ONE OF THE FIRST THINGS BATMAN WARNED ME ABOUT WHEN I STARTED OUT AS ROBIN WAS HOW EASILY A HOOD...
CAN BECOME A BLINDFOLD.
I CAN FIGHT BLIND.
I CAN HEAR YOU BREATHING AND BEAT YOU SENSELESS IN PITCH DARKNESS.
YOUR POINT IS?

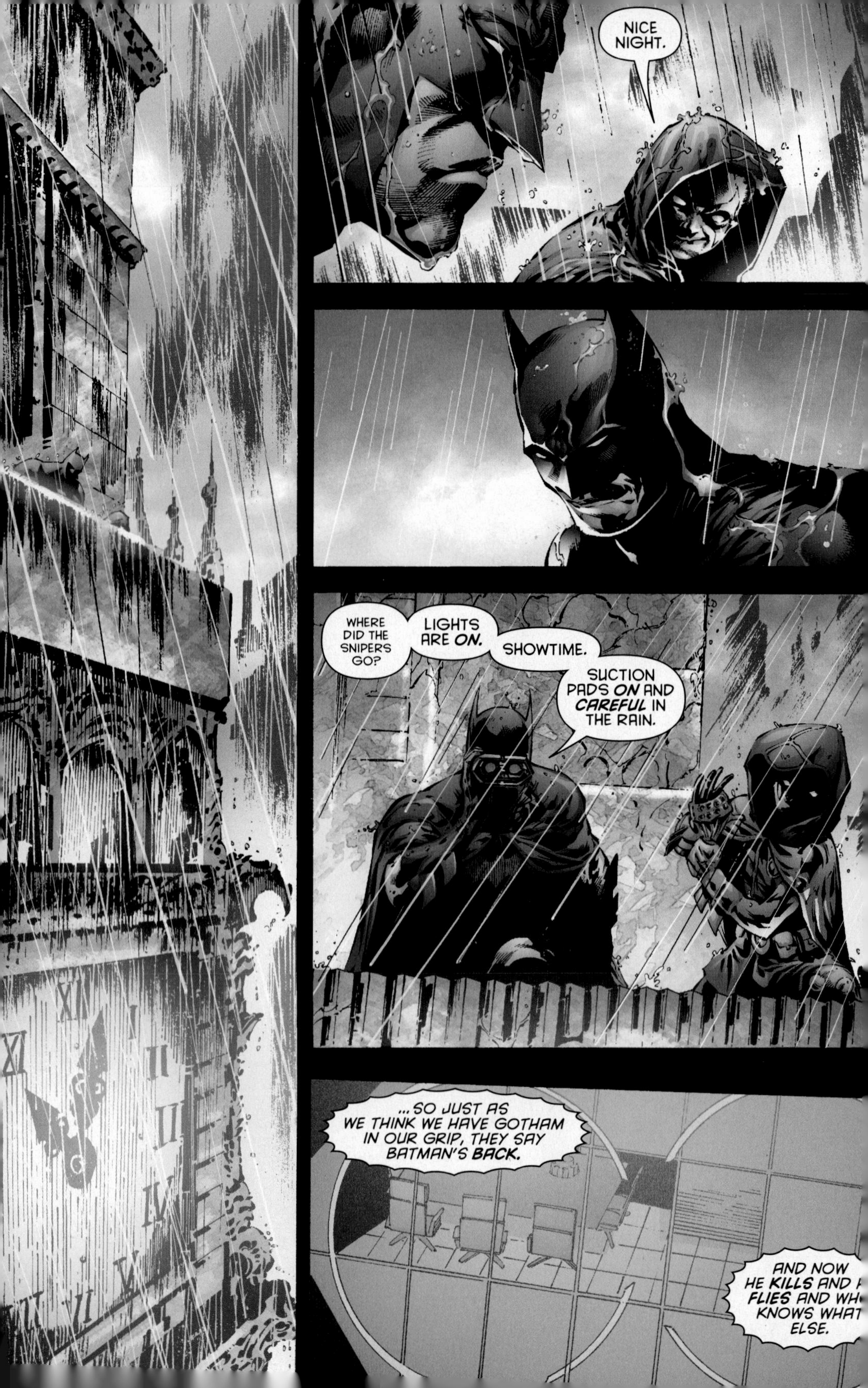
NICE NIGHT.
WHERE DID THE SNIPERS GO?
LIGHTS ARE ON.
SHOWTIME.
SUCTION PADS ON AND CAREFUL IN THE RAIN.
...SO JUST AS WE THINK WE HAVE GOTHAM IN OUR GRIP, THEY SAY BATMAN'S BACK.
AND NOW HE KILLS AND FLIES AND WH KNOWS WHAT ELSE.

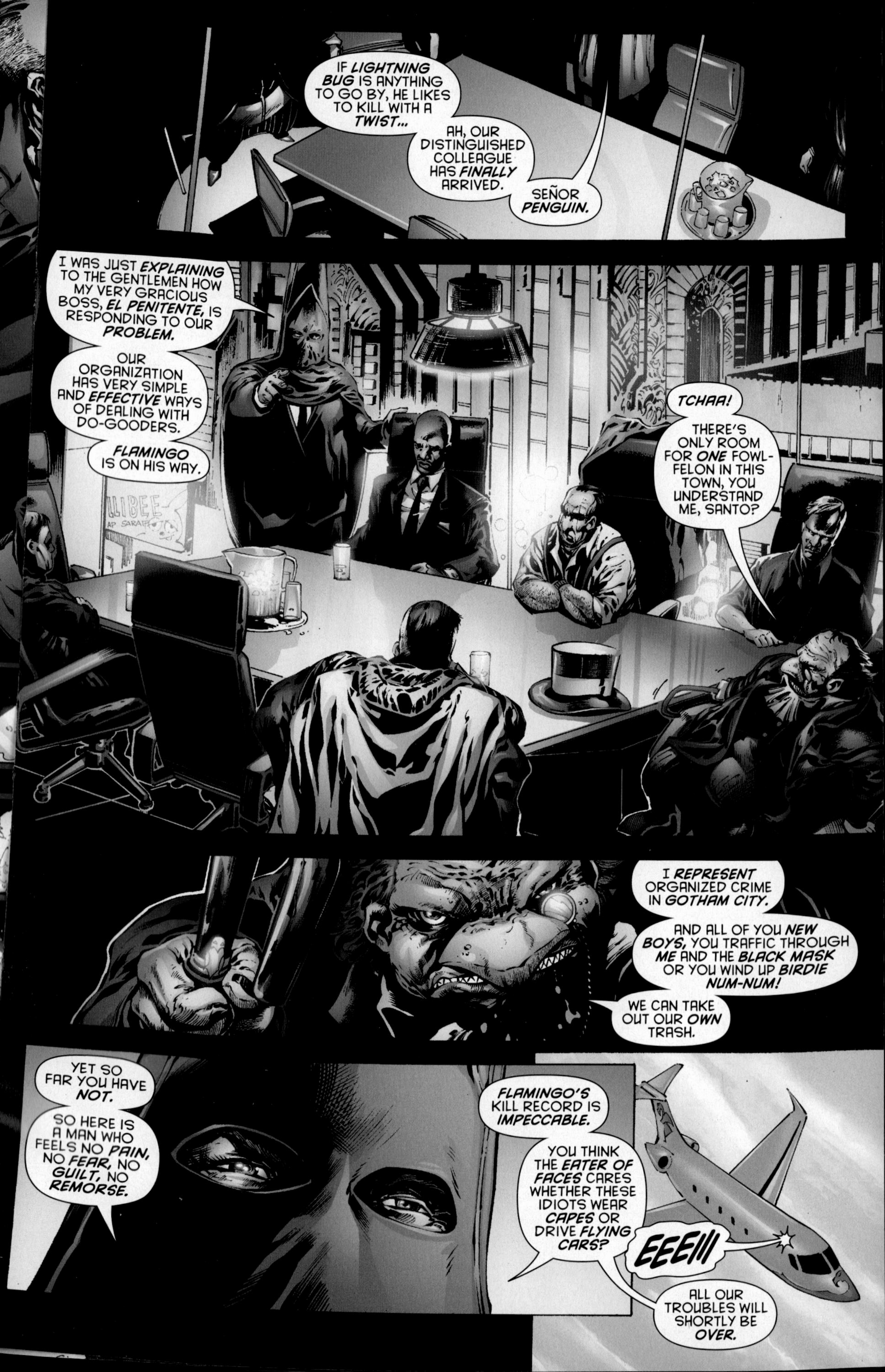
IF LIGHTNING BUG IS ANYTHING TO GO BY, HE LIKES TO KILL WITH A TWIST...
AH, OUR DISTINGUISHED COLLEAGUE HAS FINALLY ARRIVED.
SEÑOR PENGUIN.
I WAS JUST EXPLAINING TO THE GENTLEMEN HOW MY VERY GRACIOUS BOSS, EL PENITENTE, IS RESPONDING TO OUR PROBLEM.
OUR ORGANIZATION HAS VERY SIMPLE AND EFFECTIVE WAYS OF DEALING WITH DO-GOODERS.
FLAMINGO IS ON HIS WAY.
TCHAA!
THERE'S ONLY ROOM FOR ONE FOWL-FELON IN THIS TOWN, YOU UNDERSTAND ME, SANTO?
I REPRESENT ORGANIZED CRIME IN GOTHAM CITY.
AND ALL OF YOU NEW BOYS, YOU TRAFFIC THROUGH ME AND THE BLACK MASK OR YOU WIND UP BIRDIE NUM-NUM!
WE CAN TAKE OUT OUR OWN TRASH.
YET SO FAR YOU HAVE NOT.
SO HERE IS A MAN WHO FEELS NO PAIN, NO FEAR, NO GUILT, NO REMORSE.
FLAMINGO'S KILL RECORD IS IMPECCABLE.
YOU THINK THE EATER OF FACES CARES WHETHER THESE IDIOTS WEAR CAPES OR DRIVE FLYING CARS?
EEEIII
ALL OUR TROUBLES WILL SHORTLY BE OVER.

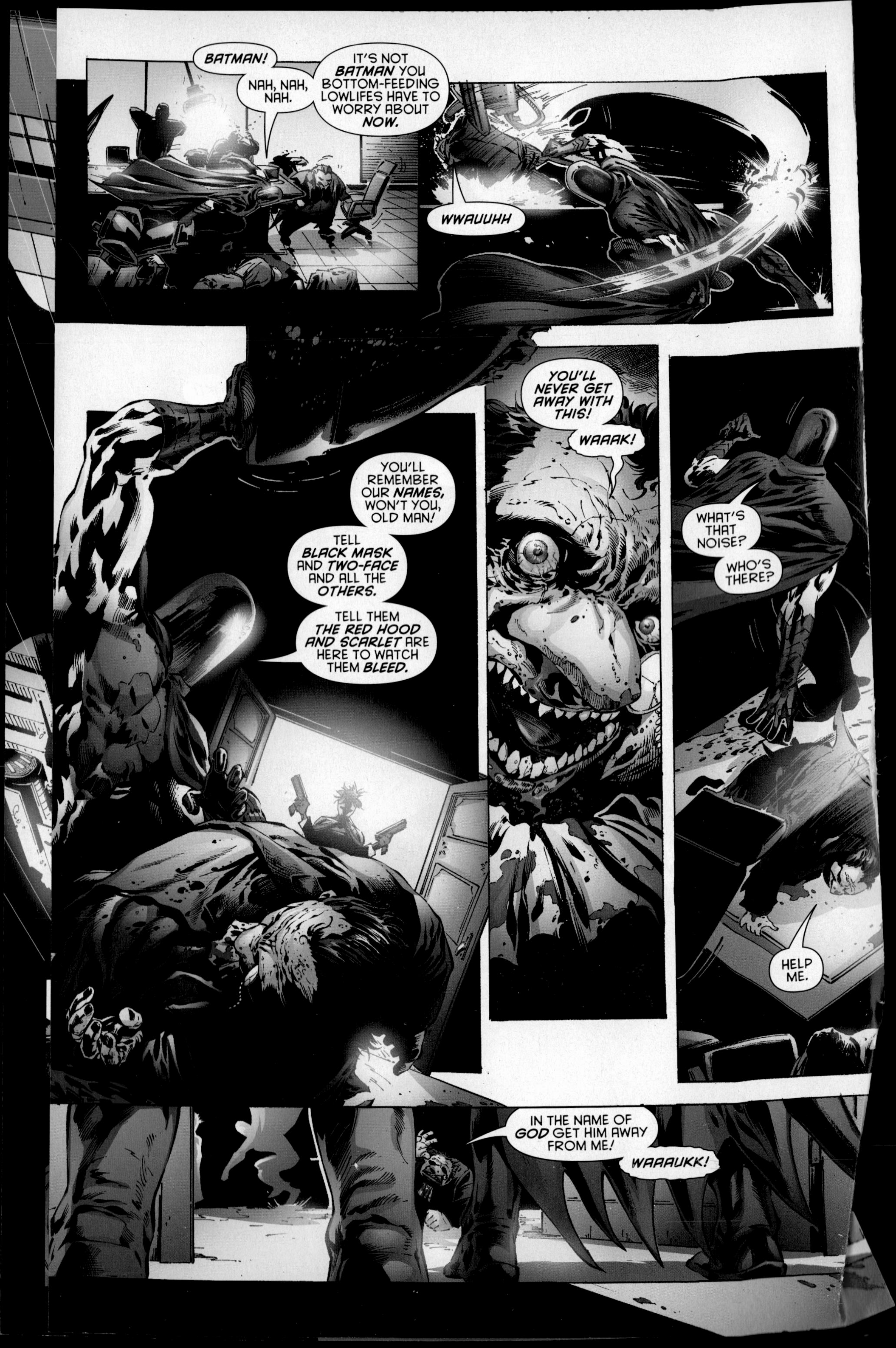
BATMAN!
NAH, NAH, NAH.
IT'S NOT BATMAN YOU BOTTOM-FEEDING LOWLIFES HAVE TO WORRY ABOUT NOW.
WWAUUHH
YOU'LL REMEMBER OUR NAMES, WON'T YOU, OLD MAN!
TELL BLACK MASK AND TWO-FACE AND ALL THE OTHERS.
TELL THEM THE RED HOOD AND SCARLET ARE HERE TO WATCH THEM BLEED.
YOU'LL NEVER GET AWAY WITH THIS!
WAAAK!
WHAT'S THAT NOISE?
WHO'S THERE?
HELP ME.
IN THE NAME OF GOD GET HIM AWAY FROM ME!
WARAUKK!

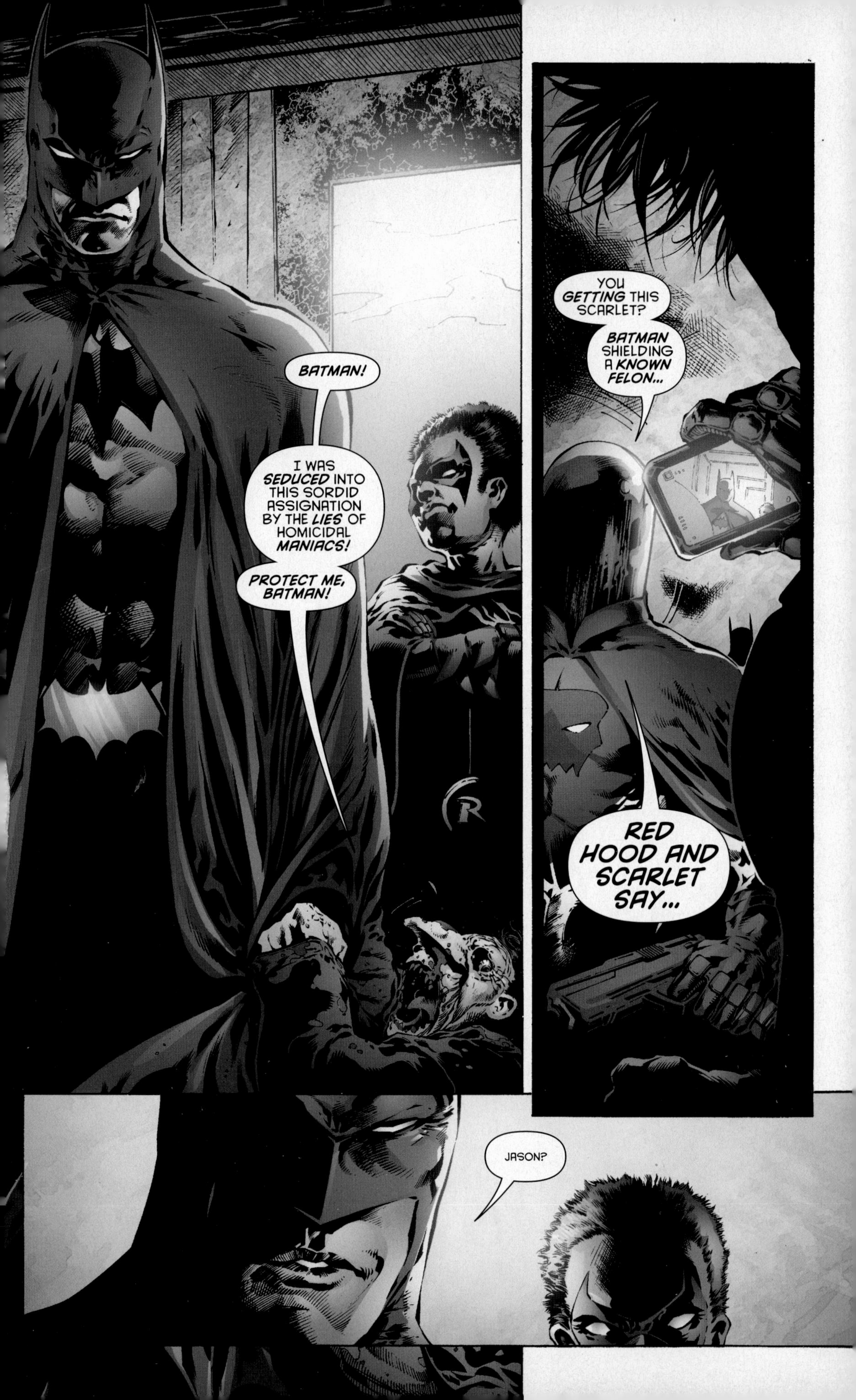
BATMAN!
I WAS SEDUCED INTO THIS SORDID ASSIGNATION BY THE LIES OF HOMICIDAL MANIACS!
PROTECT ME, BATMAN!
YOU GETTING THIS SCARLET?
BATMAN SHIELDING A KNOWN FELON...
RED HOOD AND SCARLET SAY...
JASON?

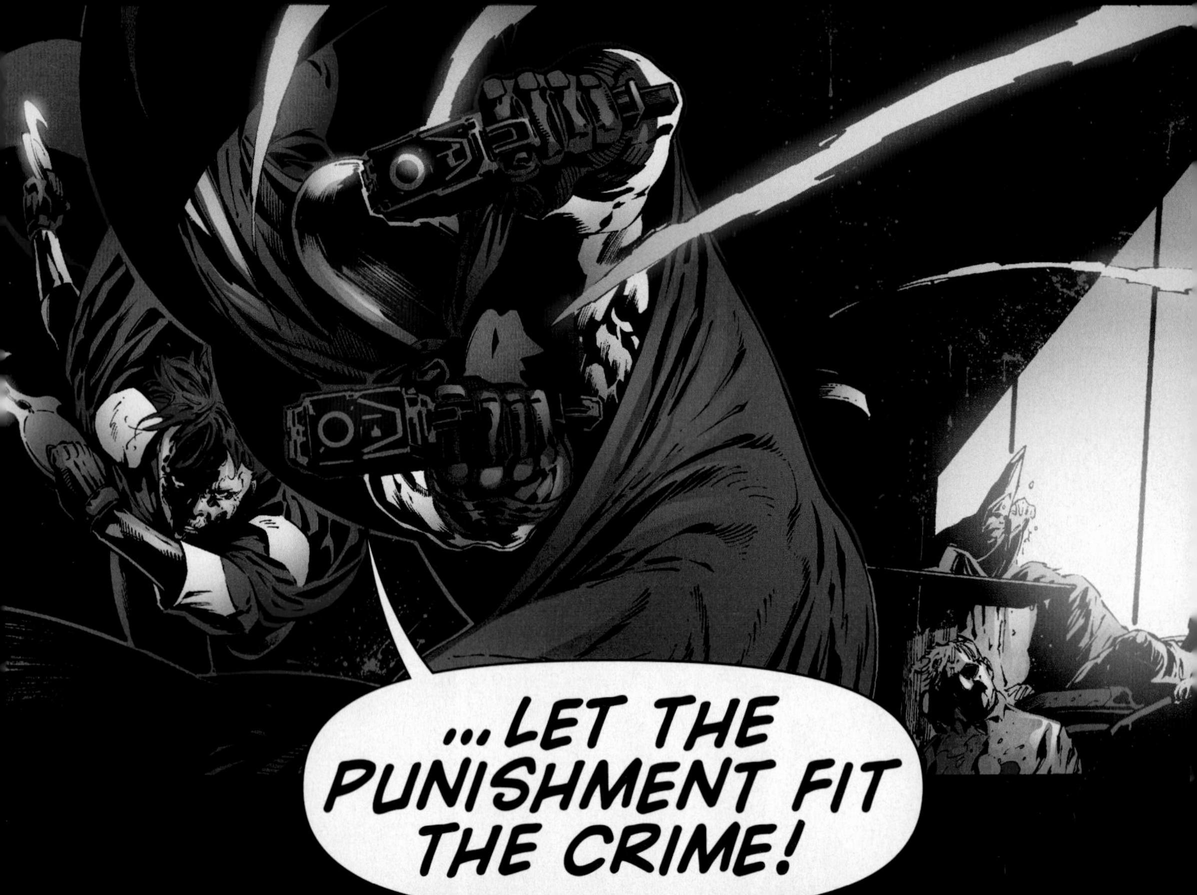
...LET THE PUNISHMENT FIT THE CRIME!

NEXT IN BATMAN AND ROBIN

SCARLET

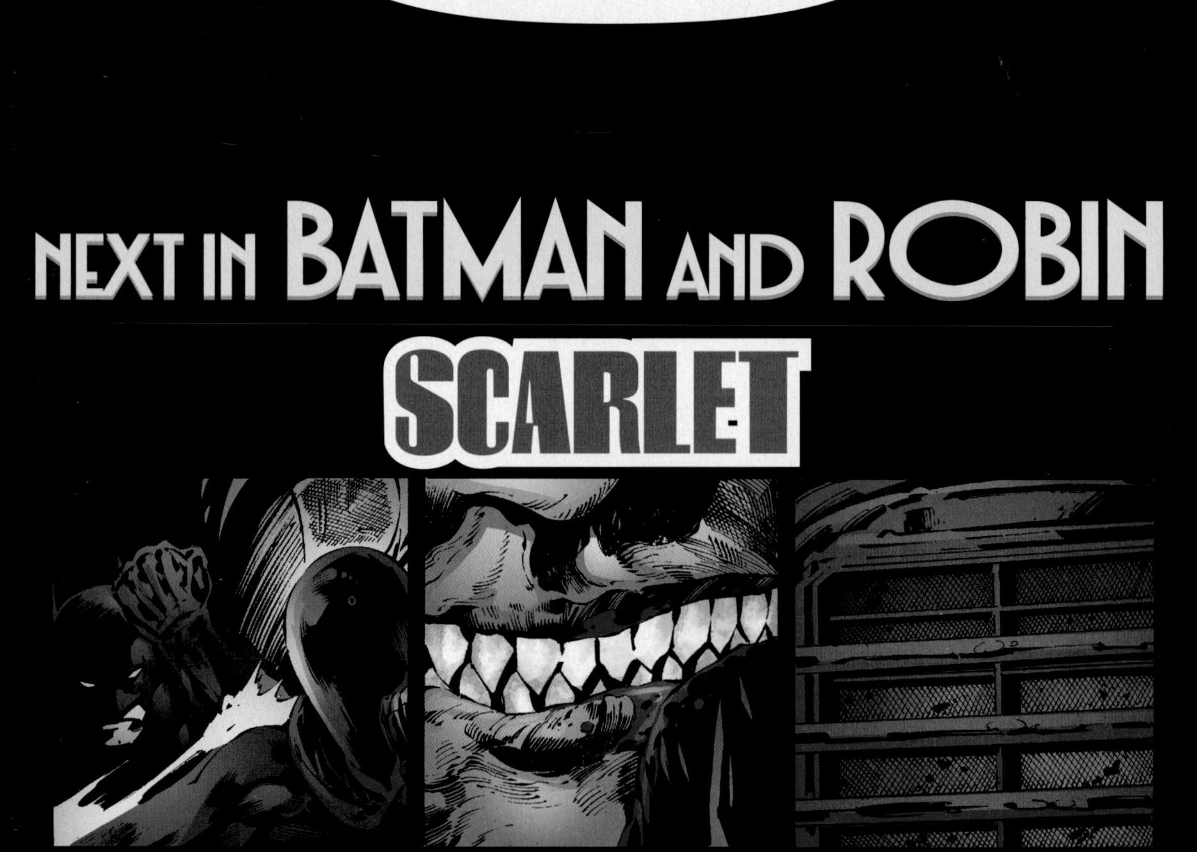

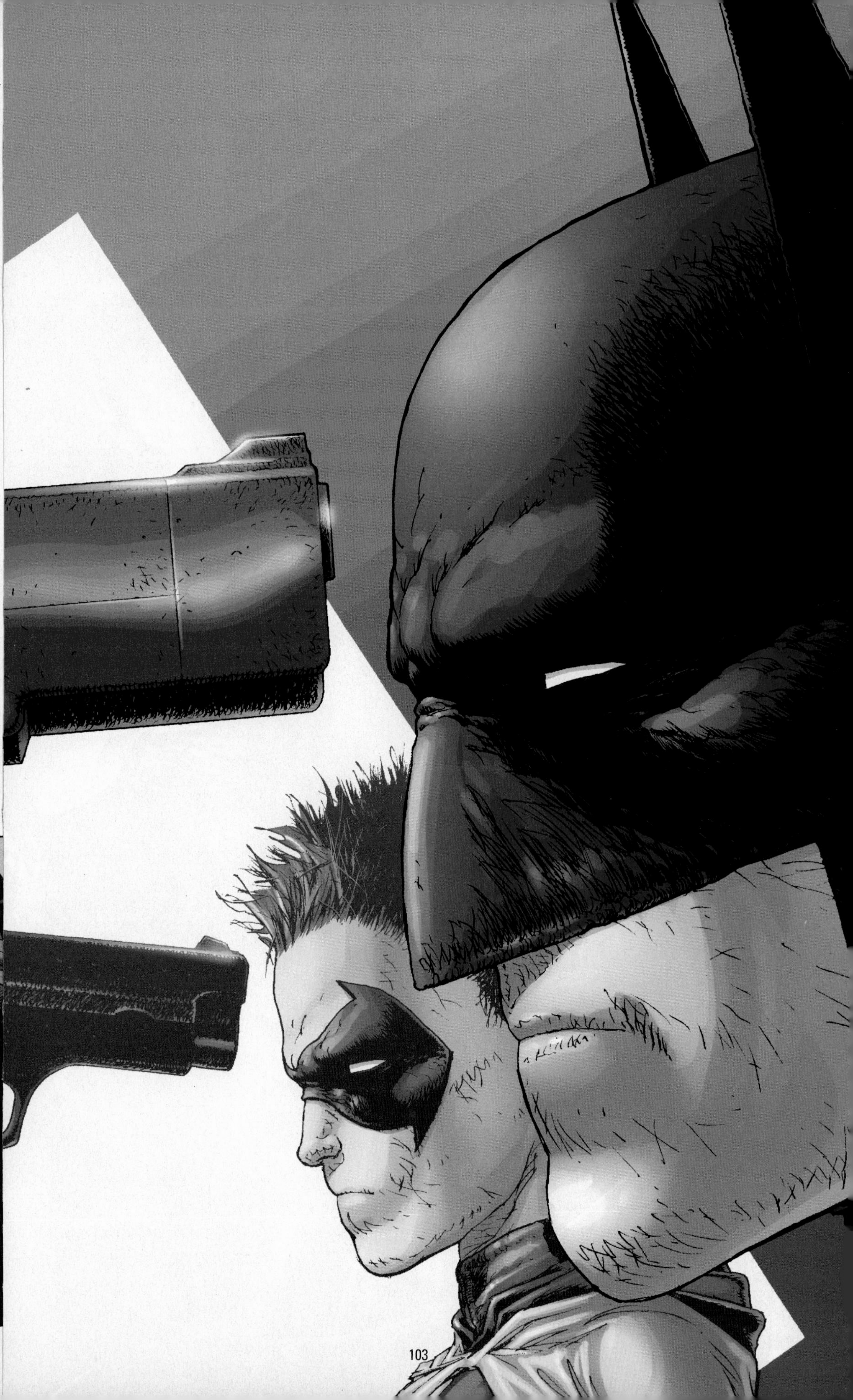

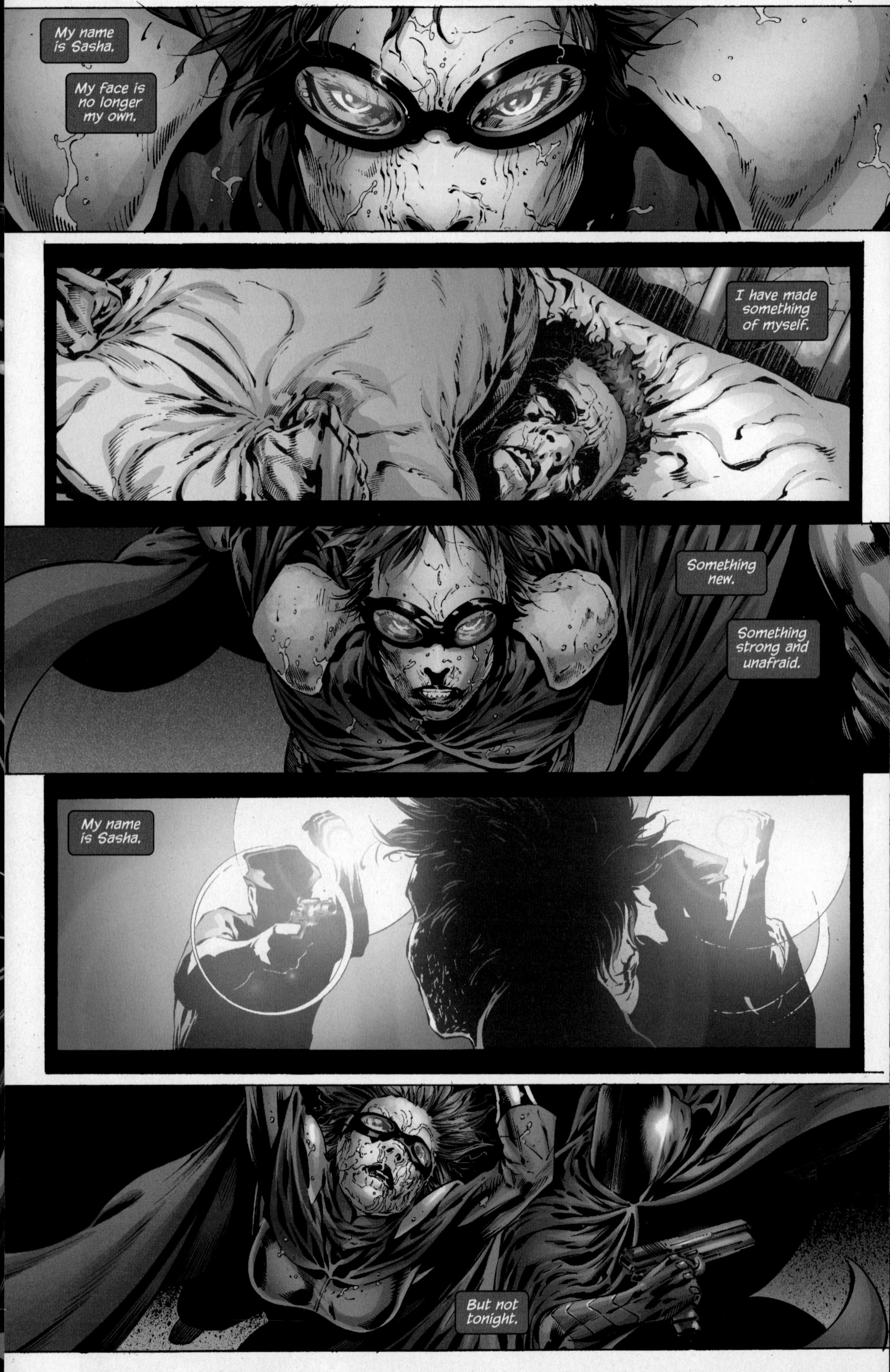
My name is Sasha.
My face is no longer my own.
I have made something of myself.
Something new.
Something strong and unafraid.
My name is Sasha.
But not tonight.

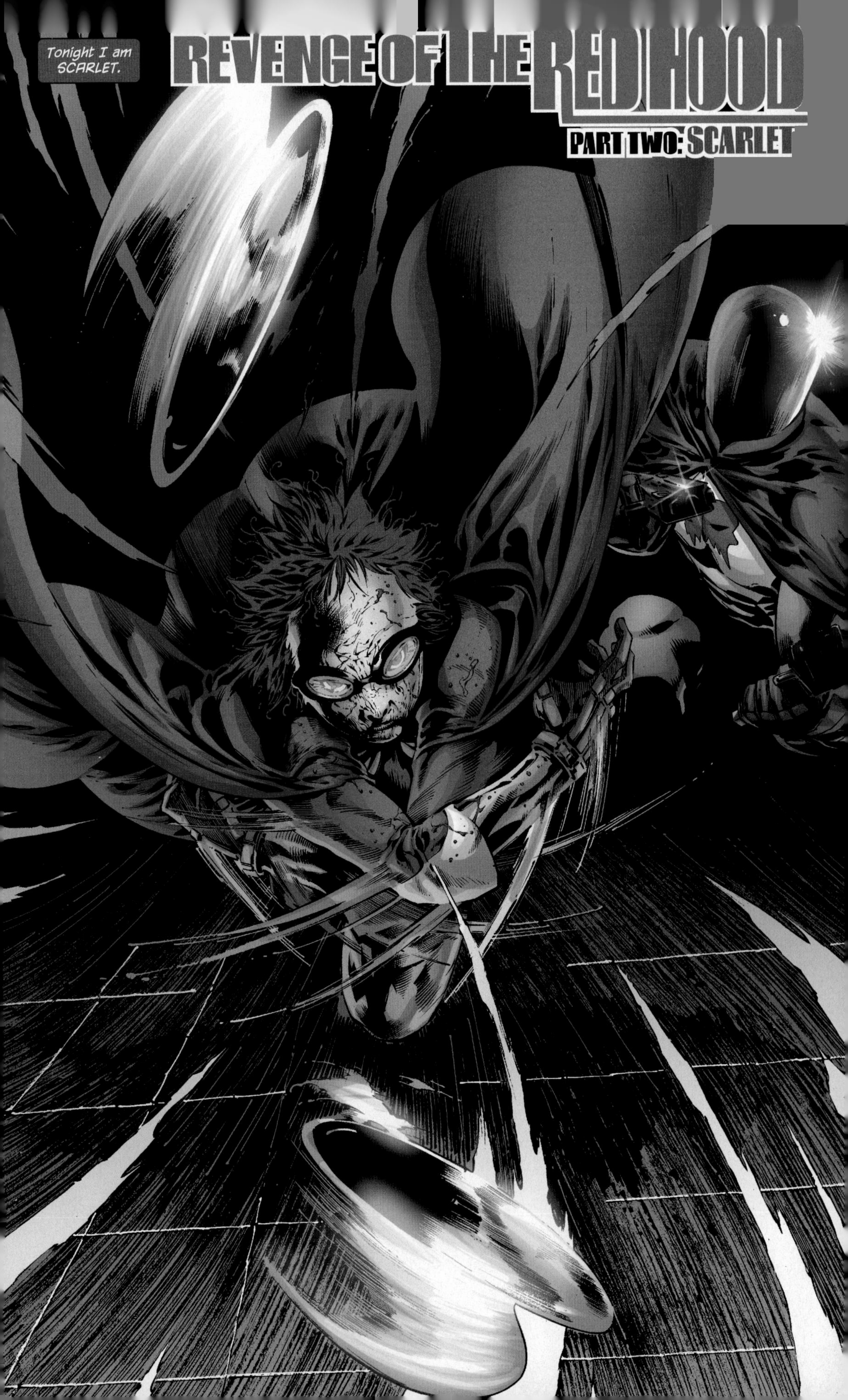

Tonight I am SCARLET.
REVENGE OF THE RED HOOD
PART TWO: SCARLET

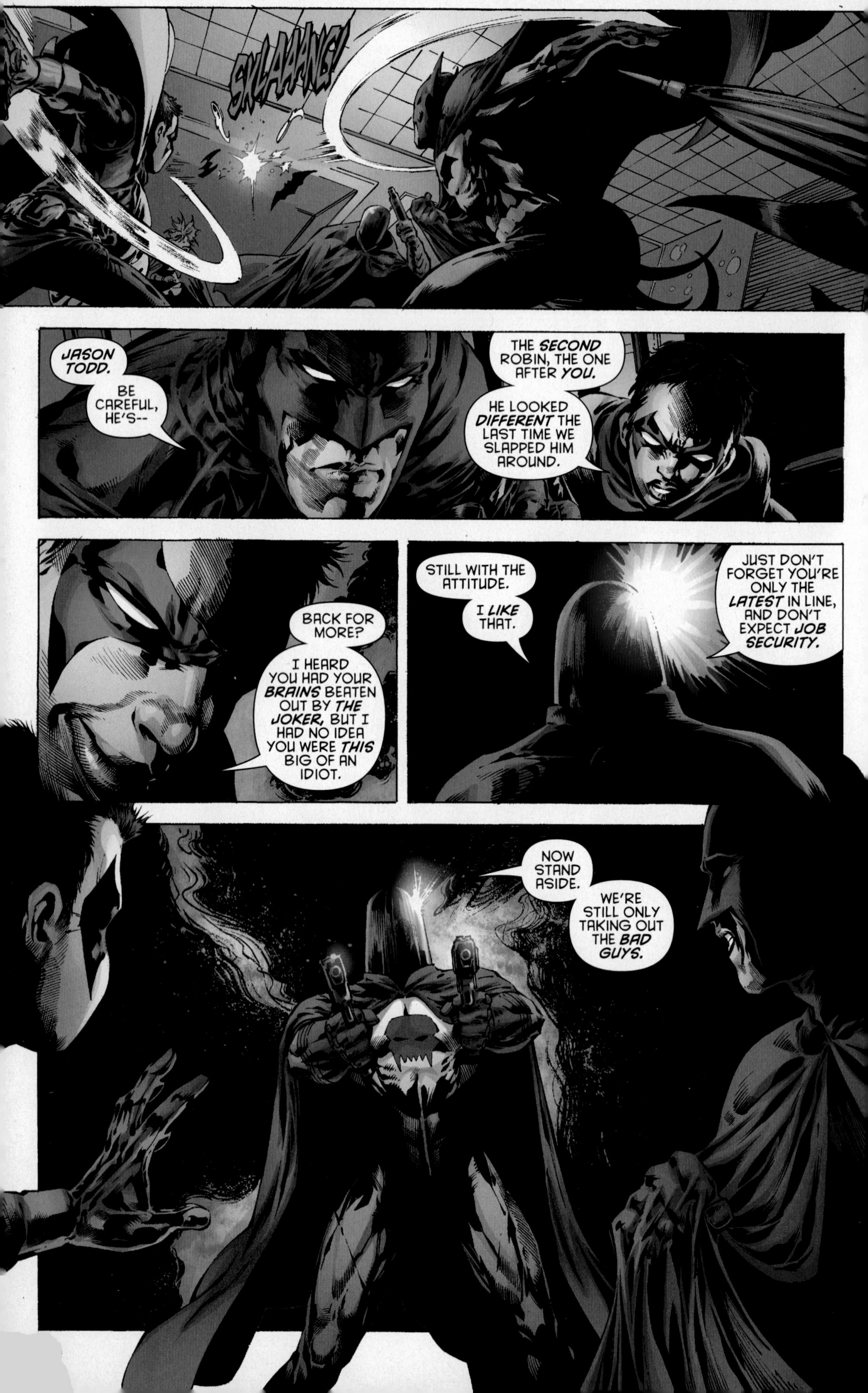
SKLAAANG!
JASON TODD.
BE CAREFUL, HE'S--
THE SECOND ROBIN, THE ONE AFTER YOU.
HE LOOKED DIFFERENT THE LAST TIME WE SLAPPED HIM AROUND.
BACK FOR MORE?
I HEARD YOU HAD YOUR BRAINS BEATEN OUT BY THE JOKER, BUT I HAD NO IDEA YOU WERE THIS BIG OF AN IDIOT.
STILL WITH THE ATTITUDE.
I LIKE THAT.
JUST DON'T FORGET YOU'RE ONLY THE LATEST IN LINE, AND DON'T EXPECT JOB SECURITY.
NOW STAND ASIDE.
WE'RE STILL ONLY TAKING OUT THE BAD GUYS.

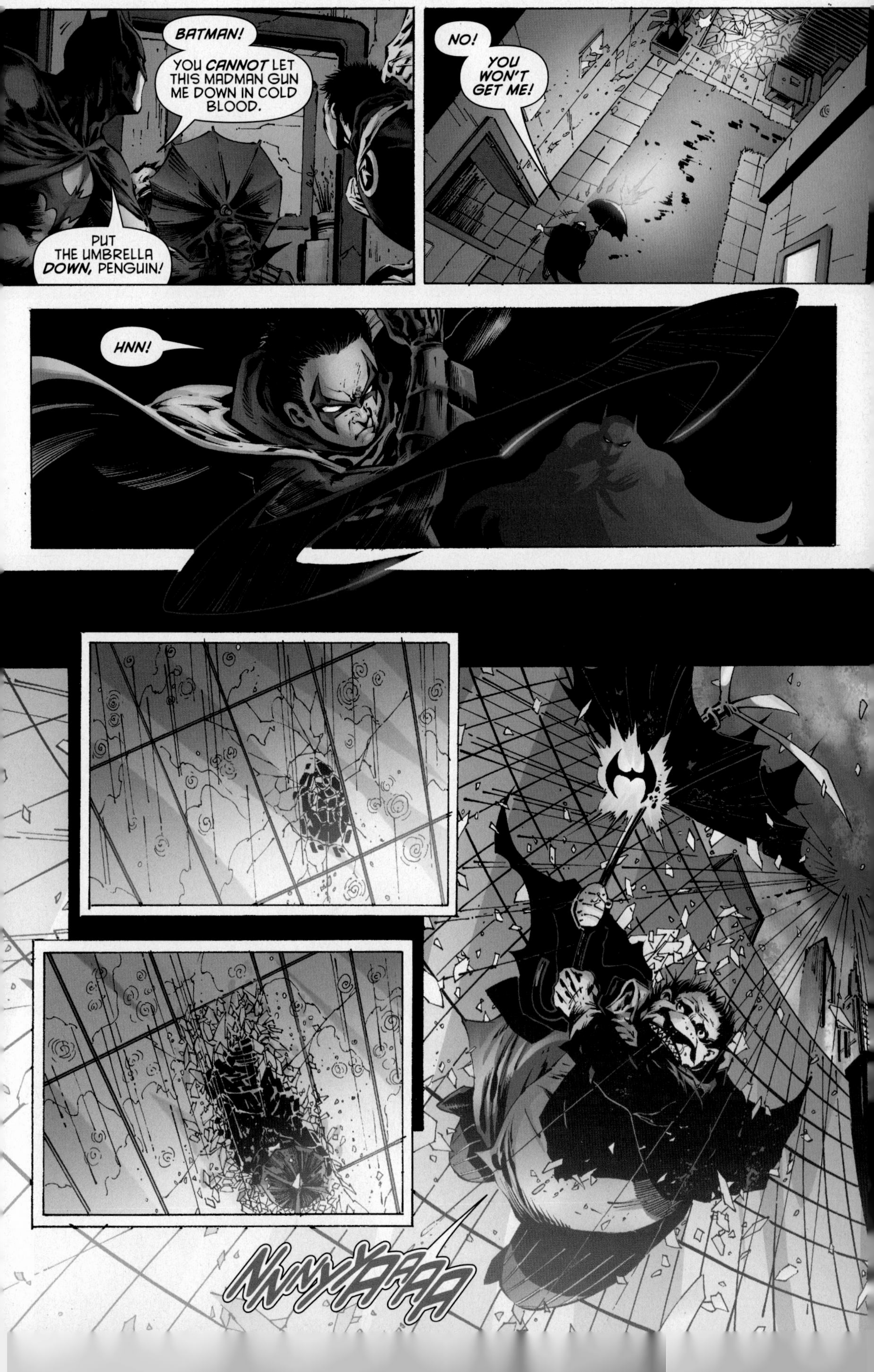
BATMAN!
YOU CANNOT LET THIS MADMAN GUN ME DOWN IN COLD BLOOD.
PUT THE UMBRELLA DOWN, PENGUIN!
NO!
YOU WON'T GET ME!
HNN!
NNNYAAAA

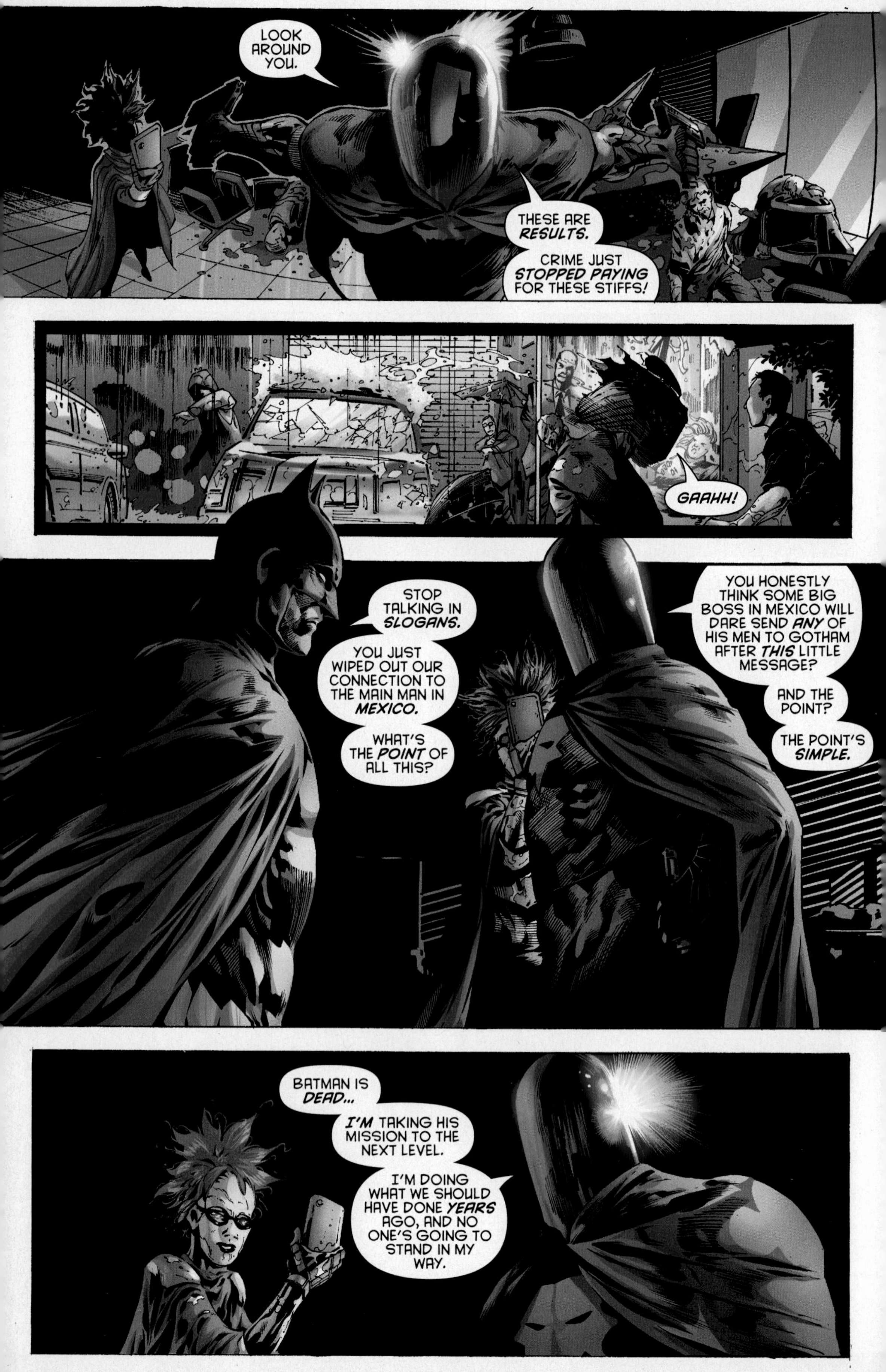
LOOK AROUND YOU.
THESE ARE RESULTS.
CRIME JUST STOPPED PAYING FOR THESE STIFFS!
GAAHH!
STOP TALKING IN SLOGANS.
YOU JUST WIPED OUT OUR CONNECTION TO THE MAIN MAN IN MEXICO.
WHAT'S THE POINT OF ALL THIS?
YOU HONESTLY THINK SOME BIG BOSS IN MEXICO WILL DARE SEND ANY OF HIS MEN TO GOTHAM AFTER THIS LITTLE MESSAGE?
AND THE POINT?
THE POINT'S SIMPLE.
BATMAN IS DEAD...
I'M TAKING HIS MISSION TO THE NEXT LEVEL.
I'M DOING WHAT WE SHOULD HAVE DONE YEARS AGO, AND NO ONE'S GOING TO STAND IN MY WAY.

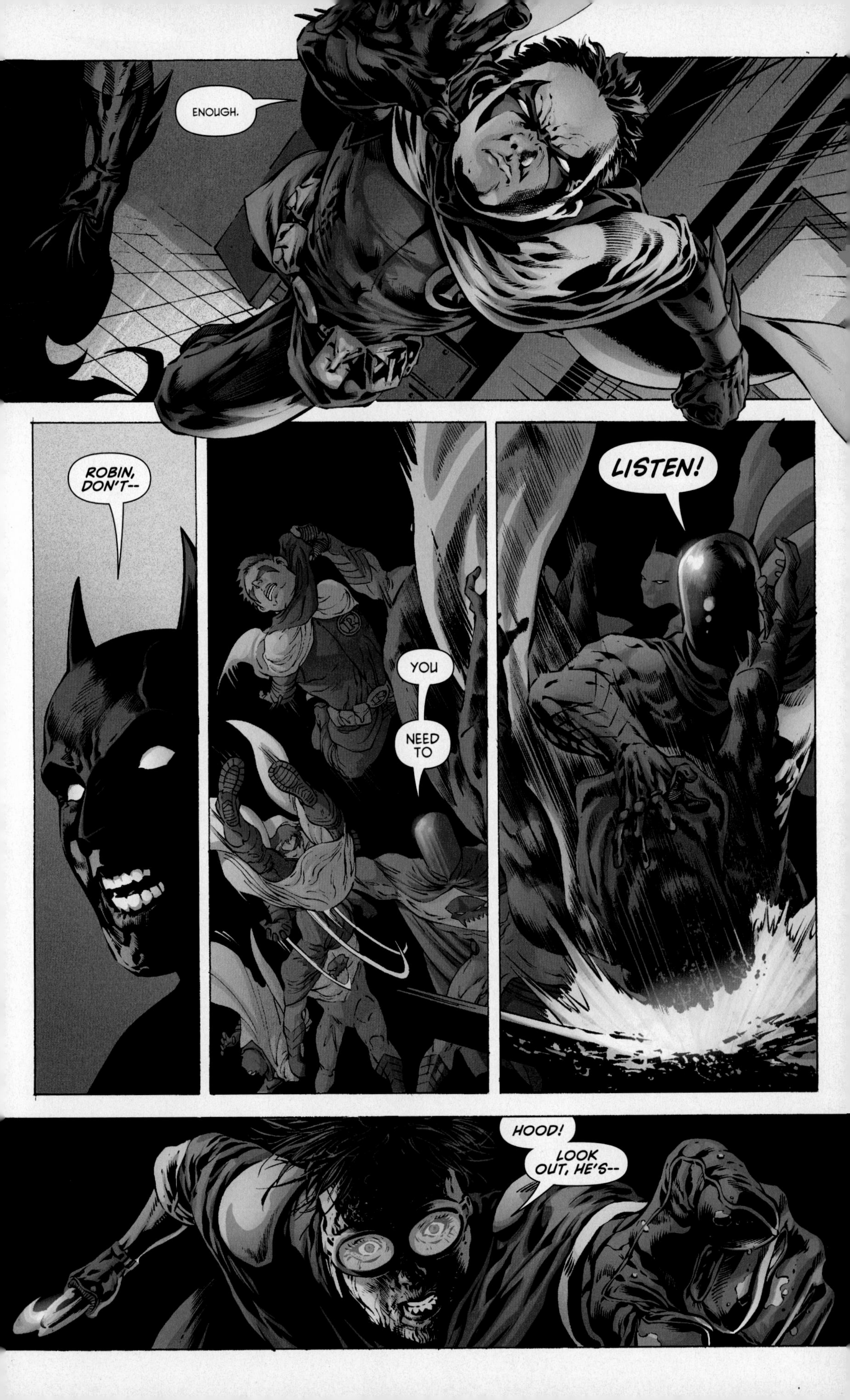
ENOUGH.
ROBIN, DON'T--
YOU
NEED TO
LISTEN!
HOOD!
LOOK OUT, HE'S--

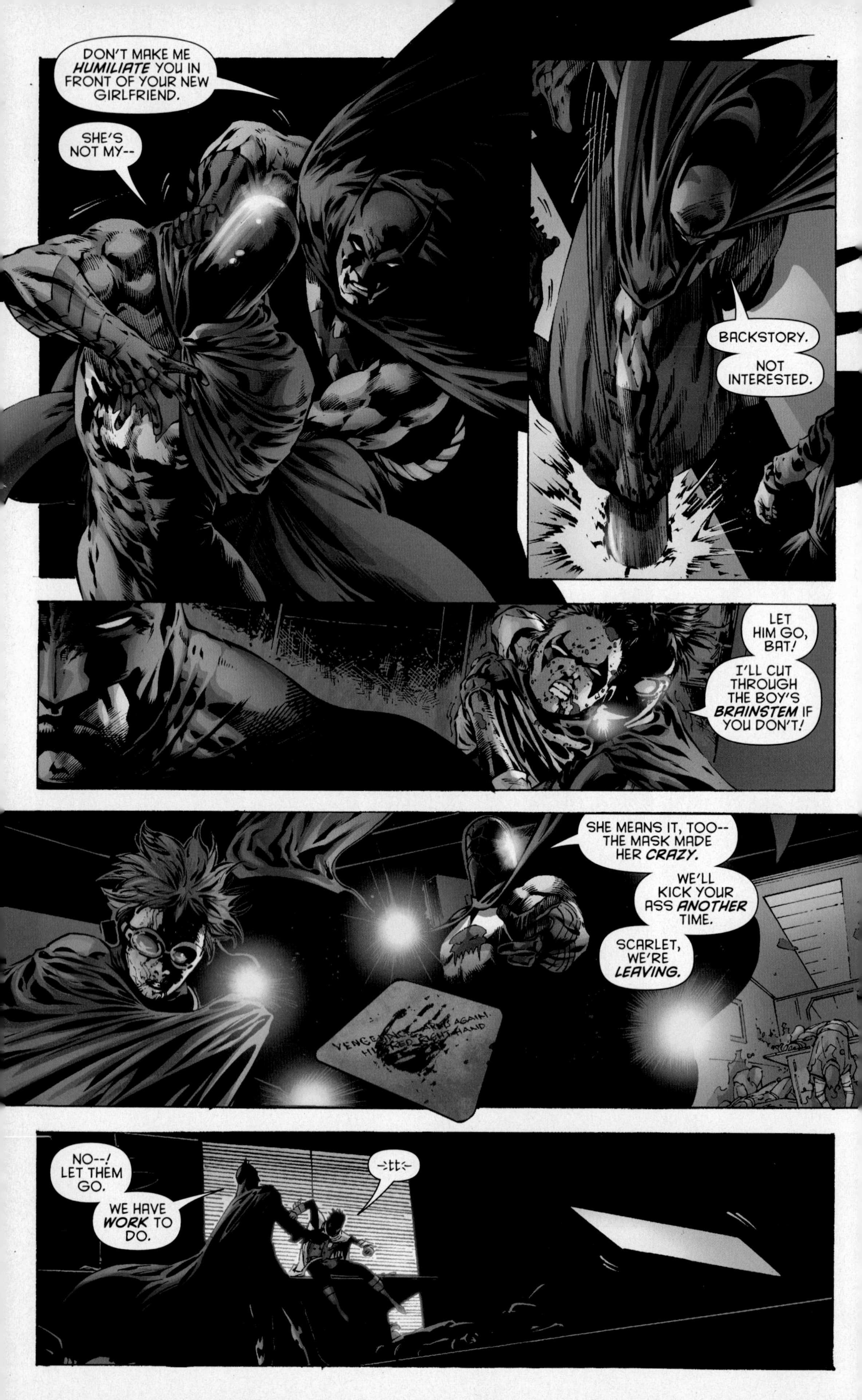
DON'T MAKE ME HUMILIATE YOU IN FRONT OF YOUR NEW GIRLFRIEND.
SHE'S NOT MY--
BACKSTORY.
NOT INTERESTED.
LET HIM GO, BAT!
I'LL CUT THROUGH THE BOY'S BRAINSTEM IF YOU DON'T!
SHE MEANS IT, TOO-- THE MASK MADE HER CRAZY.
WE'LL KICK YOUR ASS ANOTHER TIME.
SCARLET, WE'RE LEAVING.
NO--! LET THEM GO.
WE HAVE WORK TO DO.
-tt-

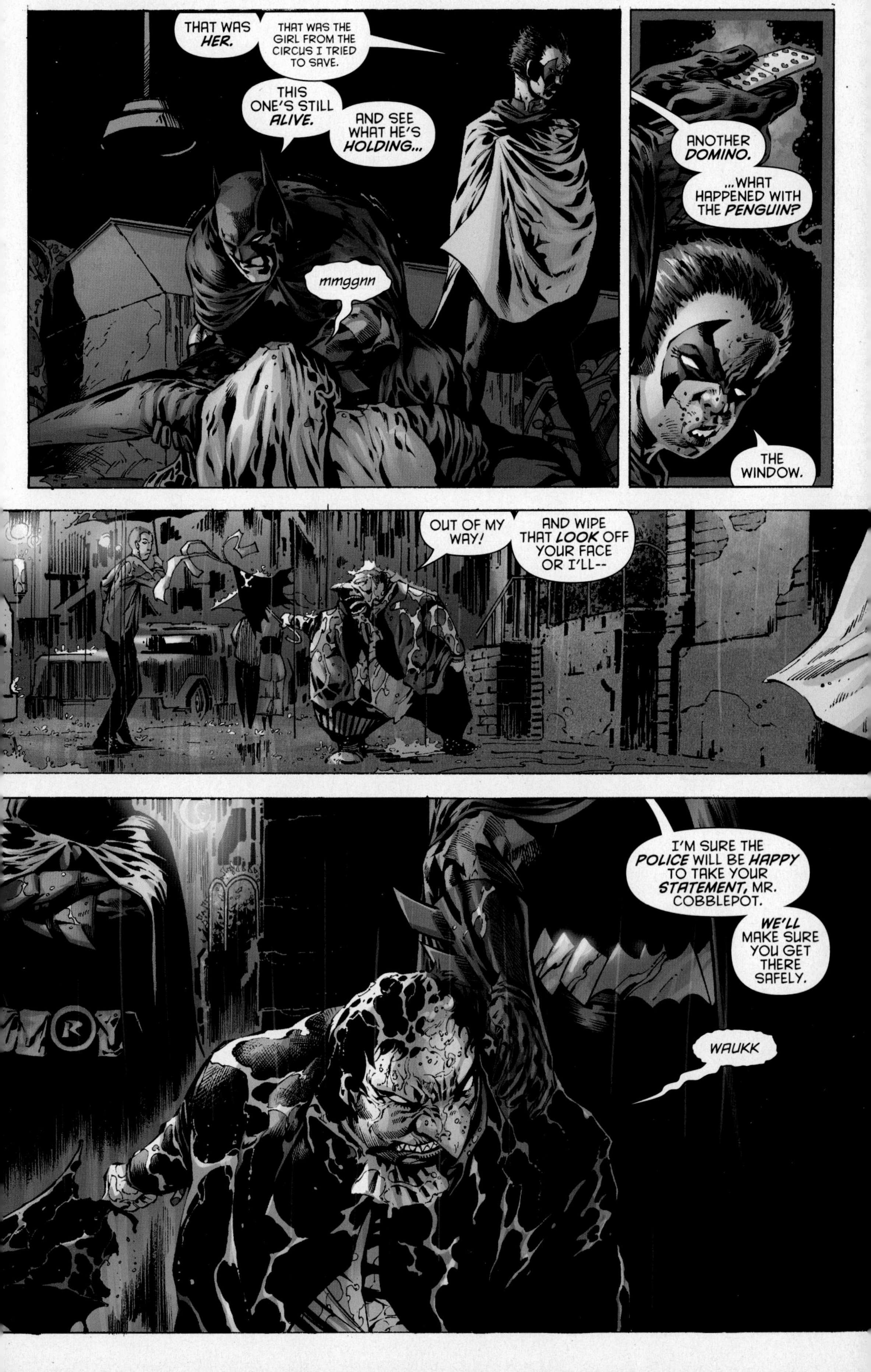
THAT WAS HER.
THAT WAS THE GIRL FROM THE CIRCUS I TRIED TO SAVE.
THIS ONE'S STILL ALIVE.
AND SEE WHAT HE'S HOLDING...
mmggnn
ANOTHER DOMINO.
...WHAT HAPPENED WITH THE PENGUIN?
THE WINDOW.
OUT OF MY WAY!
AND WIPE THAT LOOK OFF YOUR FACE OR I'LL--
I'M SURE THE POLICE WILL BE HAPPY TO TAKE YOUR STATEMENT, MR. COBBLEPOT.
WE'LL MAKE SURE YOU GET THERE SAFELY.
WAUKK

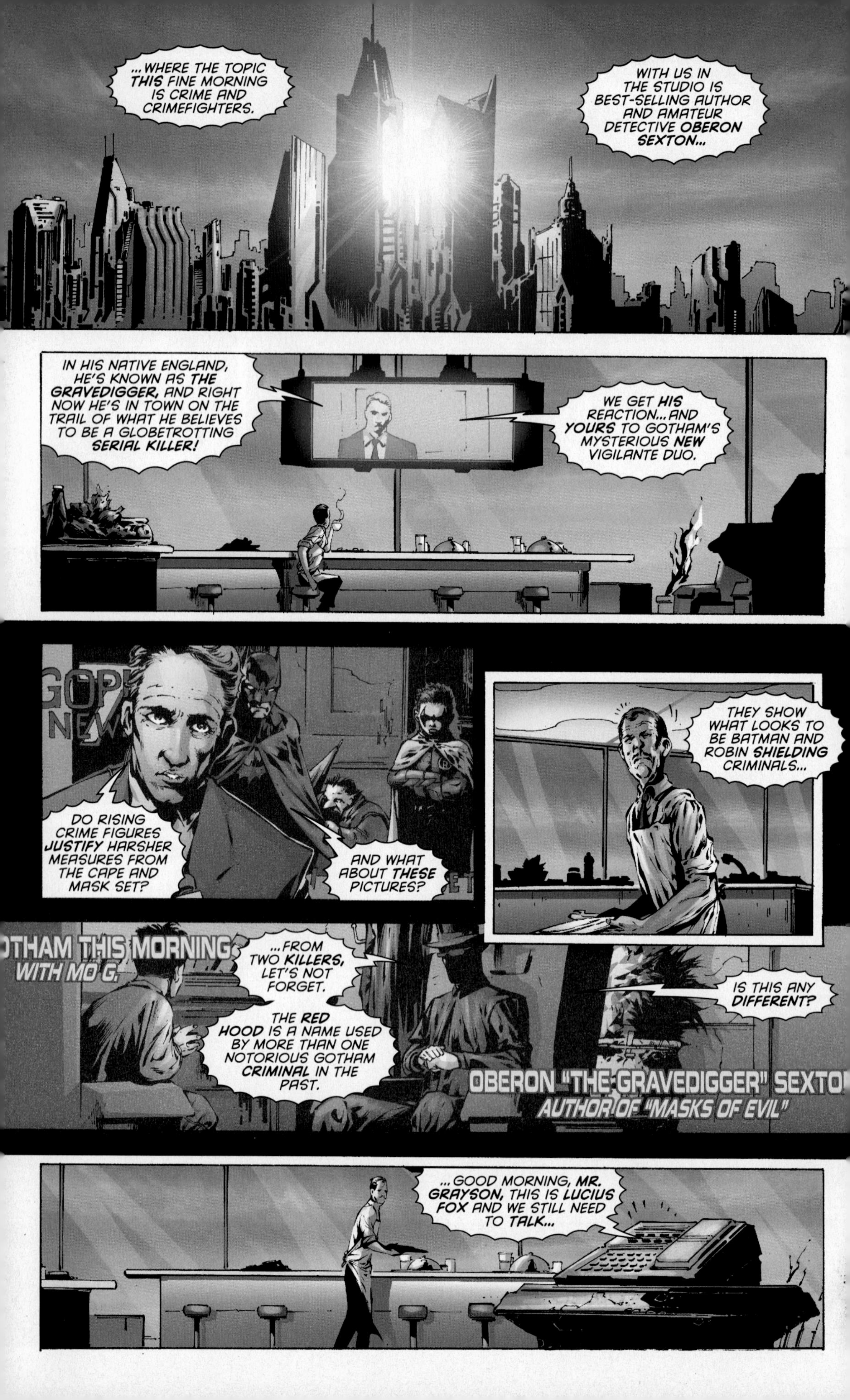
...WHERE THE TOPIC THIS FINE MORNING IS CRIME AND CRIMEFIGHTERS.
WITH US IN THE STUDIO IS BEST-SELLING AUTHOR AND AMATEUR DETECTIVE OBERON SEXTON...
IN HIS NATIVE ENGLAND, HE'S KNOWN AS THE GRAVEDIGGER, AND RIGHT NOW HE'S IN TOWN ON THE TRAIL OF WHAT HE BELIEVES TO BE A GLOBETROTTING SERIAL KILLER!
WE GET HIS REACTION...AND YOURS TO GOTHAM'S MYSTERIOUS NEW VIGILANTE DUO.
DO RISING CRIME FIGURES JUSTIFY HARSHER MEASURES FROM THE CAPE AND MASK SET?
AND WHAT ABOUT THESE PICTURES?
THEY SHOW WHAT LOOKS TO BE BATMAN AND ROBIN SHIELDING CRIMINALS...
OTHAM THIS MORNING
WITH MO G.
...FROM TWO KILLERS, LET'S NOT FORGET.
THE RED HOOD IS A NAME USED BY MORE THAN ONE NOTORIOUS GOTHAM CRIMINAL IN THE PAST.
IS THIS ANY DIFFERENT?
OBERON "THE GRAVEDIGGER" SEXTO
AUTHOR OF "MASKS OF EVIL"
...GOOD MORNING, MR. GRAYSON, THIS IS LUCIUS FOX AND WE STILL NEED TO TALK...

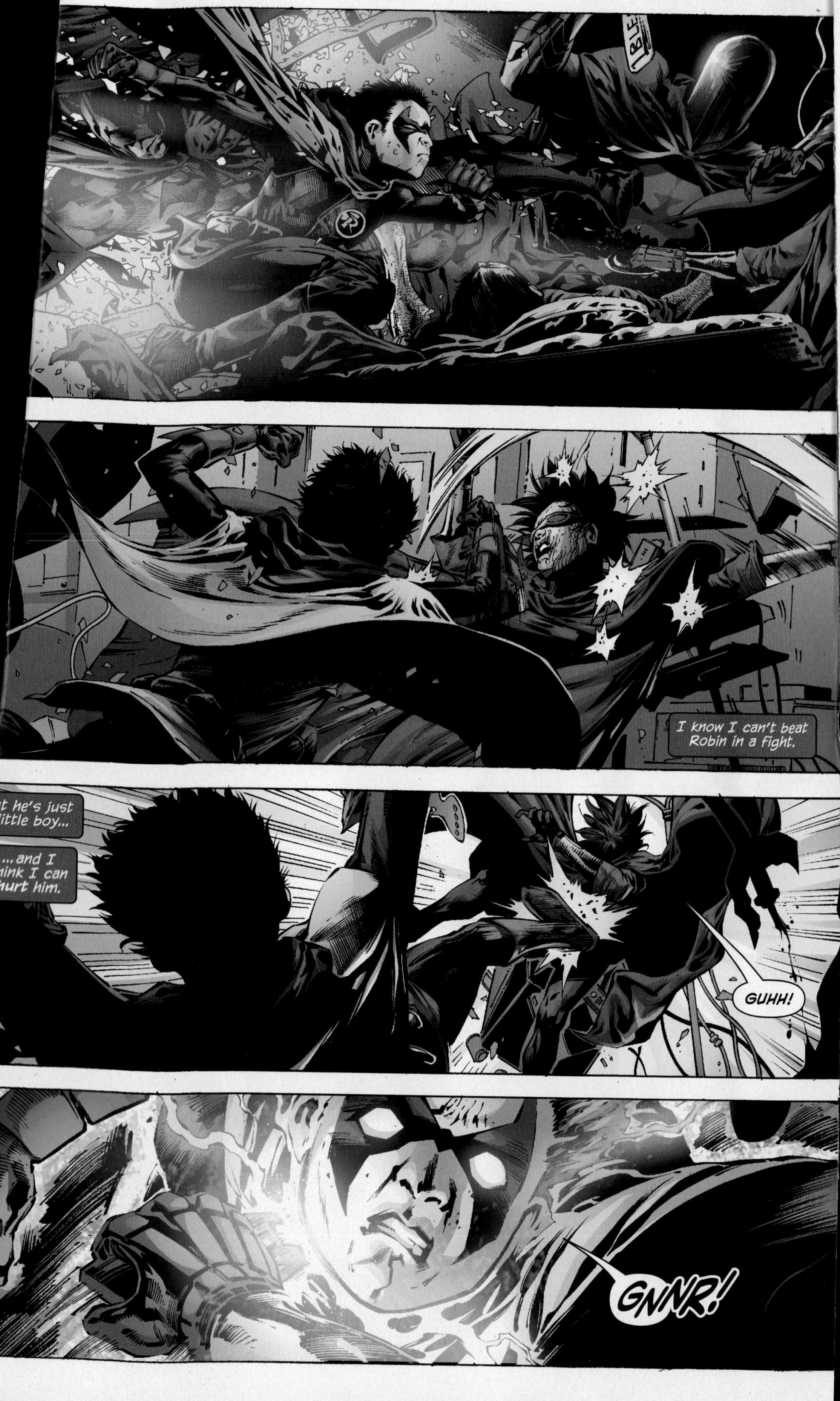

I know I can't beat Robin in a fight.
ut he's just little boy...
...and I think I can hurt him.
GUHH!
GNNR!

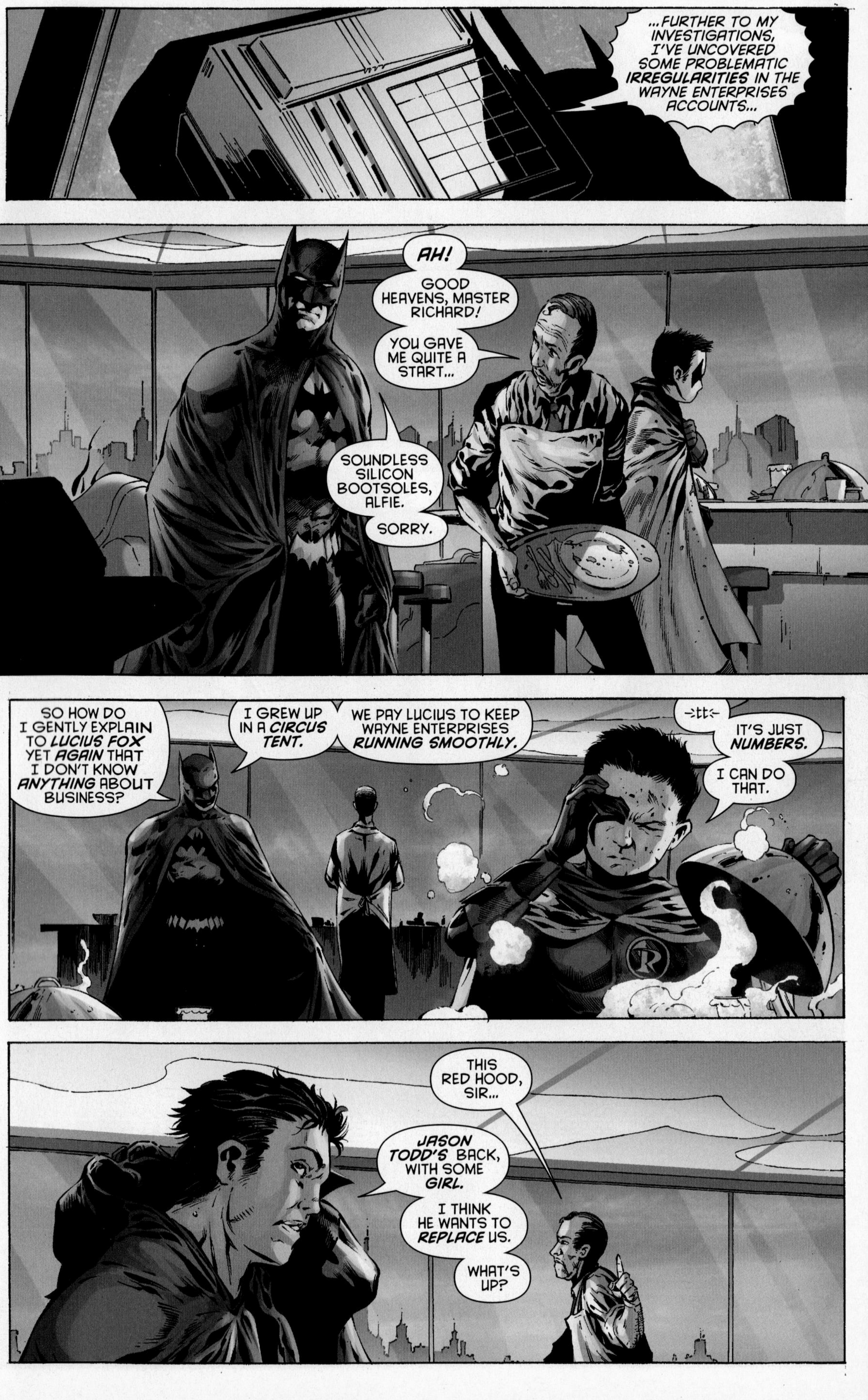

...FURTHER TO MY INVESTIGATIONS, I'VE UNCOVERED SOME PROBLEMATIC IRREGULARITIES IN THE WAYNE ENTERPRISES ACCOUNTS...
AH!
GOOD HEAVENS, MASTER RICHARD!
YOU GAVE ME QUITE A START...
SOUNDLESS SILICON BOOTSOLES, ALFIE.
SORRY.
SO HOW DO I GENTLY EXPLAIN TO LUCIUS FOX YET AGAIN THAT I DON'T KNOW ANYTHING ABOUT BUSINESS?
I GREW UP IN A CIRCUS TENT.
WE PAY LUCIUS TO KEEP WAYNE ENTERPRISES RUNNING SMOOTHLY.
-tt-
IT'S JUST NUMBERS.
I CAN DO THAT.
THIS RED HOOD, SIR...
JASON TODD'S BACK, WITH SOME GIRL.
I THINK HE WANTS TO REPLACE US.
WHAT'S UP?

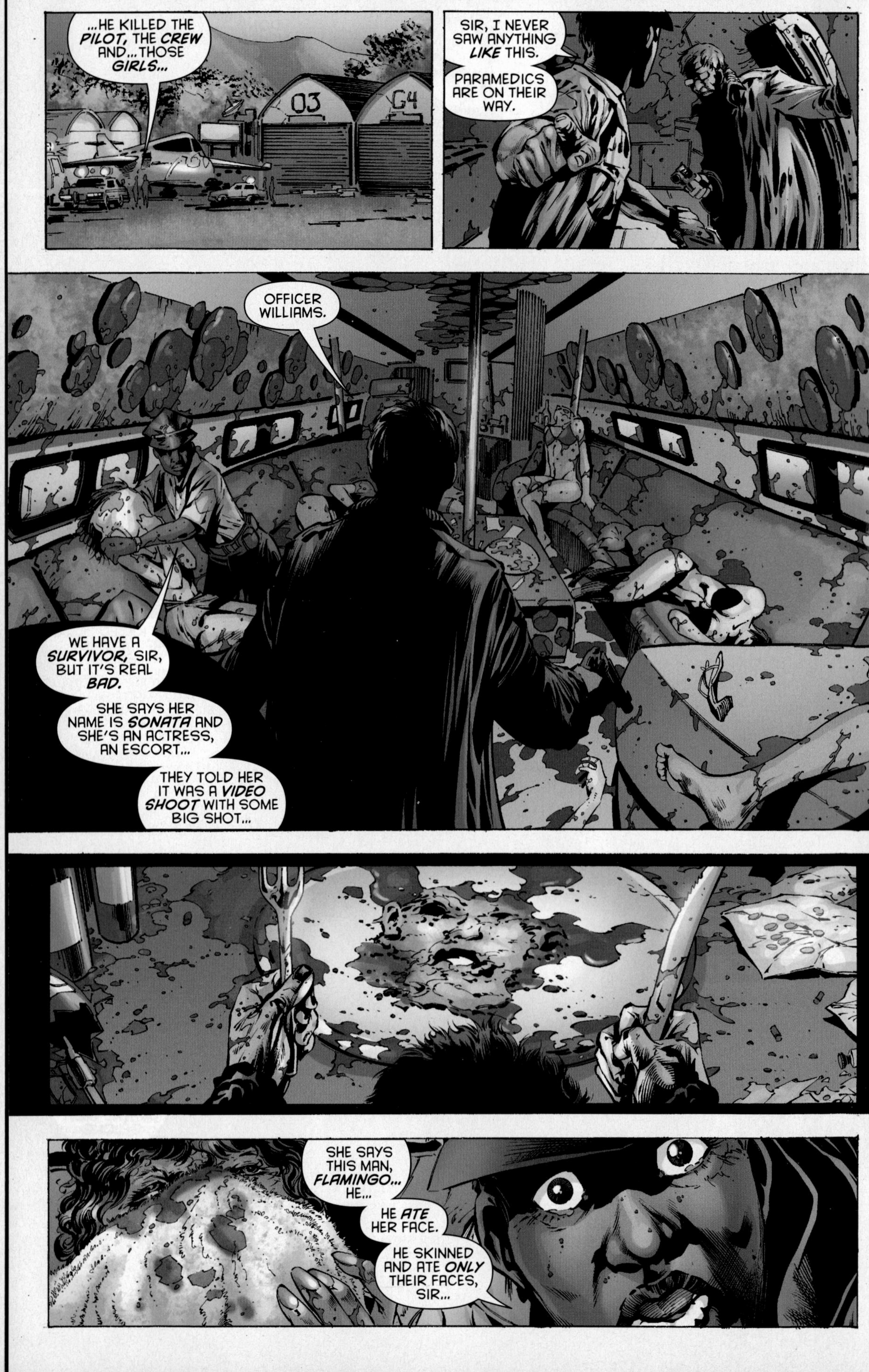

...HE KILLED THE PILOT, THE CREW AND... THOSE GIRLS...
SIR, I NEVER SAW ANYTHING LIKE THIS.
PARAMEDICS ARE ON THEIR WAY.
OFFICER WILLIAMS.
WE HAVE A SURVIVOR, SIR, BUT IT'S REAL BAD.
SHE SAYS HER NAME IS SONATA AND SHE'S AN ACTRESS, AN ESCORT...
THEY TOLD HER IT WAS A VIDEO SHOOT WITH SOME BIG SHOT...
SHE SAYS THIS MAN, FLAMINGO... HE...
HE ATE HER FACE.
HE SKINNED AND ATE ONLY THEIR FACES, SIR...

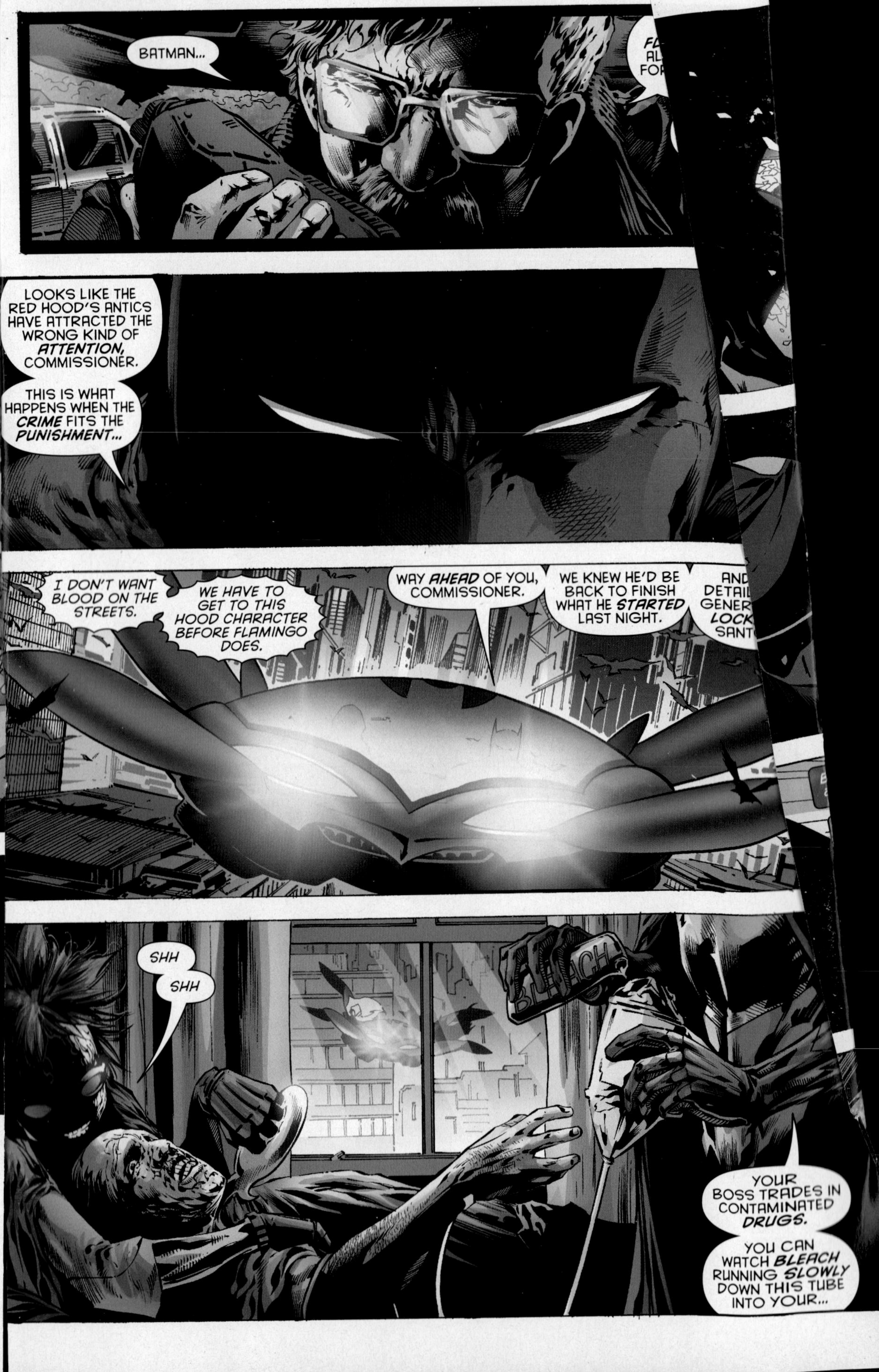

BATMAN...
LOOKS LIKE THE RED HOOD'S ANTICS HAVE ATTRACTED THE WRONG KIND OF ATTENTION, COMMISSIONER.
THIS IS WHAT HAPPENS WHEN THE CRIME FITS THE PUNISHMENT...
I DON'T WANT BLOOD ON THE STREETS.
WE HAVE TO GET TO THIS HOOD CHARACTER BEFORE FLAMINGO DOES.
WAY AHEAD OF YOU, COMMISSIONER.
WE KNEW HE'D BE BACK TO FINISH WHAT HE STARTED LAST NIGHT.
SHH
SHH
BLEACH
YOUR BOSS TRADES IN CONTAMINATED DRUGS.
YOU CAN WATCH BLEACH RUNNING SLOWLY DOWN THIS TUBE INTO YOUR...

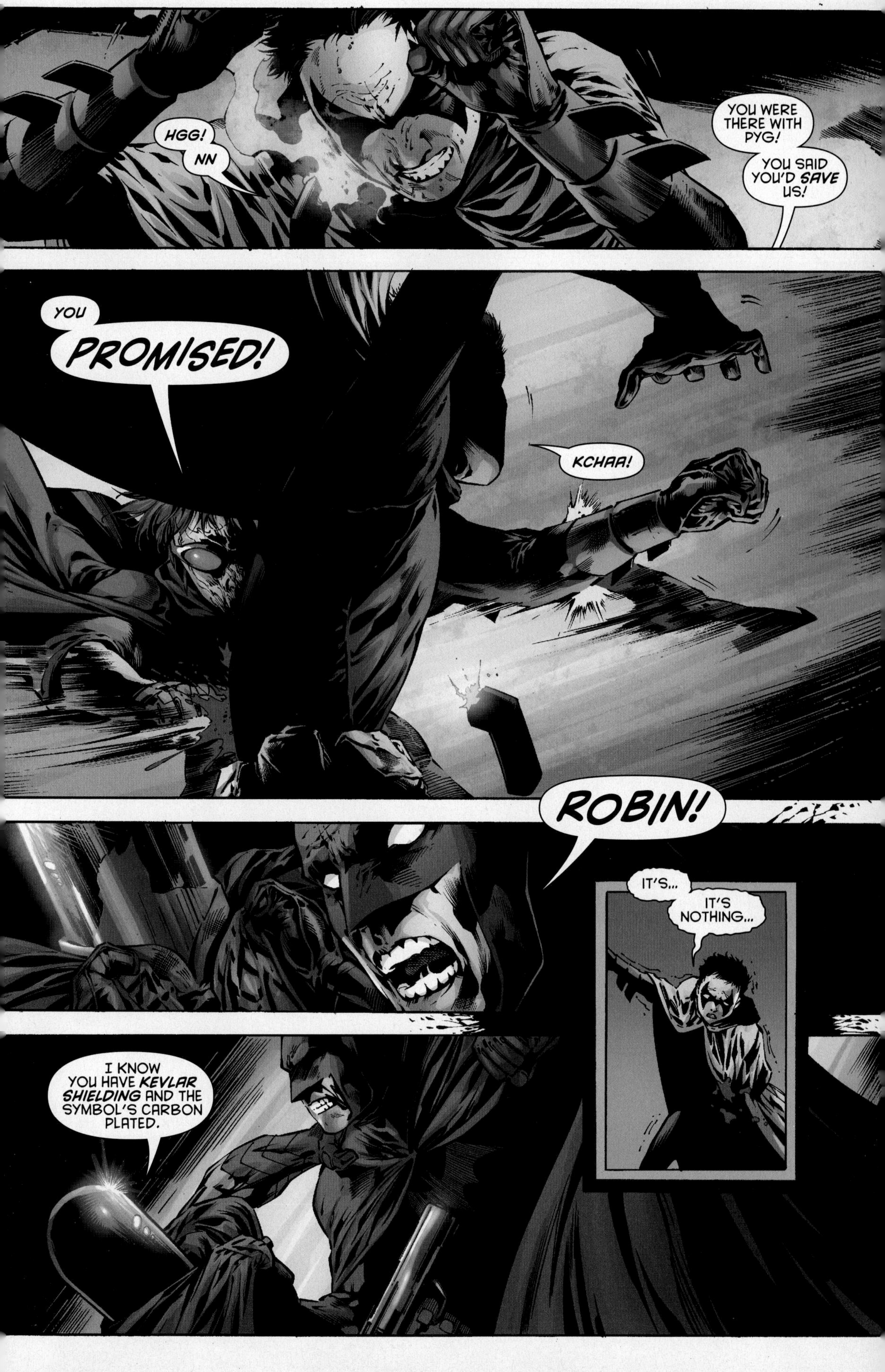

HGG!
NN
YOU WERE THERE WITH PYG!
YOU SAID YOU'D SAVE US!
YOU PROMISED!
KCHAA!
ROBIN!
IT'S...
IT'S NOTHING...
I KNOW YOU HAVE KEVLAR SHIELDING AND THE SYMBOL'S CARBON PLATED.

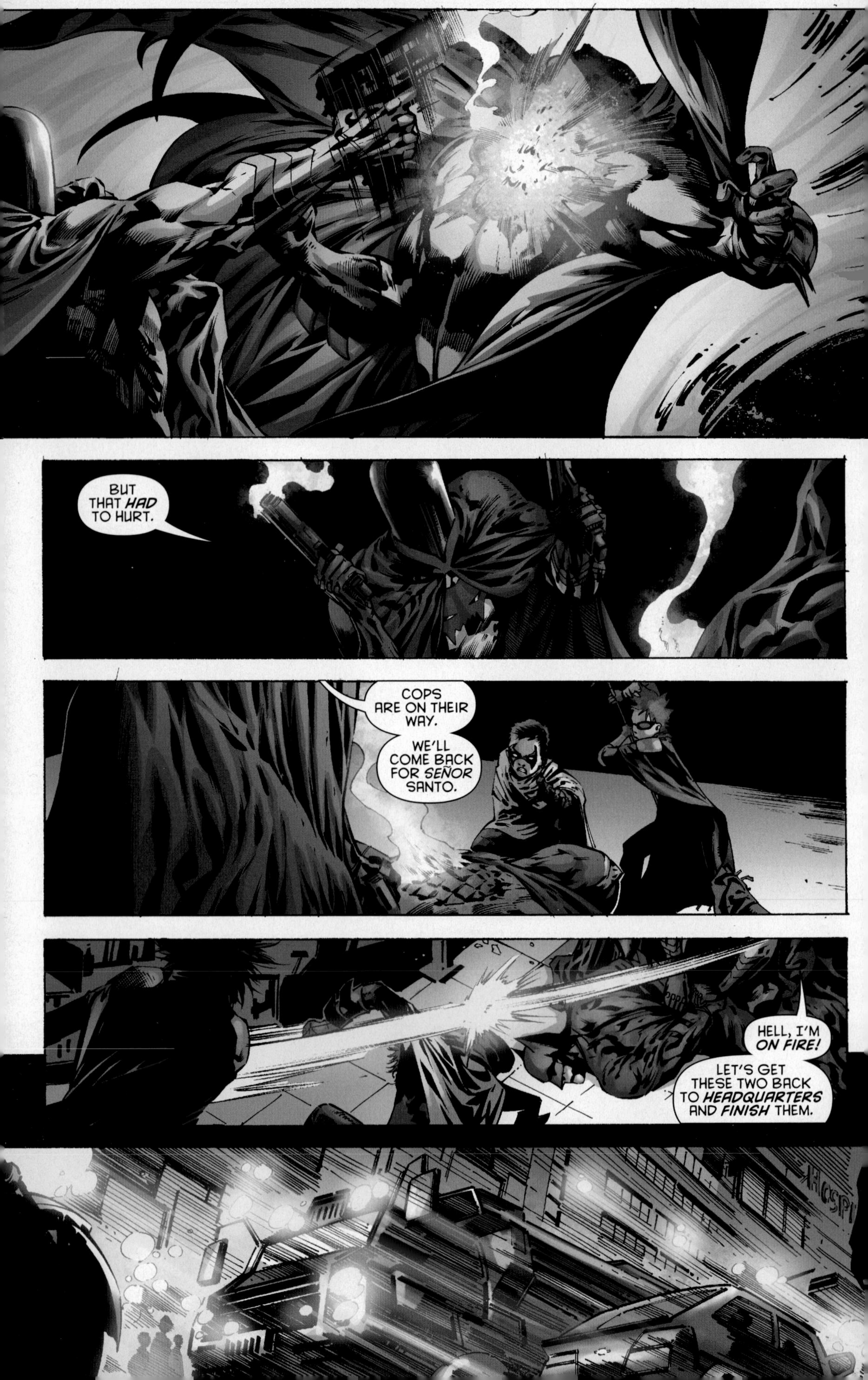
BUT THAT *HAD* TO HURT.
COPS ARE ON THEIR WAY.
WE'LL COME BACK FOR *SEÑOR* SANTO.
HELL, I'M *ON FIRE!*
LET'S GET THESE TWO BACK TO *HEADQUARTERS* AND *FINISH* THEM.

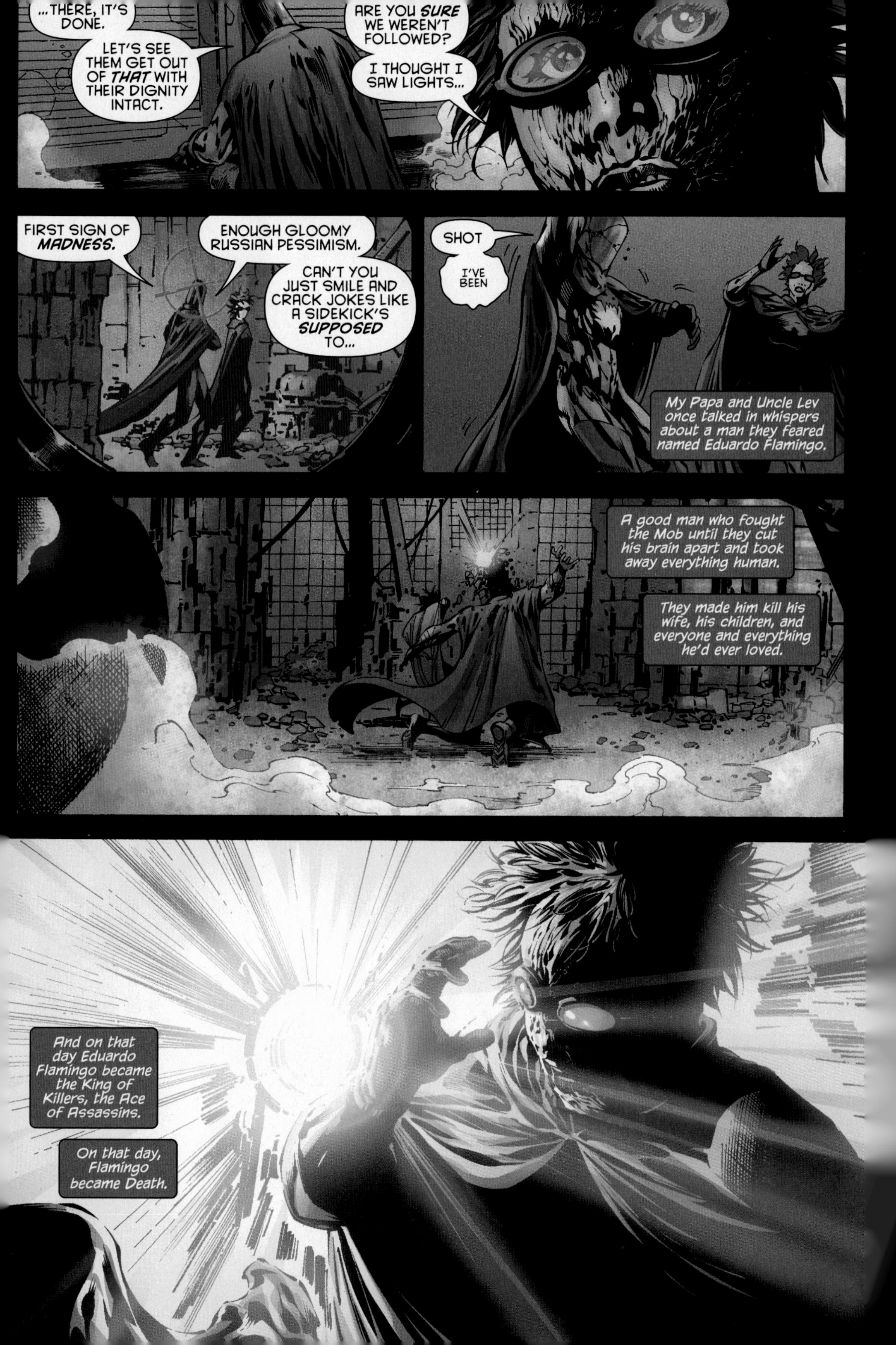
...THERE, IT'S DONE.
LET'S SEE THEM GET OUT OF THAT WITH THEIR DIGNITY INTACT.
ARE YOU SURE WE WEREN'T FOLLOWED?
I THOUGHT I SAW LIGHTS...
FIRST SIGN OF MADNESS.
ENOUGH GLOOMY RUSSIAN PESSIMISM.
CAN'T YOU JUST SMILE AND CRACK JOKES LIKE A SIDEKICK'S SUPPOSED TO...
SHOT
I'VE BEEN
My Papa and Uncle Lev once talked in whispers about a man they feared named Eduardo Flamingo.
A good man who fought the Mob until they cut his brain apart and took away everything human.
They made him kill his wife, his children, and everyone and everything he'd ever loved.
And on that day Eduardo Flamingo became the King of Killers, the Ace of Assassins.
On that day, Flamingo became Death.

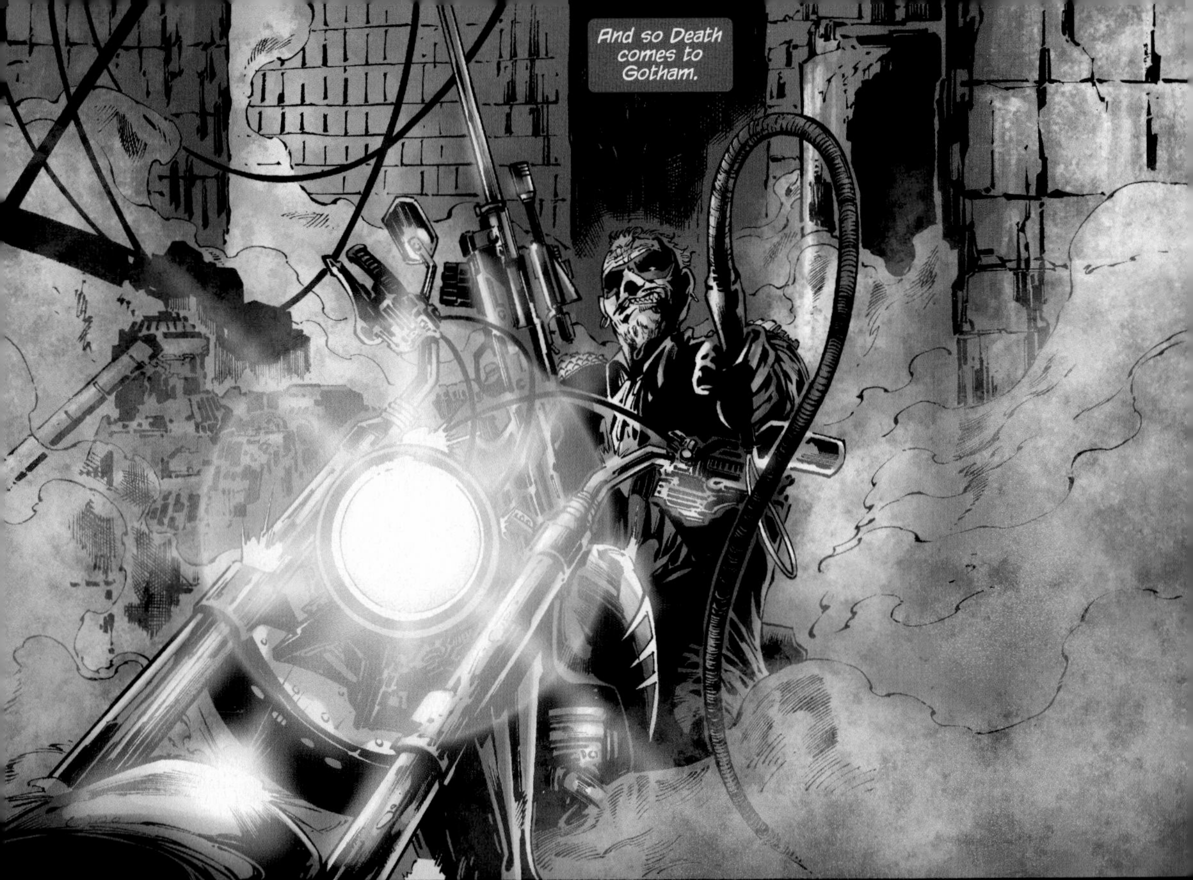
And so Death comes to Gotham.

NEXT IN BATMAN AND ROBIN

FLAMINGO IS HERE!

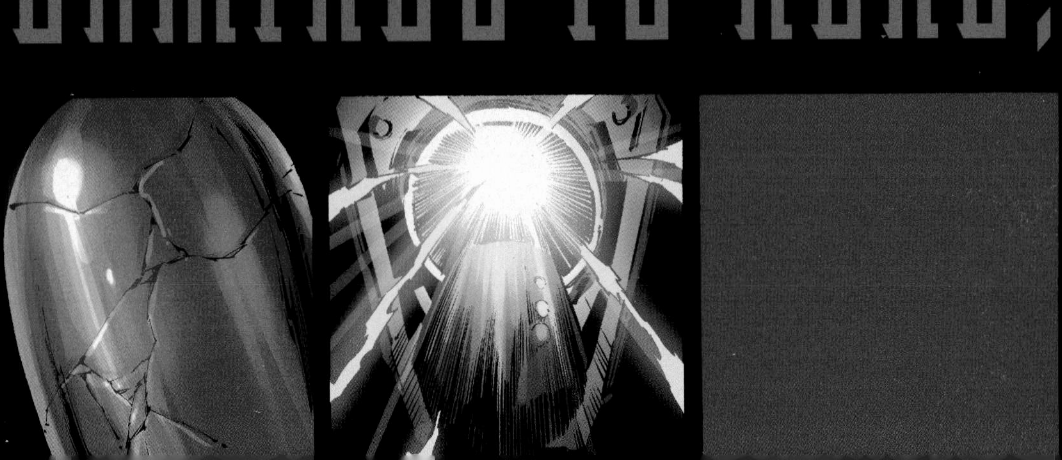

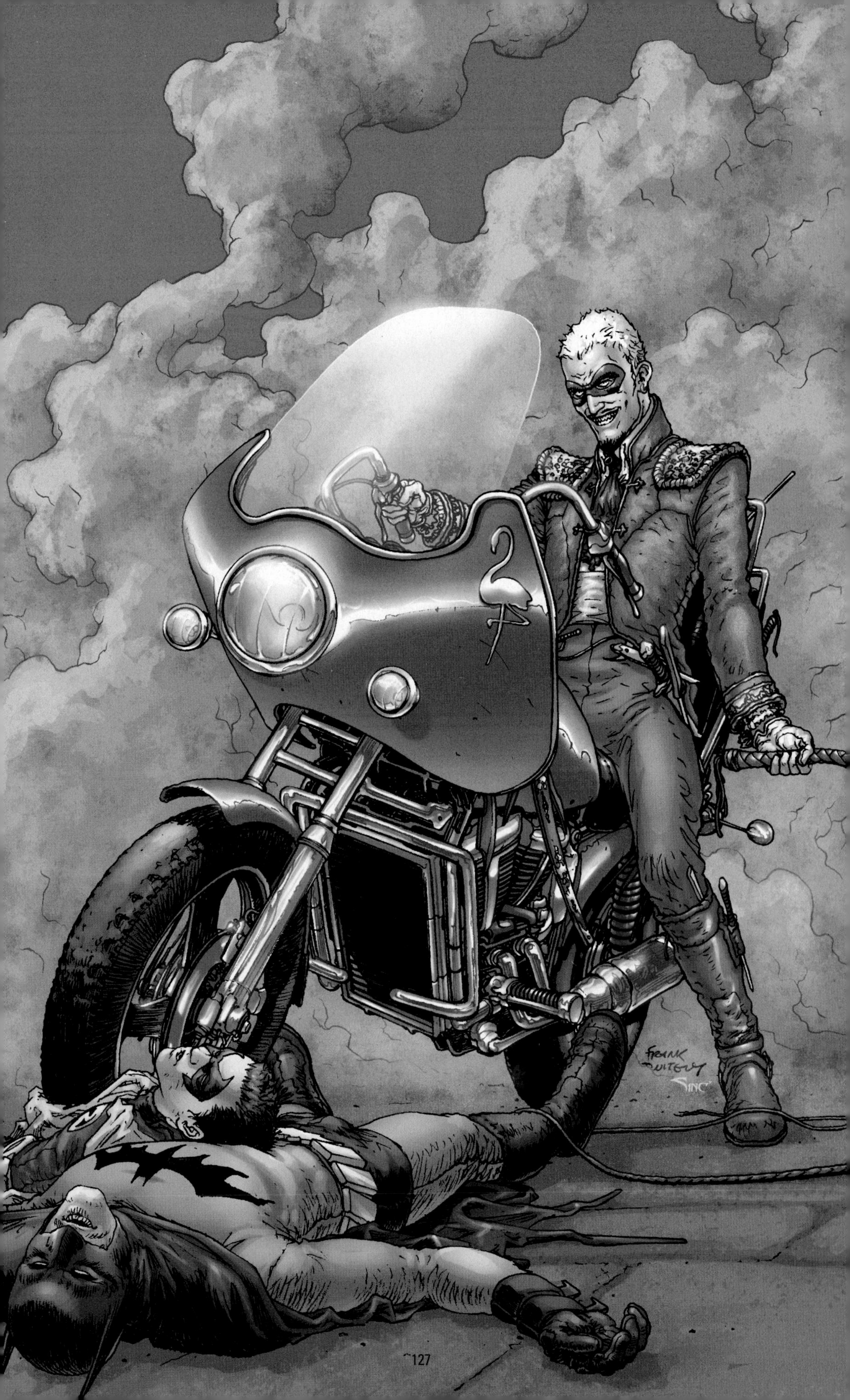
FRANK QUITELY
SINC

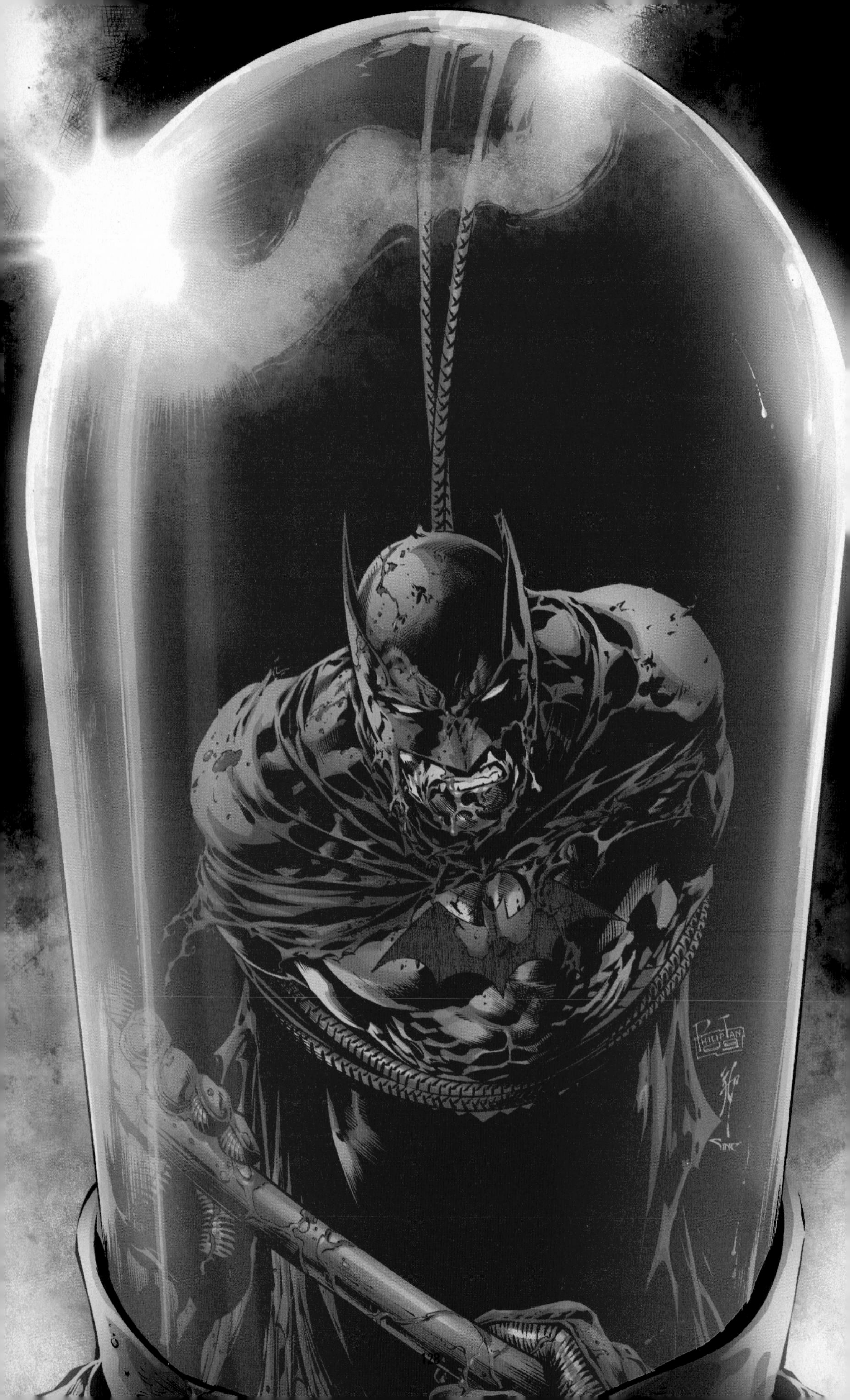

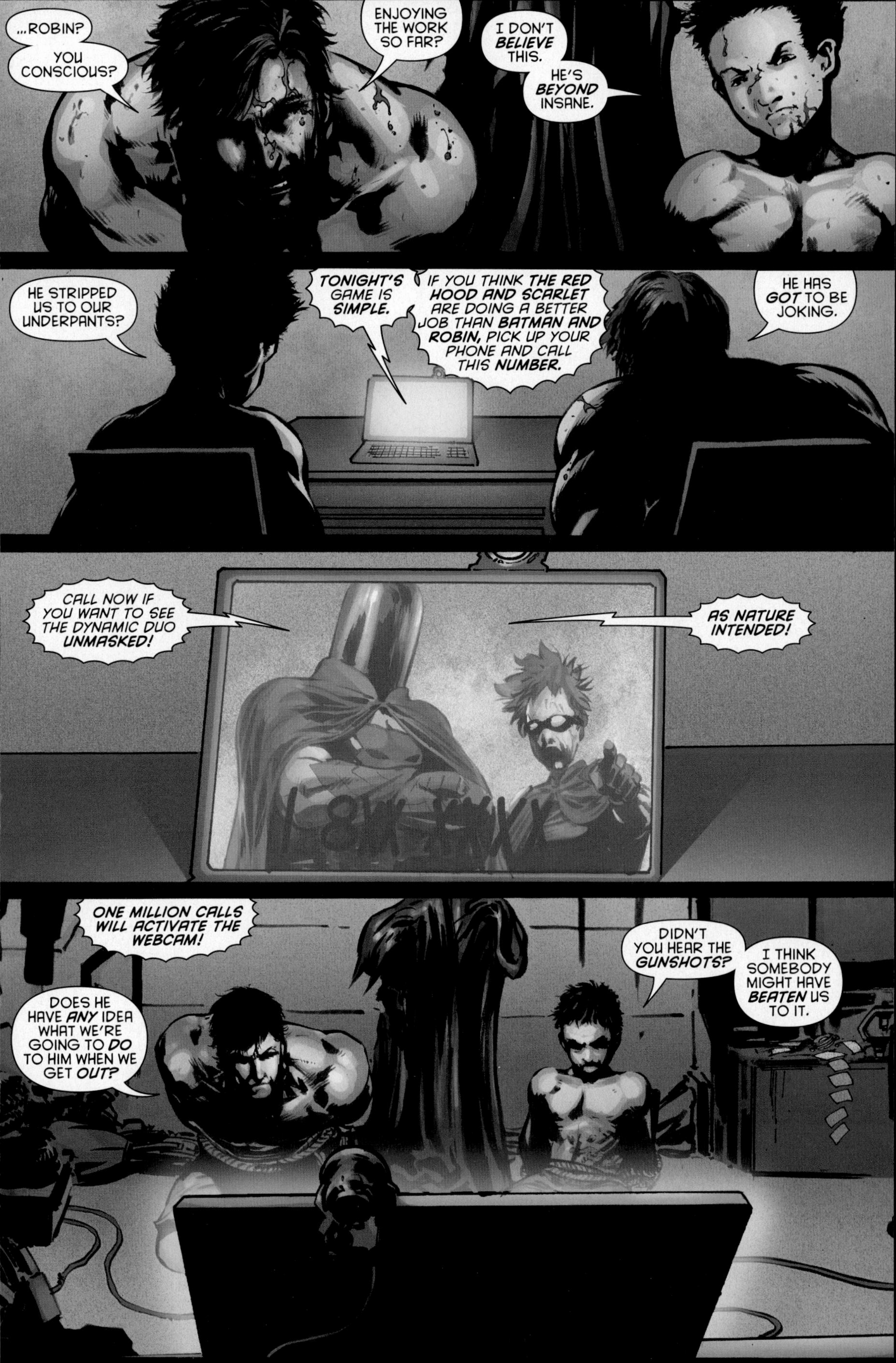
...ROBIN?
YOU CONSCIOUS?
ENJOYING THE WORK SO FAR?
I DON'T BELIEVE THIS.
HE'S BEYOND INSANE.
HE STRIPPED US TO OUR UNDERPANTS?
TONIGHT'S GAME IS SIMPLE.
IF YOU THINK THE RED HOOD AND SCARLET ARE DOING A BETTER JOB THAN BATMAN AND ROBIN, PICK UP YOUR PHONE AND CALL THIS NUMBER.
HE HAS GOT TO BE JOKING.
CALL NOW IF YOU WANT TO SEE THE DYNAMIC DUO UNMASKED!
AS NATURE INTENDED!
ONE MILLION CALLS WILL ACTIVATE THE WEBCAM!
DOES HE HAVE ANY IDEA WHAT WE'RE GOING TO DO TO HIM WHEN WE GET OUT?
DIDN'T YOU HEAR THE GUNSHOTS?
I THINK SOMEBODY MIGHT HAVE BEATEN US TO IT.

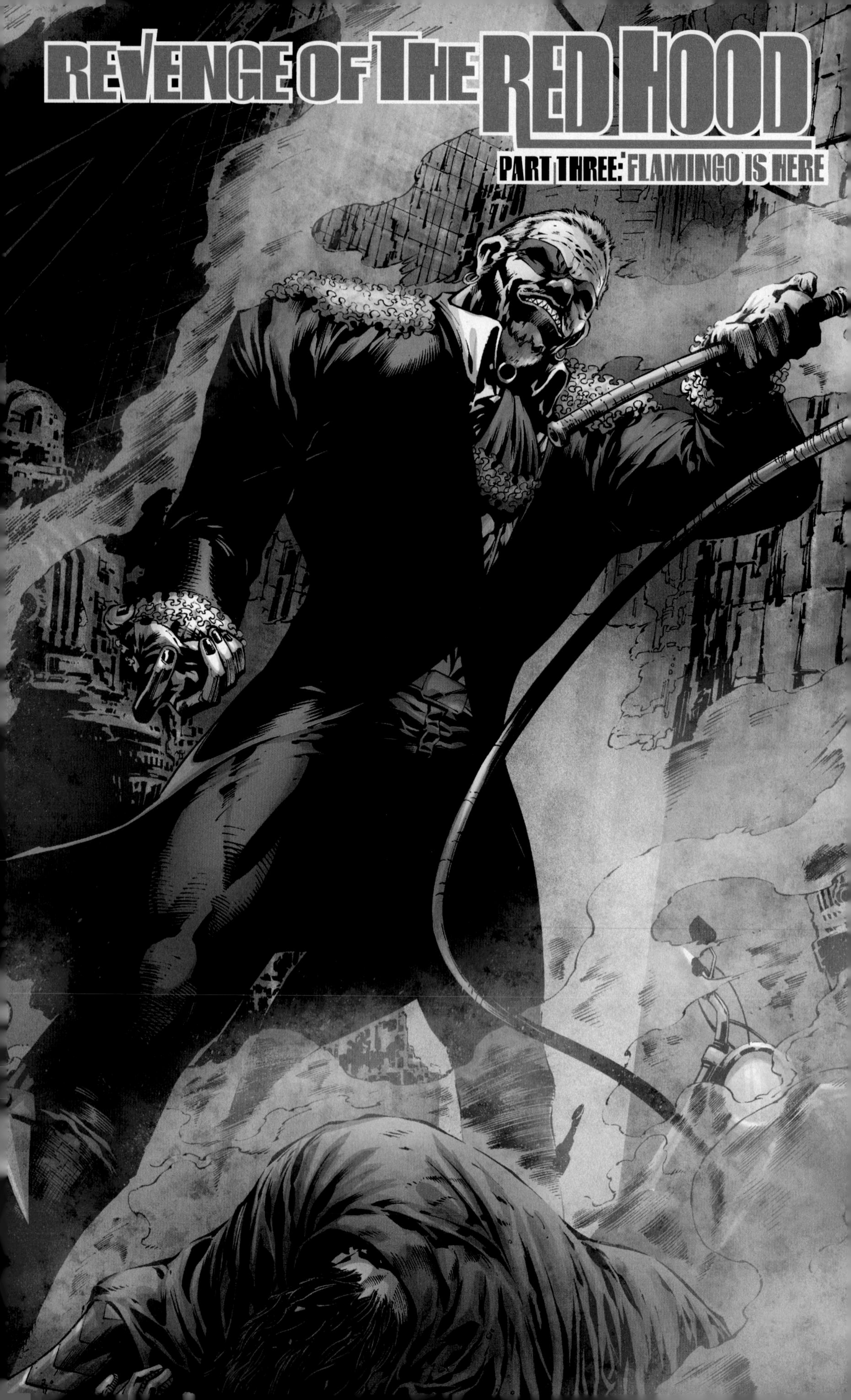
REVENGE OF THE RED HOOD
PART THREE: FLAMINGO IS HERE

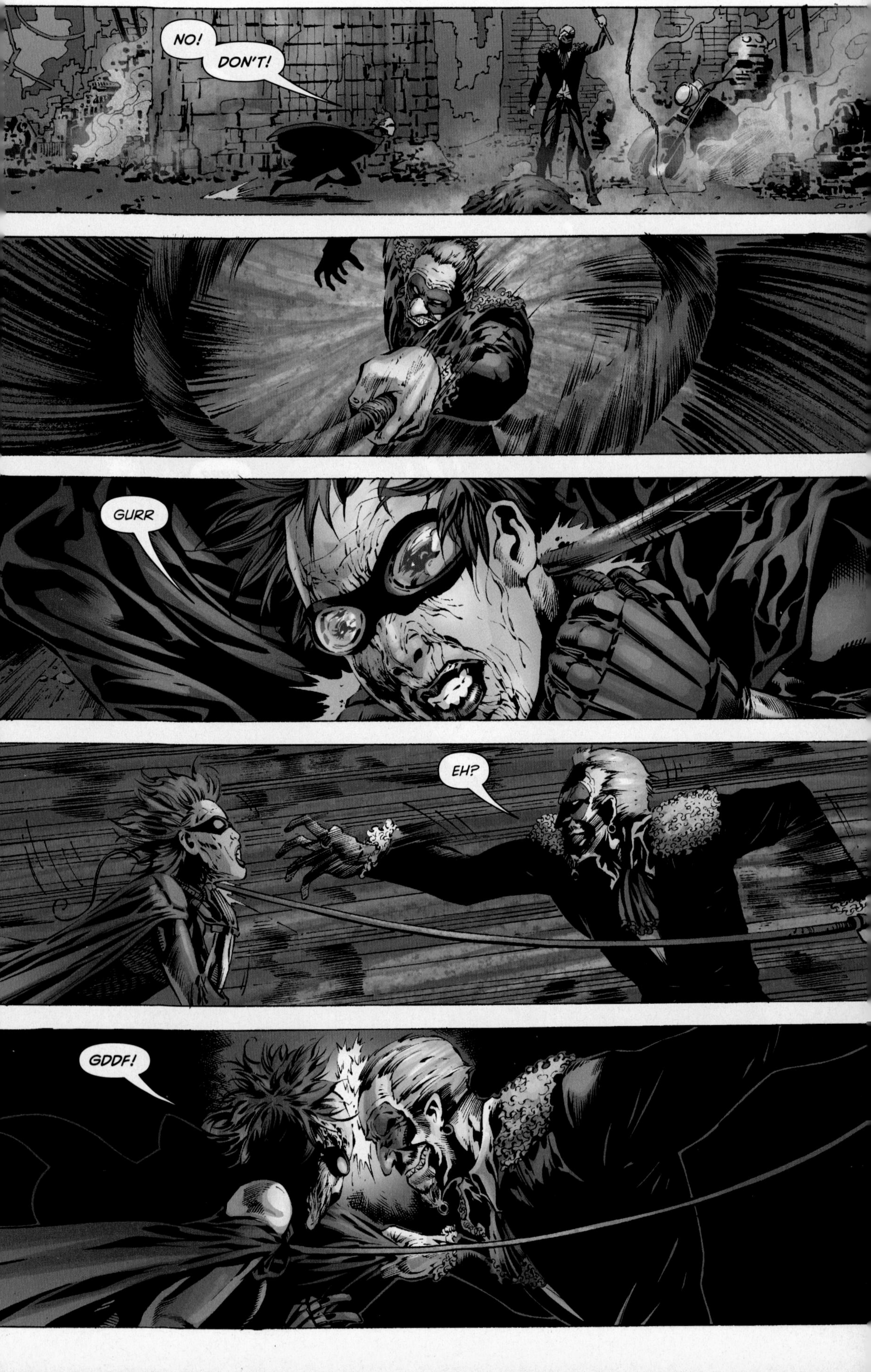
NO!
DON'T!
GURR
EH?
GDDF!

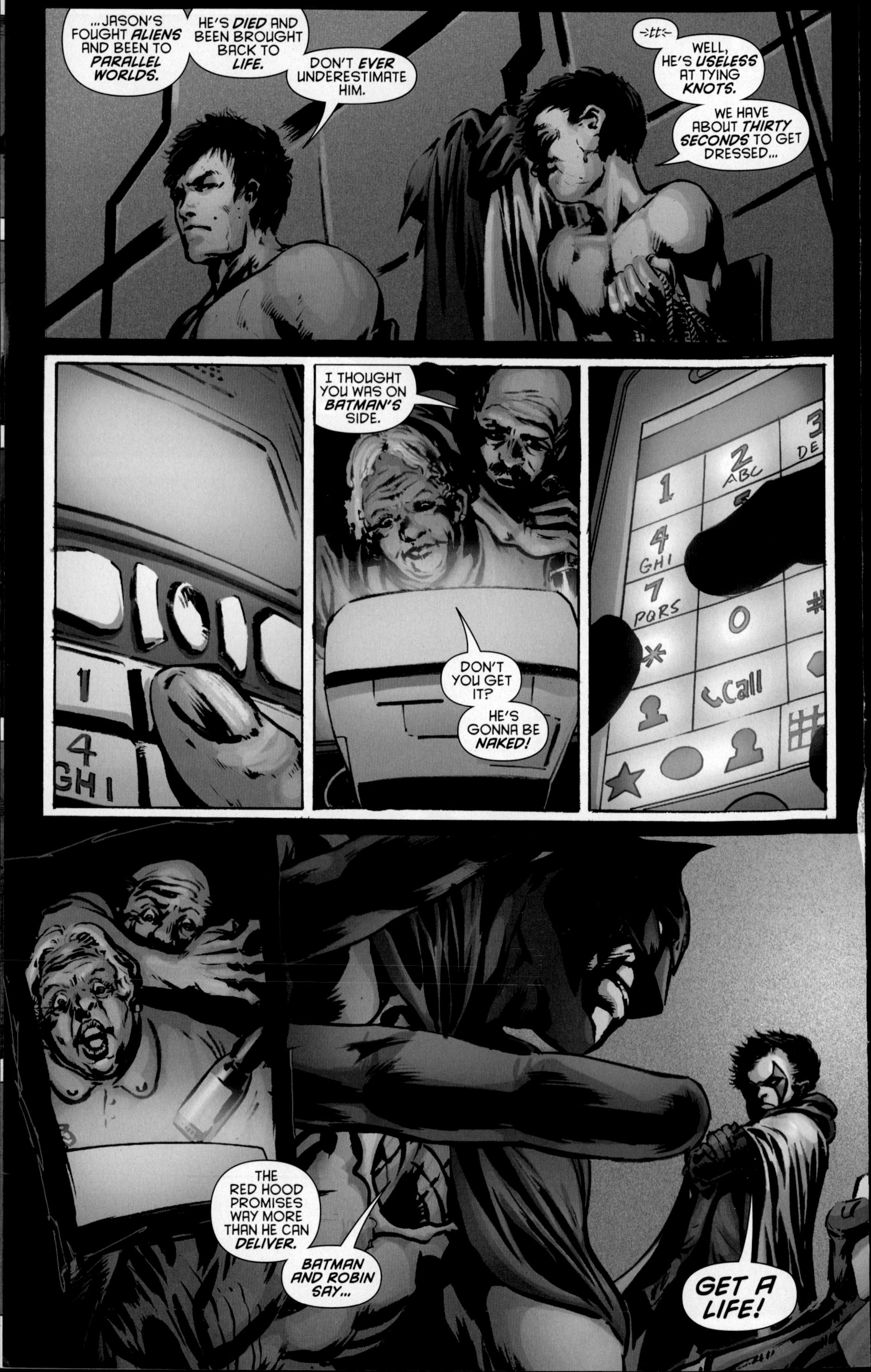
...JASON'S FOUGHT ALIENS AND BEEN TO PARALLEL WORLDS.
HE'S DIED AND BEEN BROUGHT BACK TO LIFE.
DON'T EVER UNDERESTIMATE HIM.
-tt-
WELL, HE'S USELESS AT TYING KNOTS.
WE HAVE ABOUT THIRTY SECONDS TO GET DRESSED...
I THOUGHT YOU WAS ON BATMAN'S SIDE.
DON'T YOU GET IT?
HE'S GONNA BE NAKED!
THE RED HOOD PROMISES WAY MORE THAN HE CAN DELIVER.
BATMAN AND ROBIN SAY...
GET A LIFE!

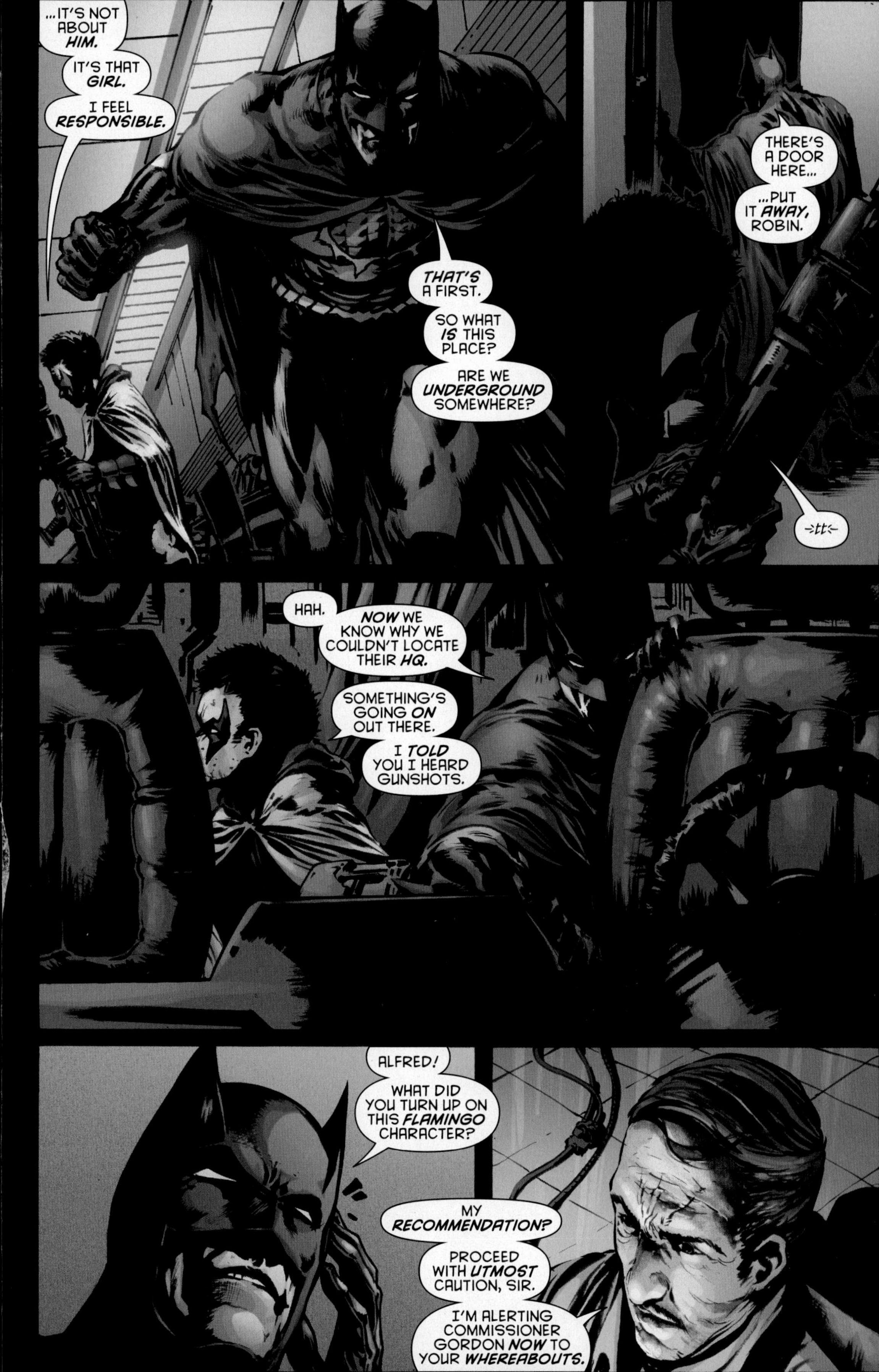
...IT'S NOT ABOUT HIM.
IT'S THAT GIRL.
I FEEL RESPONSIBLE.
THAT'S A FIRST.
SO WHAT IS THIS PLACE?
ARE WE UNDERGROUND SOMEWHERE?
THERE'S A DOOR HERE...
...PUT IT AWAY, ROBIN.
-tt-
HAH.
NOW WE KNOW WHY WE COULDN'T LOCATE THEIR HQ.
SOMETHING'S GOING ON OUT THERE.
I TOLD YOU I HEARD GUNSHOTS.
ALFRED!
WHAT DID YOU TURN UP ON THIS FLAMINGO CHARACTER?
MY RECOMMENDATION?
PROCEED WITH UTMOST CAUTION, SIR.
I'M ALERTING COMMISSIONER GORDON NOW TO YOUR WHEREABOUTS.

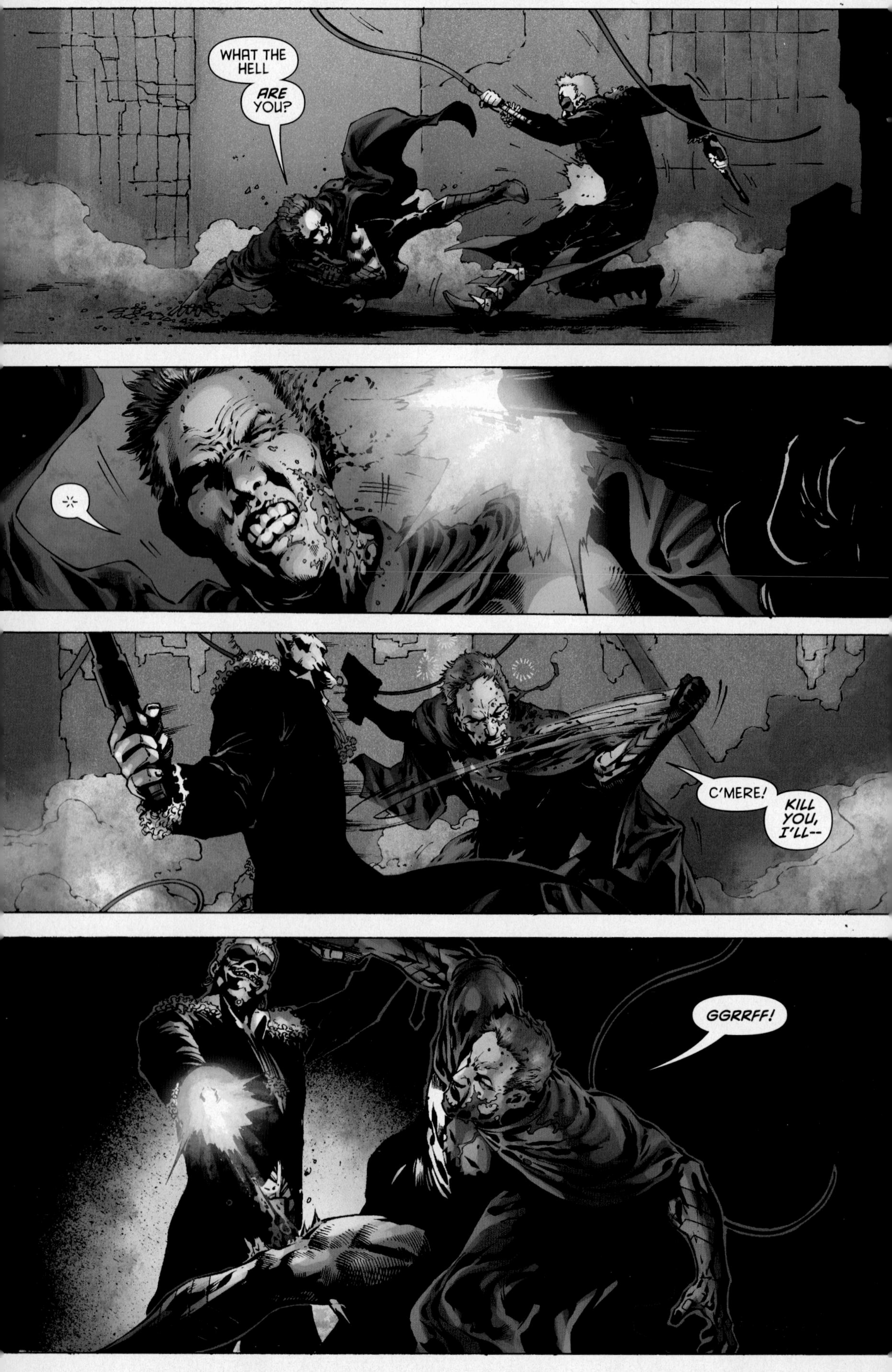
WHAT THE HELL ARE YOU?
!
C'MERE! KILL YOU, I'LL--
GGRRFF!

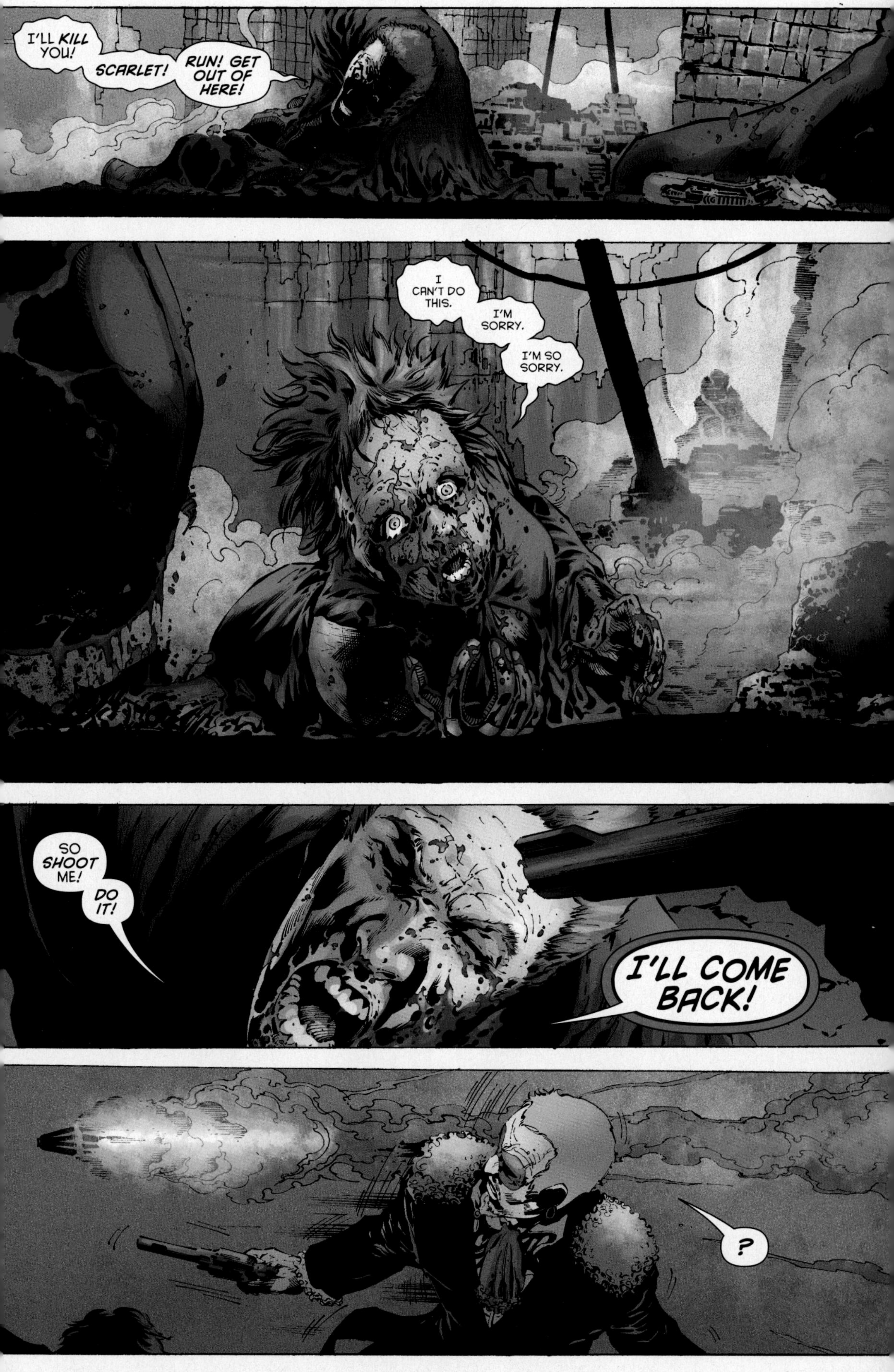
I'LL KILL YOU!
SCARLET!
RUN! GET OUT OF HERE!
I CAN'T DO THIS.
I'M SORRY.
I'M SO SORRY.
SO SHOOT ME!
DO IT!
I'LL COME BACK!
?

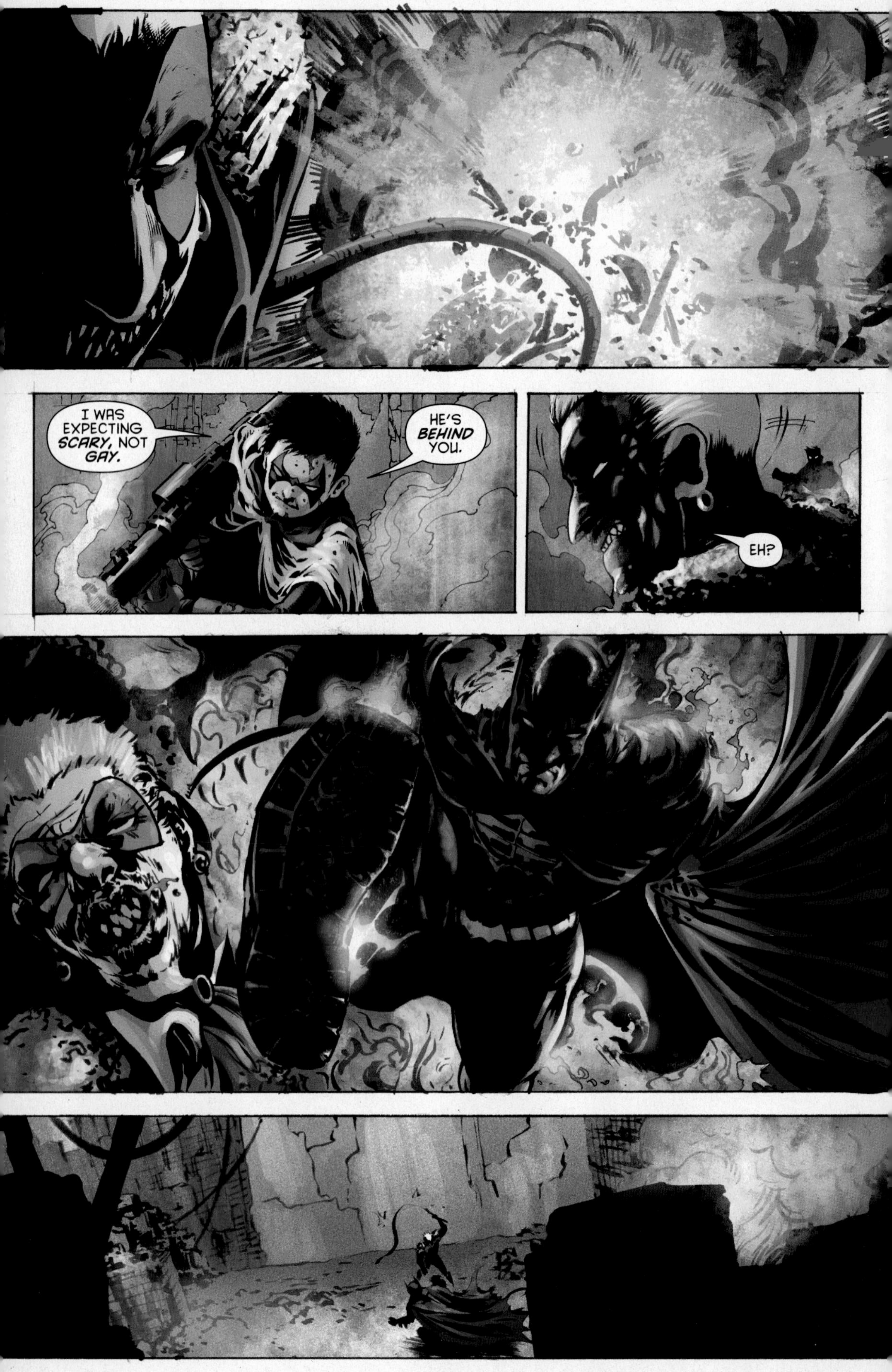
I WAS EXPECTING SCARY, NOT GAY.
HE'S BEHIND YOU.
EH?

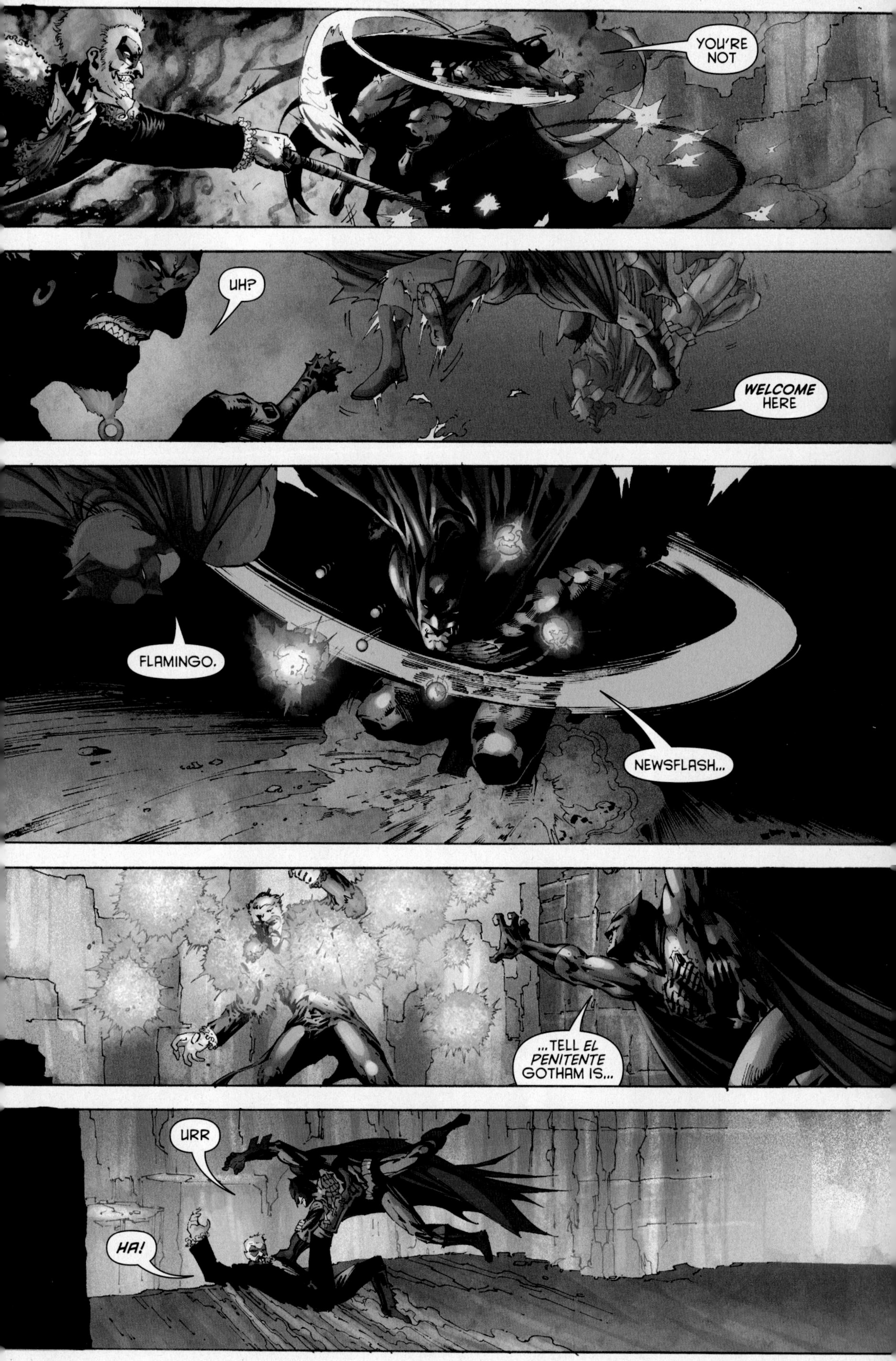
YOU'RE NOT
UH?
WELCOME HERE
FLAMINGO.
NEWSFLASH...
...TELL EL PENITENTE GOTHAM IS...
URR
HA!

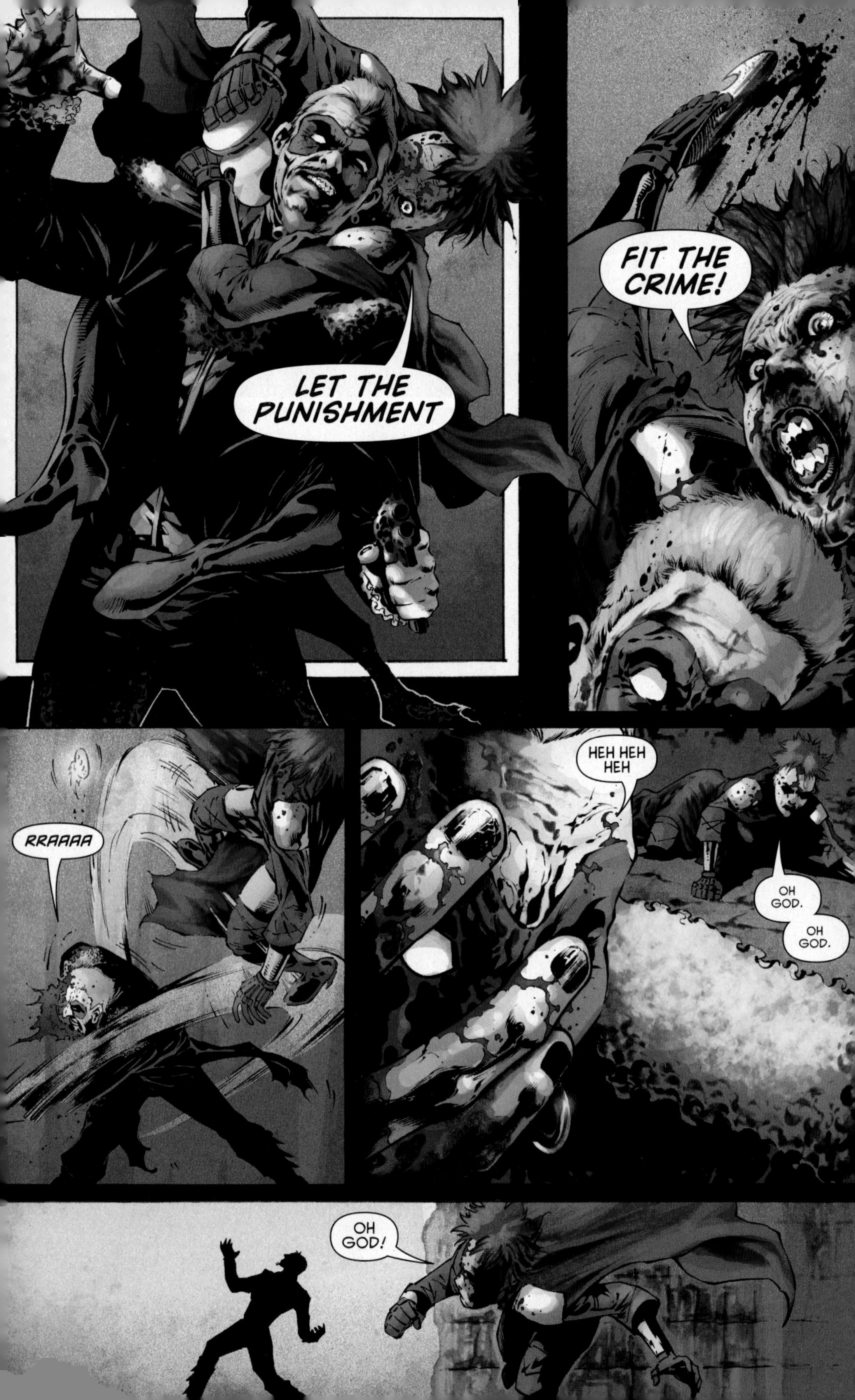
LET THE PUNISHMENT
FIT THE CRIME!
RRAAAA
HEH HEH HEH
OH GOD.
OH GOD.
OH GOD!

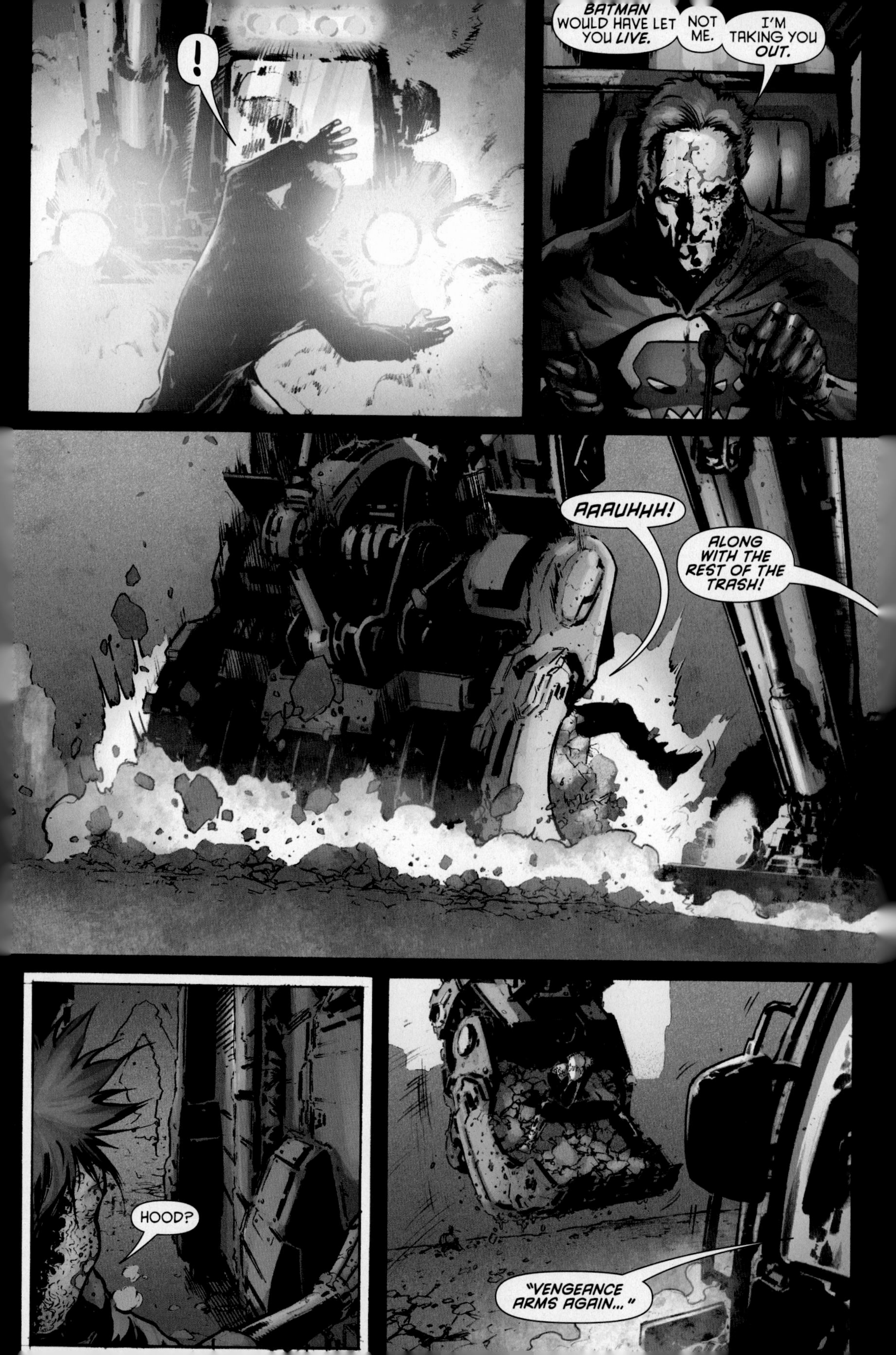

!
BATMAN WOULD HAVE LET YOU LIVE.
NOT ME.
I'M TAKING YOU OUT.
AAAUHHH!
ALONG WITH THE REST OF THE TRASH!
HOOD?
"VENGEANCE ARMS AGAIN..."

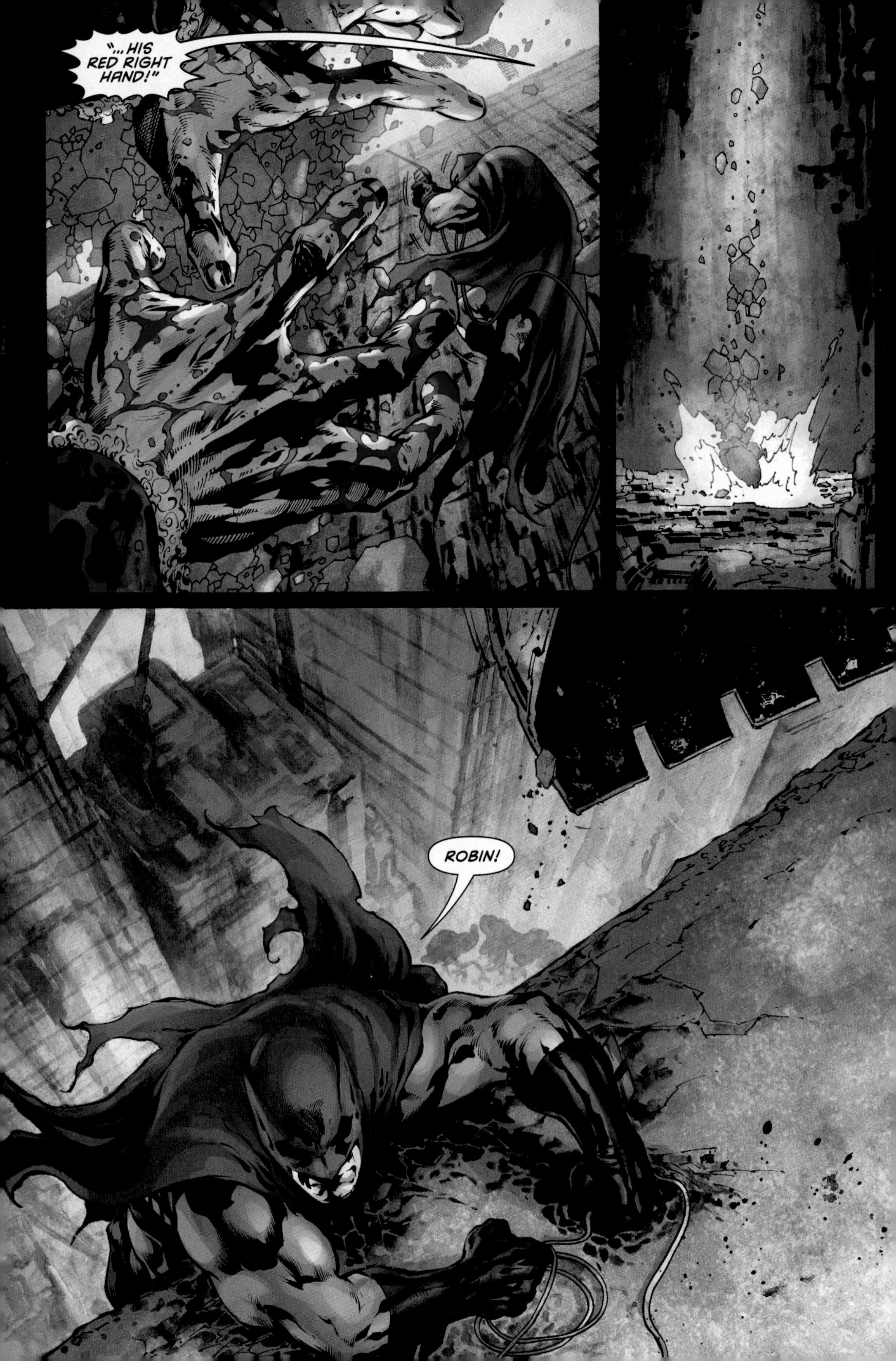
"...HIS RED RIGHT HAND!"
ROBIN!

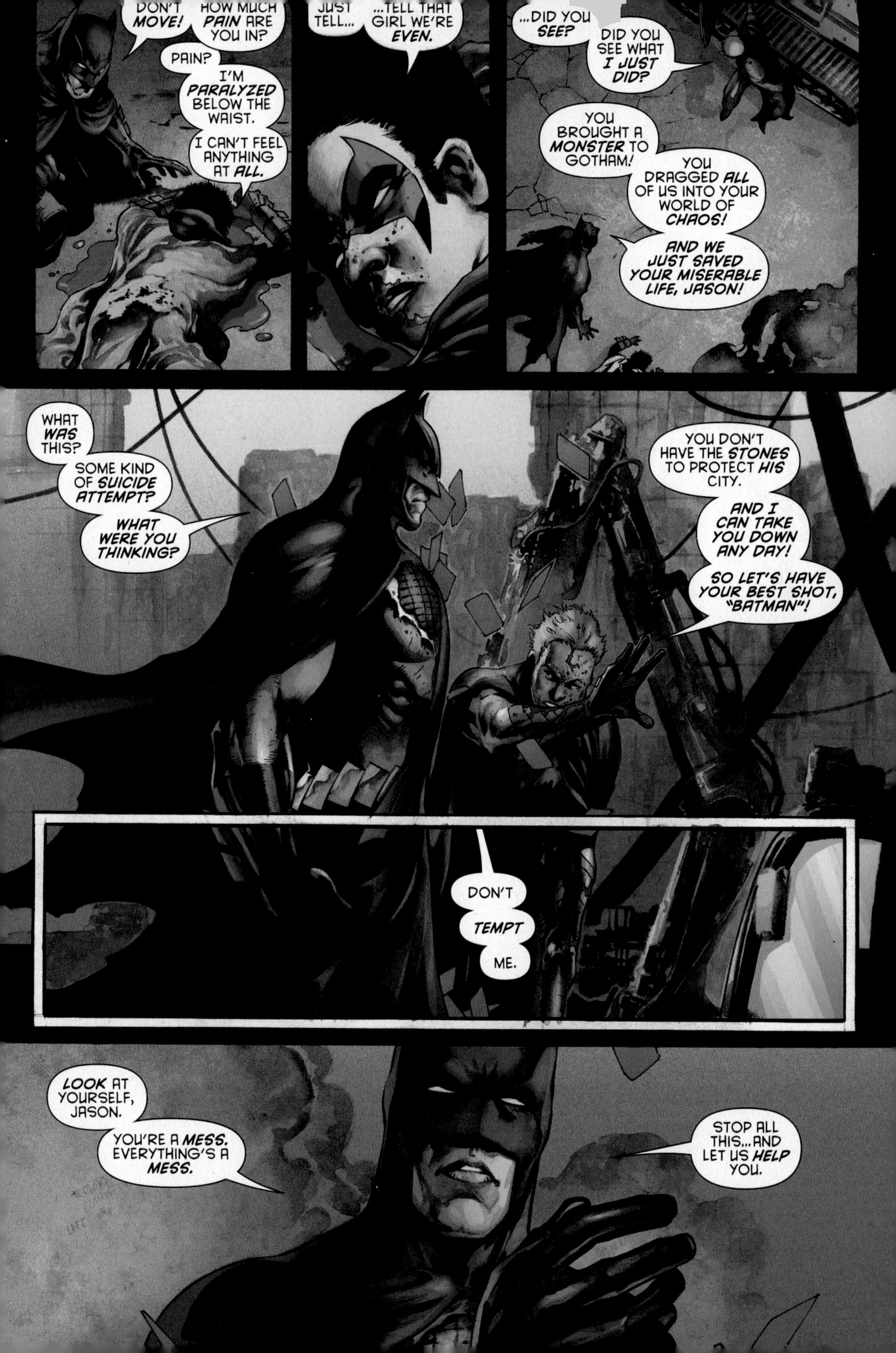
DON'T MOVE!
HOW MUCH PAIN ARE YOU IN?
PAIN?
I'M PARALYZED BELOW THE WAIST.
I CAN'T FEEL ANYTHING AT ALL.
JUST TELL...
...TELL THAT GIRL WE'RE EVEN.
...DID YOU SEE?
DID YOU SEE WHAT I JUST DID?
YOU BROUGHT A MONSTER TO GOTHAM!
YOU DRAGGED ALL OF US INTO YOUR WORLD OF CHAOS!
AND WE JUST SAVED YOUR MISERABLE LIFE, JASON!
WHAT WAS THIS?
SOME KIND OF SUICIDE ATTEMPT?
WHAT WERE YOU THINKING?
YOU DON'T HAVE THE STONES TO PROTECT HIS CITY.
AND I CAN TAKE YOU DOWN ANY DAY!
SO LET'S HAVE YOUR BEST SHOT, "BATMAN"!
DON'T
TEMPT
ME.
LOOK AT YOURSELF, JASON.
YOU'RE A MESS. EVERYTHING'S A MESS.
STOP ALL THIS...AND LET US HELP YOU.

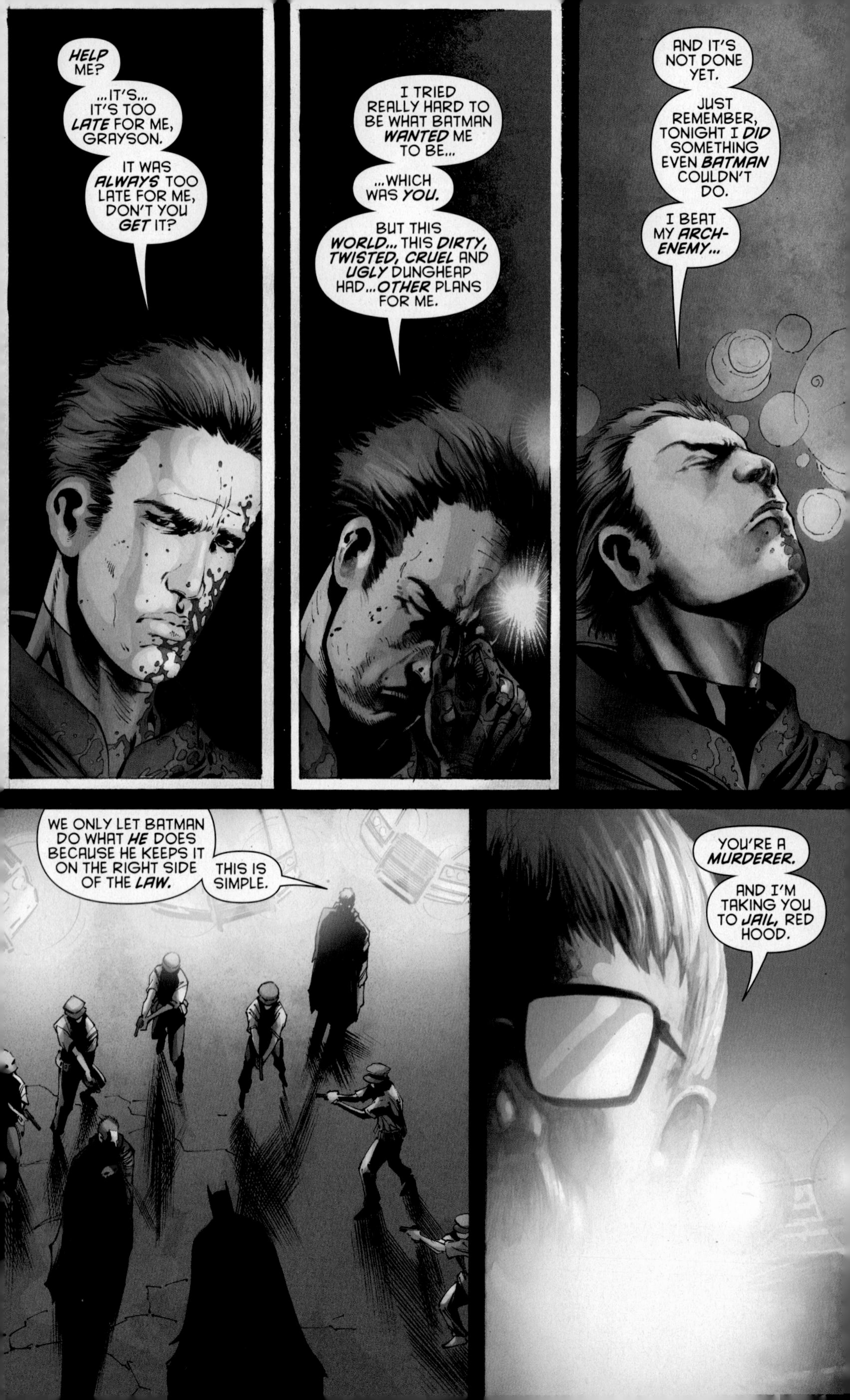
HELP ME?
...IT'S... IT'S TOO LATE FOR ME, GRAYSON.
IT WAS ALWAYS TOO LATE FOR ME, DON'T YOU GET IT?
I TRIED REALLY HARD TO BE WHAT BATMAN WANTED ME TO BE...
...WHICH WAS YOU.
BUT THIS WORLD... THIS DIRTY, TWISTED, CRUEL AND UGLY DUNGHEAP HAD...OTHER PLANS FOR ME.
AND IT'S NOT DONE YET.
JUST REMEMBER, TONIGHT I DID SOMETHING EVEN BATMAN COULDN'T DO.
I BEAT MY ARCH-ENEMY...
WE ONLY LET BATMAN DO WHAT HE DOES BECAUSE HE KEEPS IT ON THE RIGHT SIDE OF THE LAW.
THIS IS SIMPLE.
YOU'RE A MURDERER.
AND I'M TAKING YOU TO JAIL, RED HOOD.

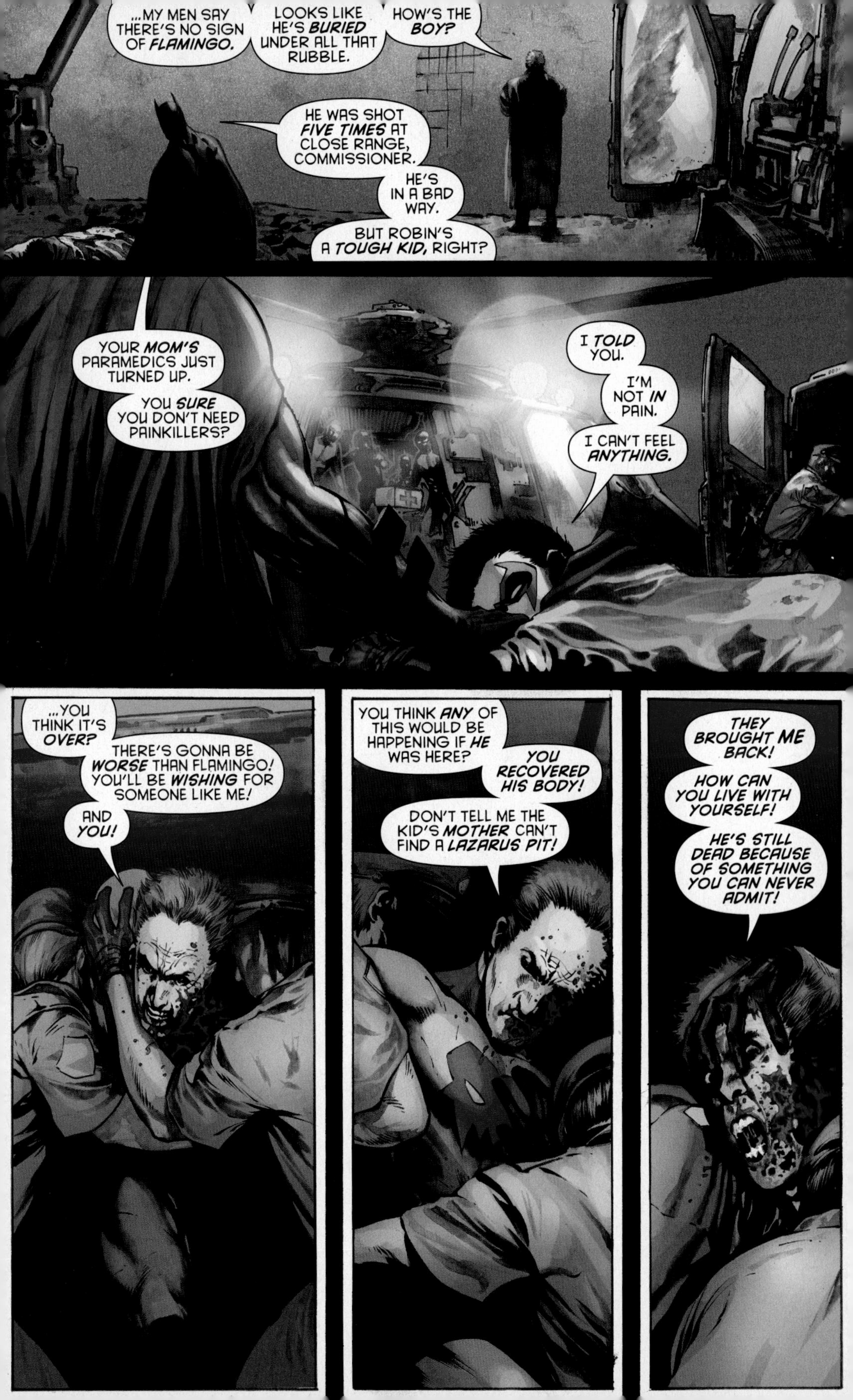

...MY MEN SAY THERE'S NO SIGN OF FLAMINGO.
LOOKS LIKE HE'S BURIED UNDER ALL THAT RUBBLE.
HOW'S THE BOY?
HE WAS SHOT FIVE TIMES AT CLOSE RANGE, COMMISSIONER.
HE'S IN A BAD WAY.
BUT ROBIN'S A TOUGH KID, RIGHT?
YOUR MOM'S PARAMEDICS JUST TURNED UP.
YOU SURE YOU DON'T NEED PAINKILLERS?
I TOLD YOU.
I'M NOT IN PAIN.
I CAN'T FEEL ANYTHING.
...YOU THINK IT'S OVER?
THERE'S GONNA BE WORSE THAN FLAMINGO! YOU'LL BE WISHING FOR SOMEONE LIKE ME!
AND YOU!
YOU THINK ANY OF THIS WOULD BE HAPPENING IF HE WAS HERE?
YOU RECOVERED HIS BODY!
DON'T TELL ME THE KID'S MOTHER CAN'T FIND A LAZARUS PIT!
THEY BROUGHT ME BACK!
HOW CAN YOU LIVE WITH YOURSELF!
HE'S STILL DEAD BECAUSE OF SOMETHING YOU CAN NEVER ADMIT!

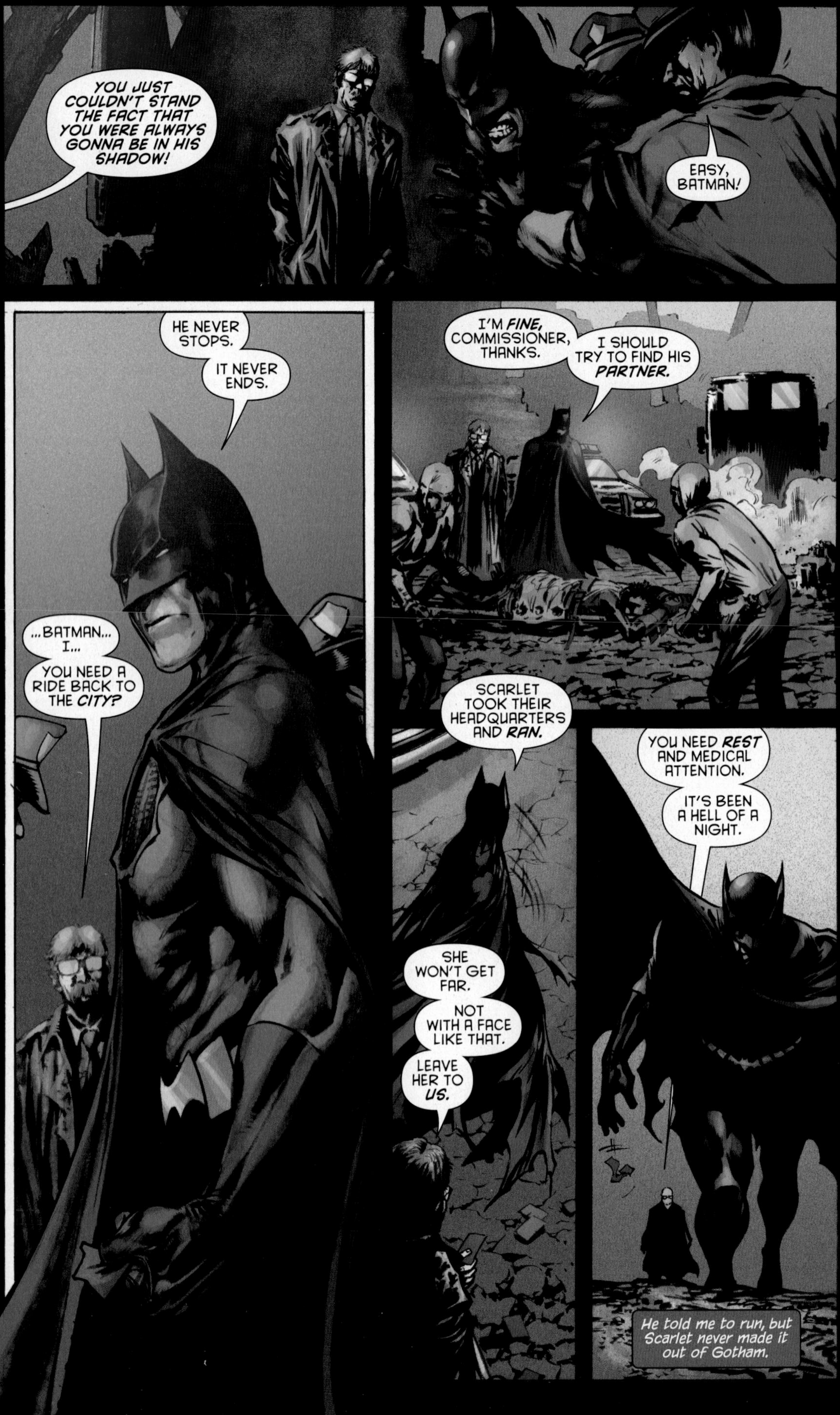
YOU JUST COULDN'T STAND THE FACT THAT YOU WERE ALWAYS GONNA BE IN HIS SHADOW!
EASY, BATMAN!
HE NEVER STOPS.
IT NEVER ENDS.
...BATMAN... I...
YOU NEED A RIDE BACK TO THE CITY?
I'M FINE, COMMISSIONER, THANKS.
I SHOULD TRY TO FIND HIS PARTNER.
SCARLET TOOK THEIR HEADQUARTERS AND RAN.
SHE WON'T GET FAR.
NOT WITH A FACE LIKE THAT.
LEAVE HER TO US.
YOU NEED REST AND MEDICAL ATTENTION.
IT'S BEEN A HELL OF A NIGHT.
He told me to run, but Scarlet never made it out of Gotham.

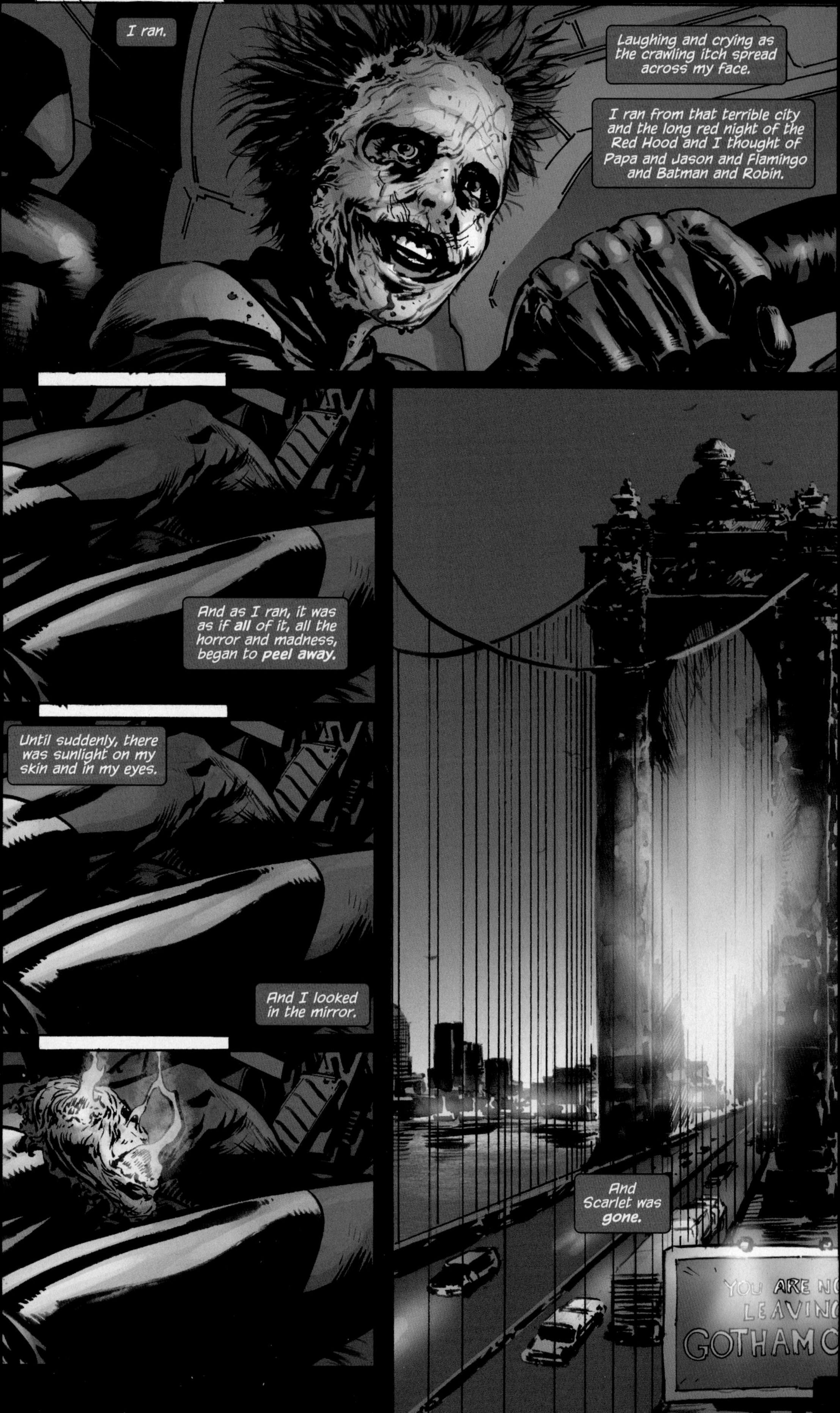
I ran.
Laughing and crying as the crawling itch spread across my face.
I ran from that terrible city and the long red night of the Red Hood and I thought of Papa and Jason and Flamingo and Batman and Robin.
And as I ran, it was as if **all** of it, all the horror and madness, began to **peel away.**
Until suddenly, there was sunlight on my skin and in my eyes.
And I looked in the mirror.
And Scarlet was **gone.**
YOU ARE NO
LEAVIN
GOTHAM

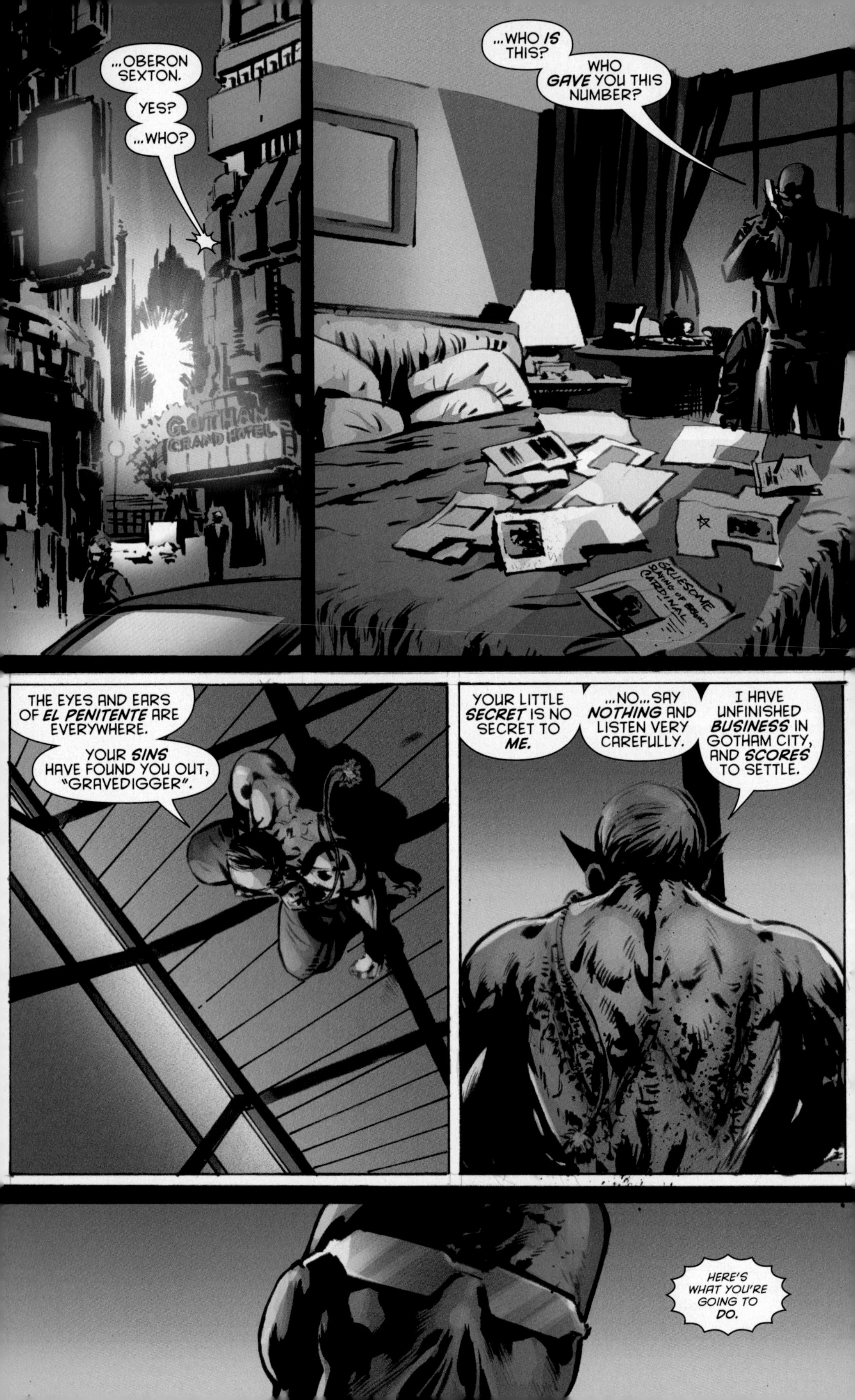
...OBERON SEXTON.
YES?
...WHO?
GOTHAM GRAND HOTEL
...WHO *IS* THIS?
WHO *GAVE* YOU THIS NUMBER?
GRUESOME
CARDINAL
THE EYES AND EARS OF *EL PENITENTE* ARE EVERYWHERE.
YOUR *SINS* HAVE FOUND YOU OUT, "GRAVEDIGGER".
YOUR LITTLE *SECRET* IS NO SECRET TO *ME.*
...NO...SAY *NOTHING* AND LISTEN VERY CAREFULLY.
I HAVE UNFINISHED *BUSINESS* IN GOTHAM CITY, AND *SCORES* TO SETTLE.
HERE'S WHAT YOU'RE GOING TO *DO.*

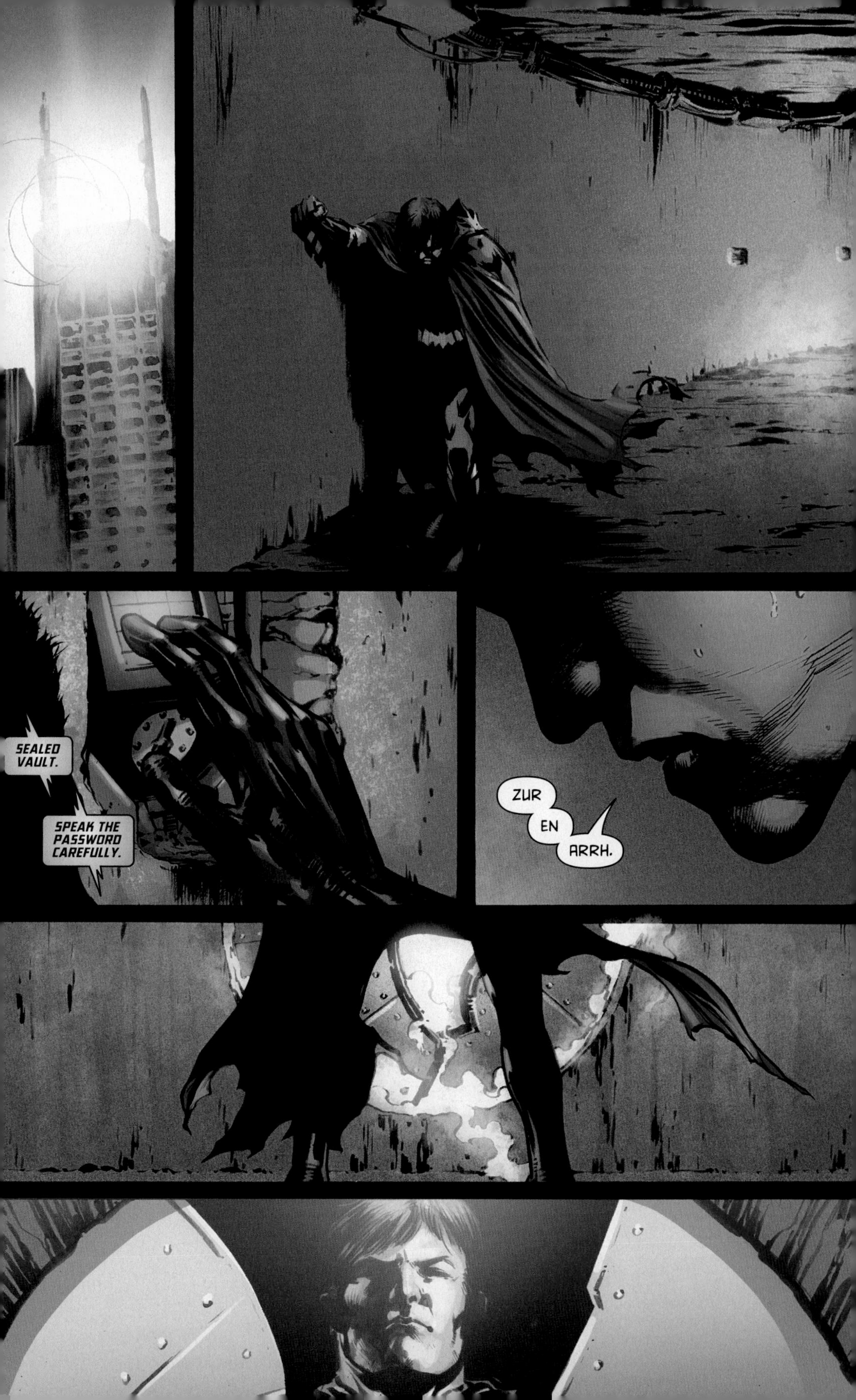
SEALED VAULT.
SPEAK THE PASSWORD CAREFULLY.
ZUR
EN
ARRH.

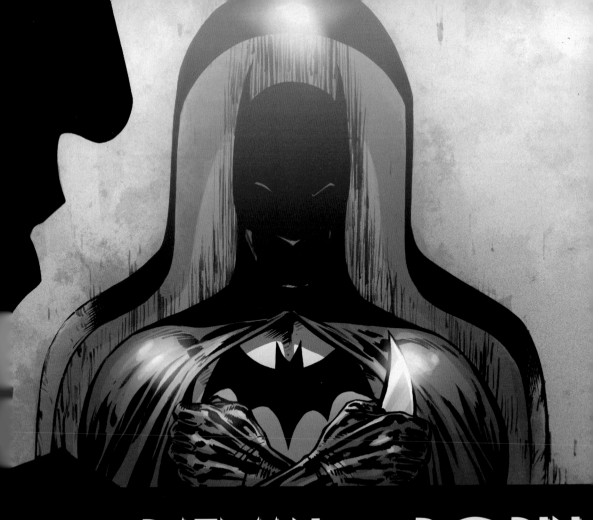

NEXT IN BATMAN AND ROBIN
BLACKEST KNIGHT

BATMAN REDRAWN

A guided tour through the creation of BATMAN AND ROBIN by Grant Morrison, Frank Quitely and Philip Tan

THE COVERS

issue one

Bruce Wayne was gone, but Batman could not die.

With Dick Grayson and Damian Wayne taking the lead roles, we wanted to make the new book instantly feel and look different from the Bruce Wayne/Tim Drake team we'd be replacing.

Since starting this run of Batman stories in 2006, I've been drawing inspiration from some of the most neglected areas of Batman's long publishing and screen history — like the 1950s "sci-fi" Batman and the '60s TV show. The color palette of the "Batman R.I.P." storyline which preceded BATMAN AND ROBIN was built around red and black and was mostly grimly funereal and somber, so we chose brighter colors for BATMAN AND ROBIN to reflect the change in tone.

Looking at the 1950s covers in particular, there's an obvious vogue for intense, clashing colors in the logos, so we were able to do something ostensibly un-Batman-like while quoting Batman's graphic past — the vibrating contrast of purple and green, or blue and yellow, and the big, flat expanses of background color that were popular during that era of design all seemed ripe for a comeback. Unlike the flowing lines and paisley fronds of '60s psychedelia, the '50s brand of op/pop art in comics was straight, no frills, linear, modernist and, we felt, contemporary once more.

The idea was to intensify the trashy, pulpy energy of the book, but where "Batman R.I.P." had been inspired by industrial music, the Tibetan Book of the Dead and pop psychology, the reborn BATMAN AND ROBIN would be fast-moving, twisty and physical, like paint flung around a room by chimps in a gabba gabba frenzy of violence without consequence — as garish, sensational and flippant as we could make it.

In publishing circles, the color yellow is considered taboo (according to market research, yellow covers sell less than any other color, while covers with a lot of red tend to sell the best), so right up until the last second the yellow background for the first issue's cover was being debated, but it went out as originally intended and was one the best-selling comics of the decade, running to four printings (each of which used a different background color).

The image had to be simple and iconic — the modern equivalent of Batman holding up the ringmaster's hoop on the cover of DETECTIVE COMICS #38 which introduced Robin as "The sensational character find of 1940!" — and, as this original sketch shows, the cover idea didn't change much from conception to publication.

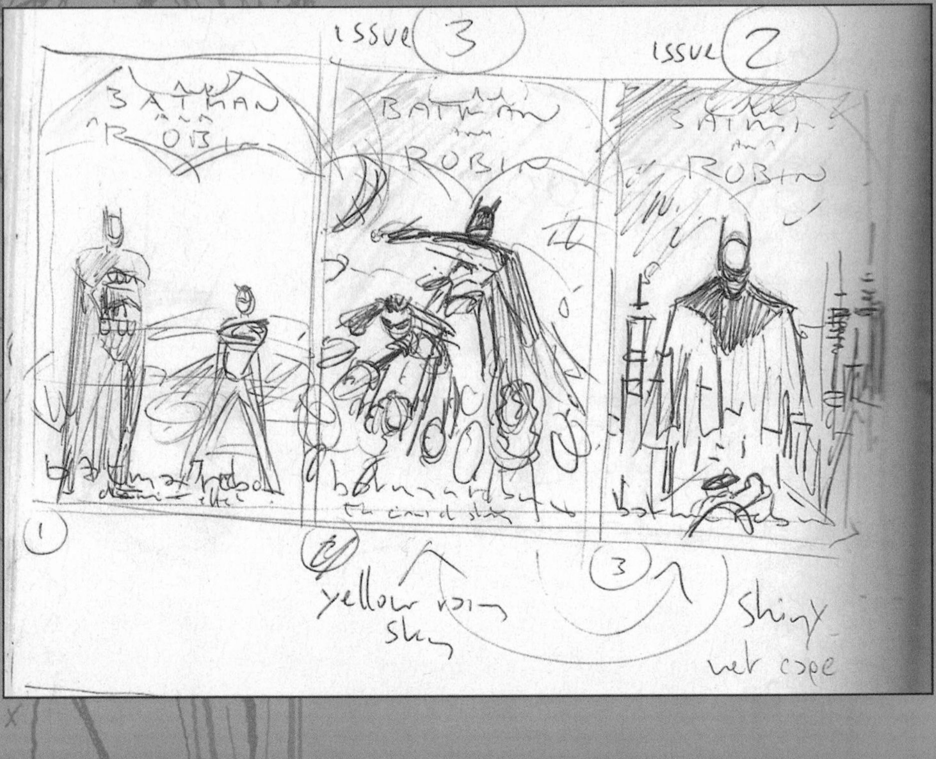
ISSUE 3
ISSUE 2
yellow
Shiny

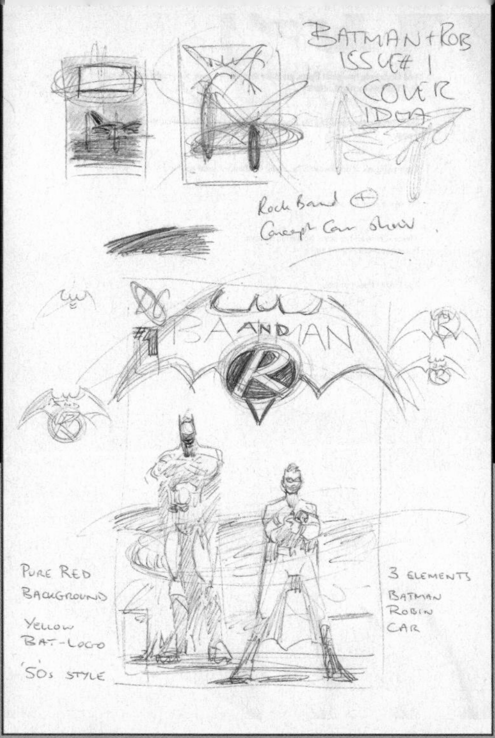
BATMAN + ROB ISSUE # 1 COVER IDEA
Rock Band + Concept Car show
PURE RED BACKGROUND
YELLOW BAT-LOGO
'50s STYLE
3 ELEMENTS BATMAN ROBIN CAR

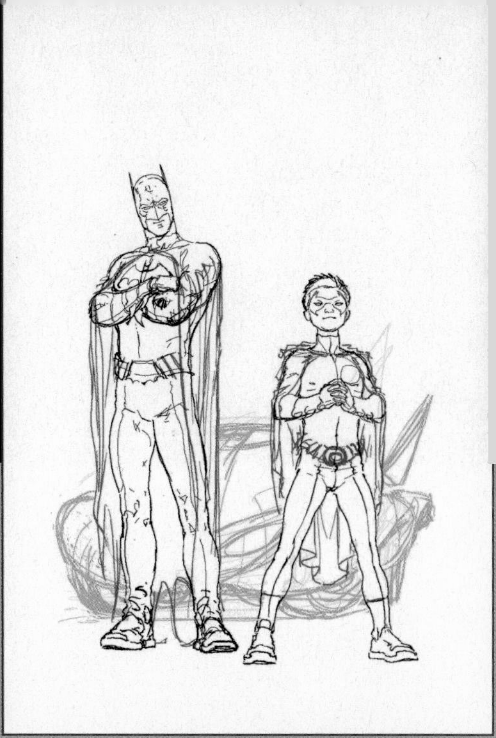

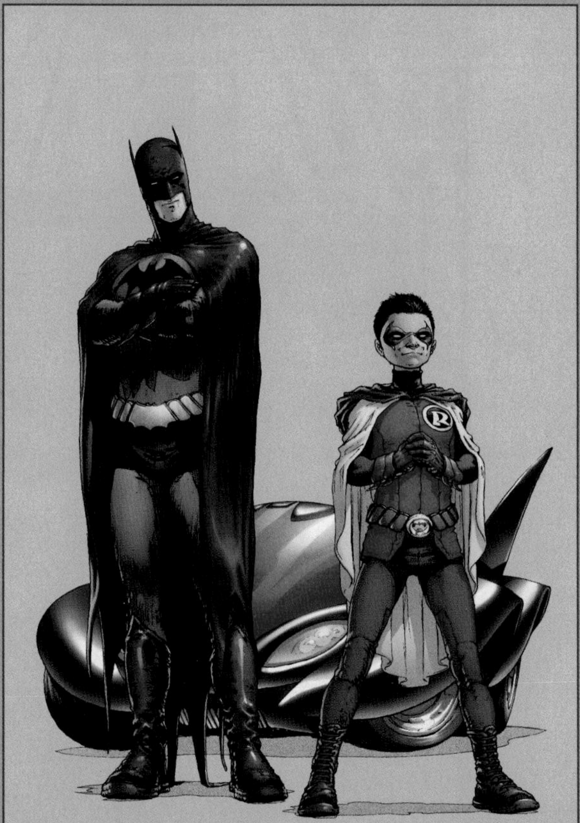

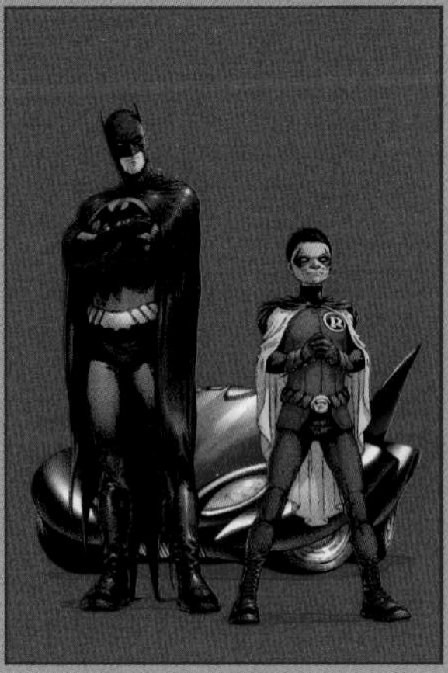

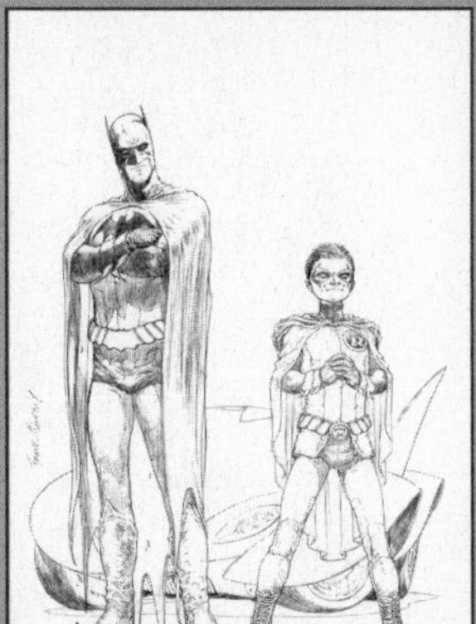

issue two

The original idea for this cover was to do a visual gag based on covers like these, which depict a huge, symbolic Batman towering over the scene of his latest adventure.

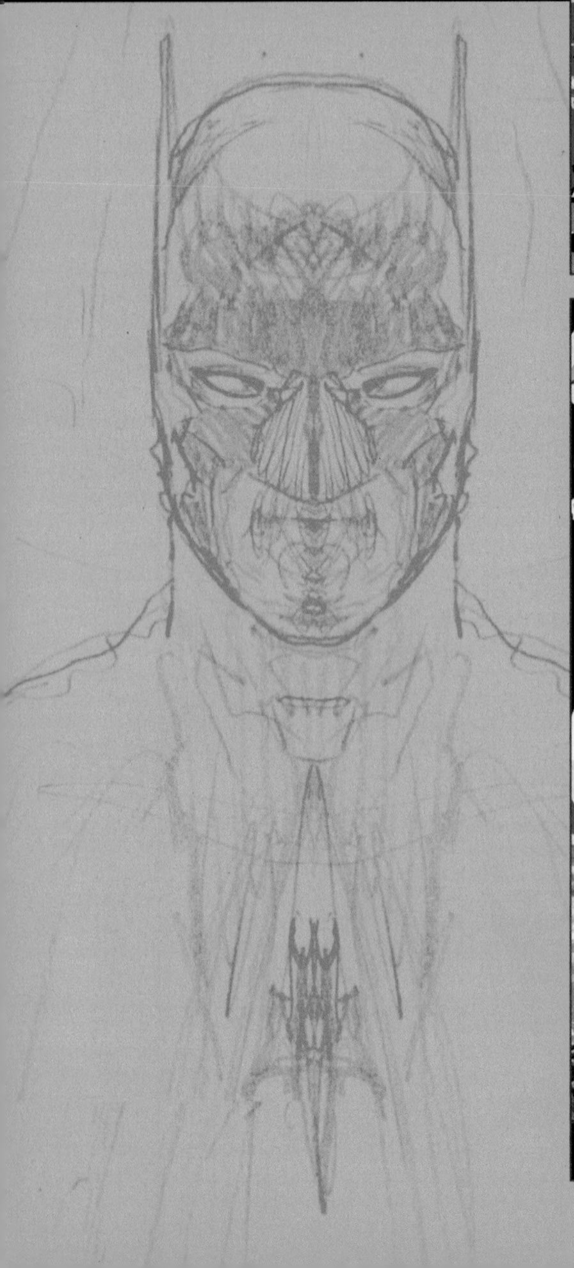

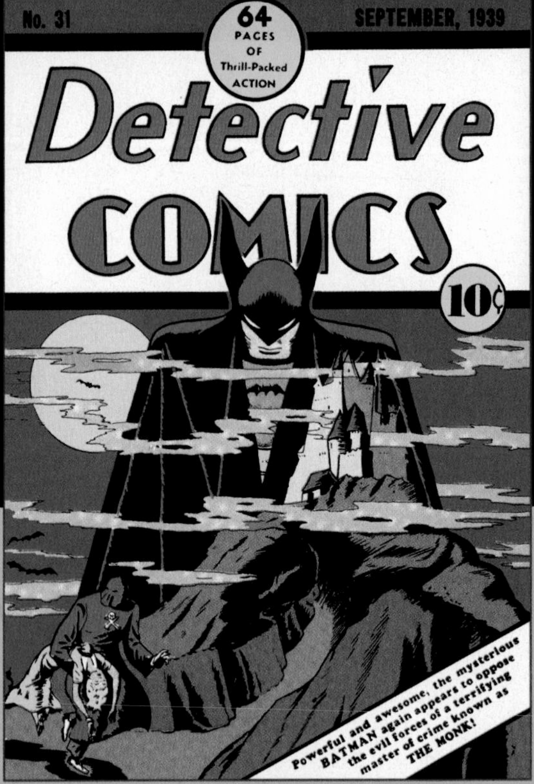
No. 31
64 PAGES OF Thrill-Packed ACTION
SEPTEMBER, 1939
Detective COMICS
10¢
Powerful and awesome, the mysterious BATMAN again appears to oppose the evil forces of a terrifying master of crime known as THE MONK!

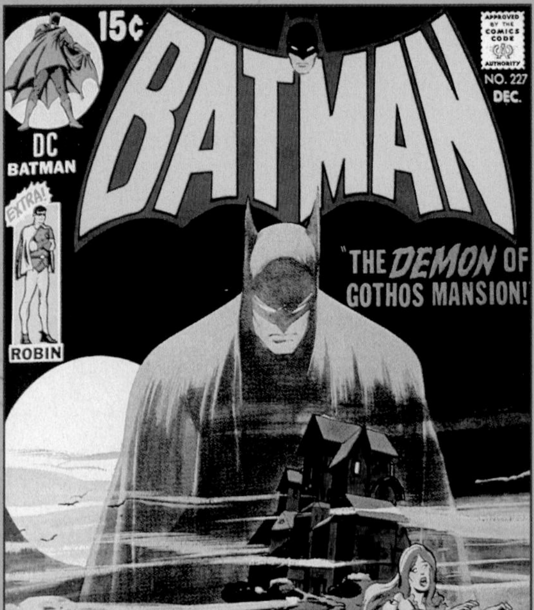
15¢
BATMAN
APPROVED BY THE COMICS CODE AUTHORITY
NO. 227
DEC.
DC
BATMAN
EXTRA!
ROBIN
"THE DEMON OF GOTHOS MANSION!"

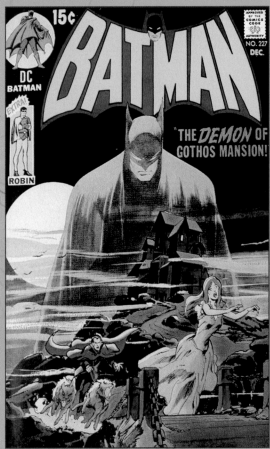

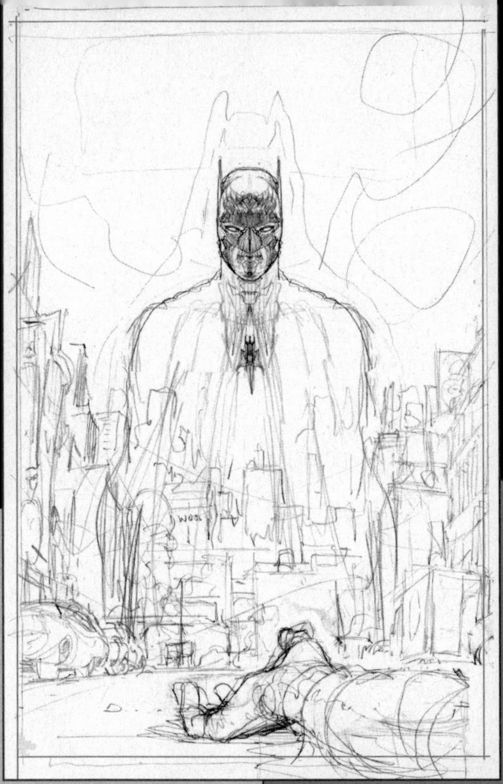

It seemed an interesting twist to make the "giant" Batman a *normal*-sized man looming over a *model* city — an architect's presentation piece made of balsa wood. In the middle of Main Street, we would see a dead man's arm and hand holding a domino, flattening buildings and crushing toy cars. Somehow I failed to convey any of this to Frank Quitely, but fortunately the finished cover was still a classic, which again went through several re-printings, each with its own different background color.

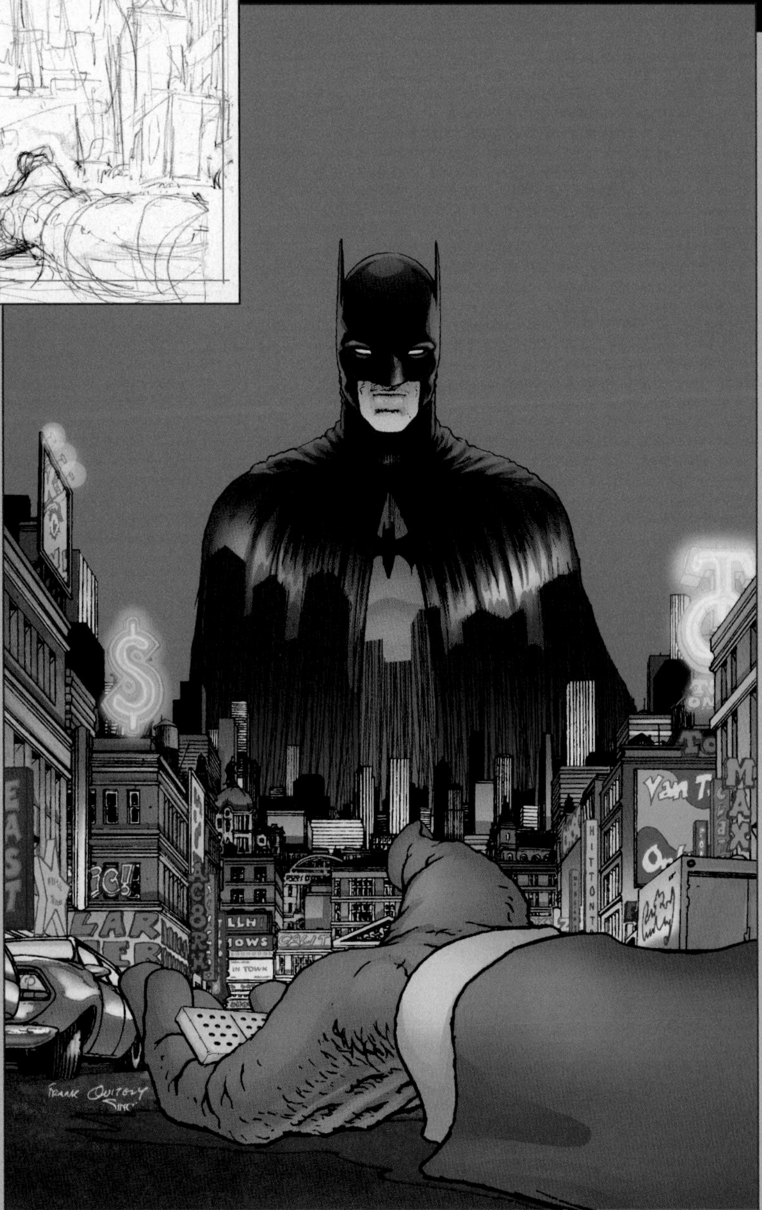
EAST
Van T
MAX
IN TOWN
FRANK QUITELY

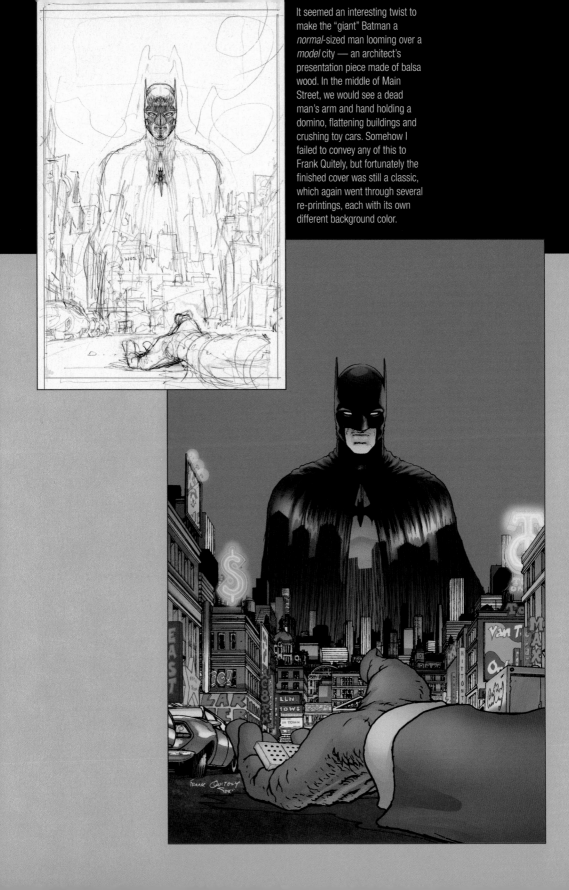

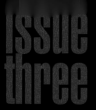

Issue three

This was commissioned as part of DC's "weird cover month" (as far as I'm aware, there were no other weird covers that month, leading us to suspect some elaborate practical joke), so Frank took the opportunity to create this Dollotron's-eye view of the conflict. The whirling vortex that spirals towards the tiny, battling figures of Batman and Robin creates a sense of lurching, unstoppable motion. Combined with the purple and lime green logo the result is purest necrodelia!

FRANK
QUITELY
SINC

FRANK
QUITELY

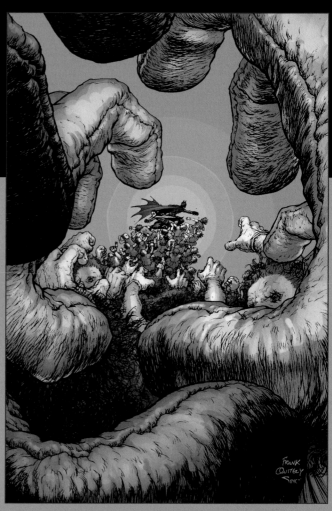

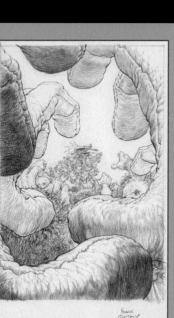

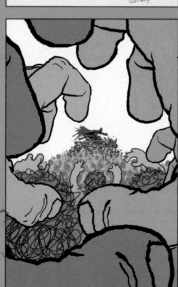

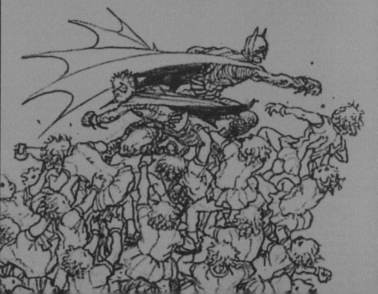

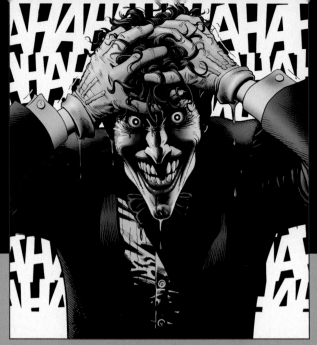

In a wonderfully Beatles-esque moment, this cover became the subject of frenzied conspiracy theory and fan interpretation when a reader, for unimaginable reasons of his own — perhaps goaded by Professor Pyg's obsession with upside-down-ness — rotated it through 180° only to find an eerie ghost of *this* famous image, as drawn by Brian Bolland in his and Alan Moore's graphic novel BATMAN: THE KILLING JOKE.

I'm sad to say that none of this was planned, but the undeniable apparition of a faceless face — a mask and a personality made of vertiginous space and scraps of meaning, all spiraling down into the ineluctable singularity of a Batman right hook — was so absolutely emblematic of the Joker that it surely had to be the work of some Cosmic Trickster.

What makes it odder and somehow more perfect is that BATMAN AND ROBIN *was* intended to feel "haunted" by the Joker from the very beginning. Although he does not appear in person in this volume, you will find numerous deliberate and carefully inserted traces of the Clown Prince of Crime's sinister presence throughout the series, some in the form of scenes that hint at or recall famous Joker moments of the past.

GRANT
MORRISON
FRANK
QUITELY
BATMAN
AND
ROBIN
3
OCT '09
BATMAN:
REBIRTH

So, if Quitely's hidden Joker image is *completely* unintended yet somehow perfectly complements the themes of the stories themselves, can it truly be described as "coincidence"? Is coincidence just our name for those moments when we are most truly aware of the fearful symmetry of existence? I don't know. Go ask your mom.

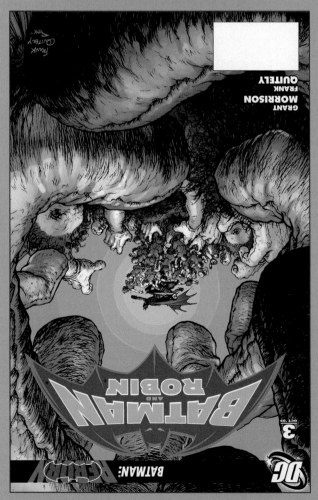

issues four five & six

With these covers, we returned to my design suggestions and there were no more "Magical Mystery Tour" moments of weird serendipity.

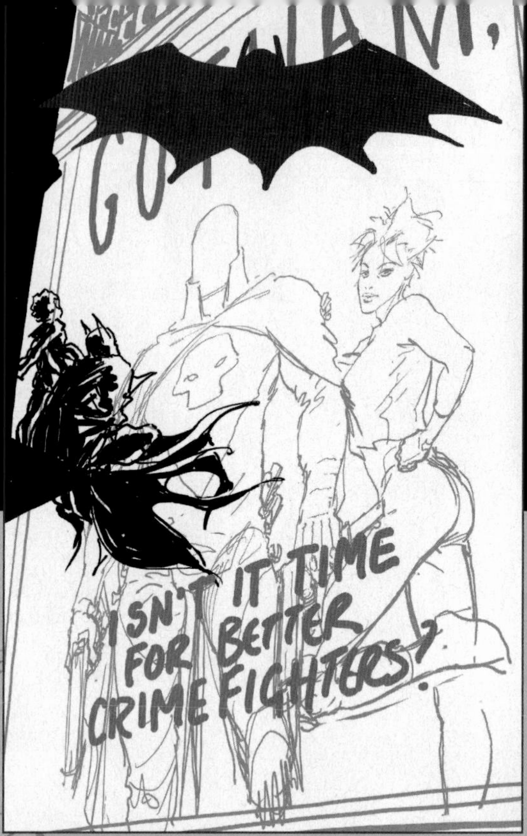
ISN'T IT TIME
FOR BETTER
CRIME FIGHTERS?

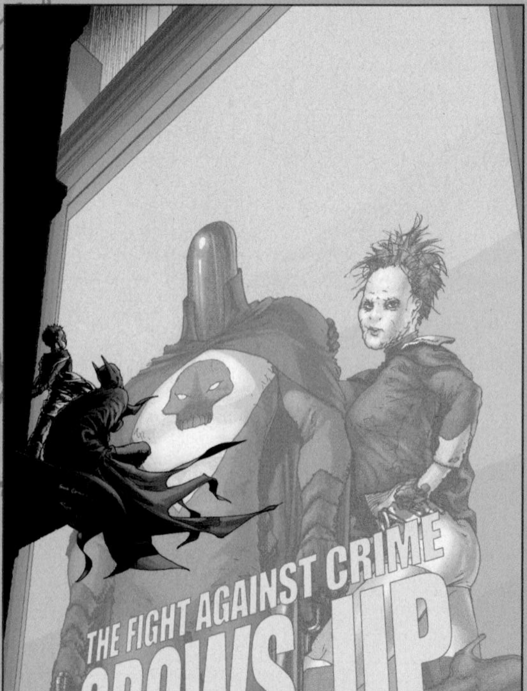
THE FIGHT AGAINST CRIME
GROWS UP

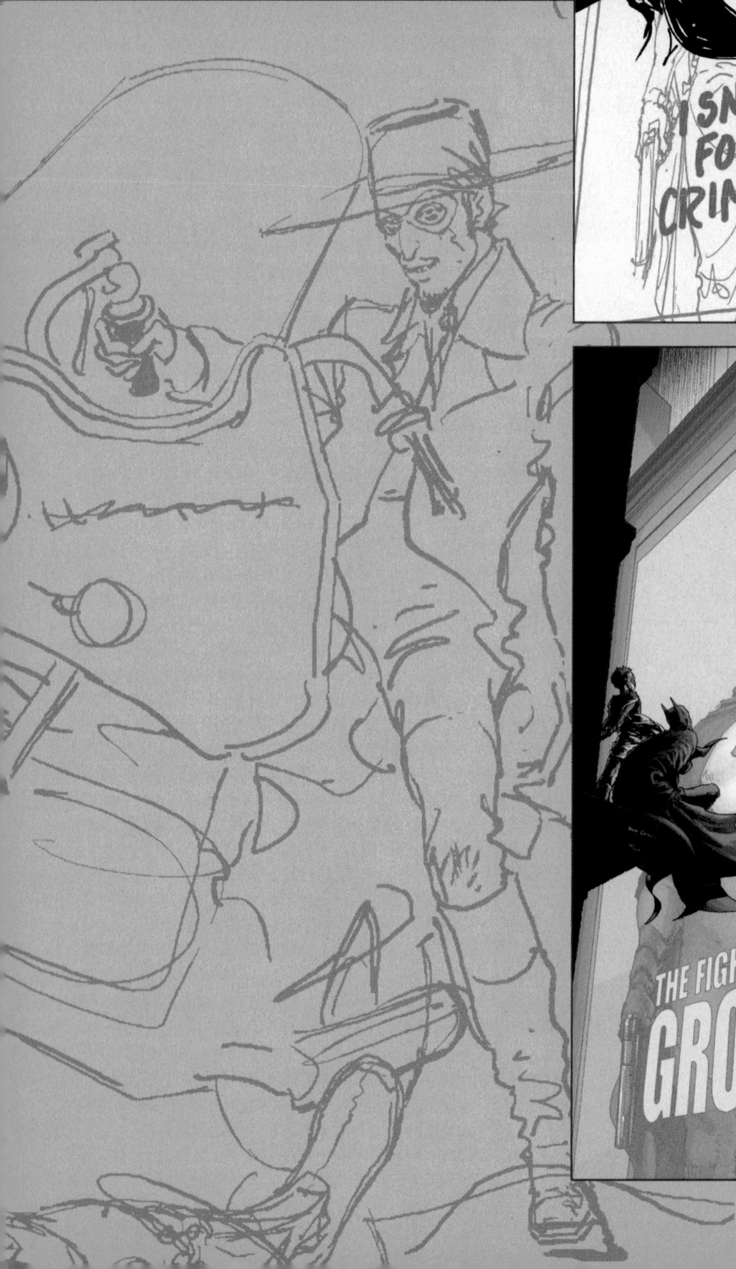

On issue 5, Frank was sick and laboring under an oncoming deadline, so we went with a strong, simple-to-draw head shot in an effort to make his life a little easier. It's a very direct image — the fearless heroes facing a flamboyantly colored threat to their brains, as usual.

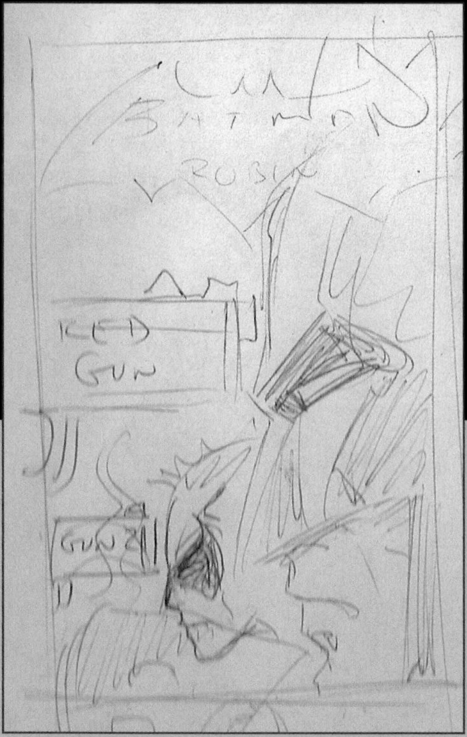
BATMAN
ROBIN

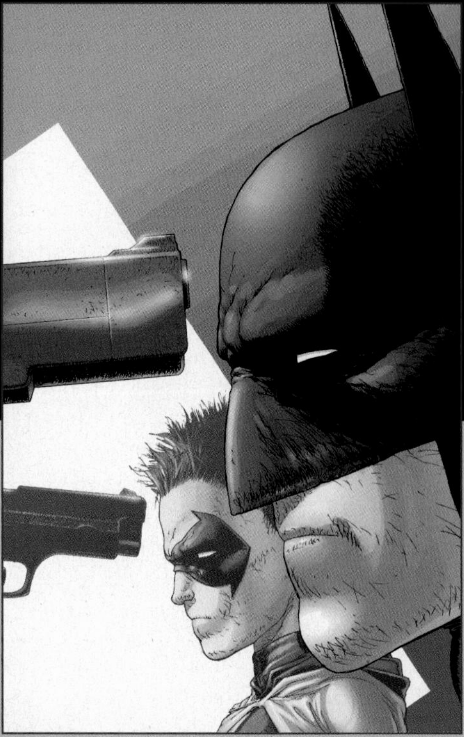

Cover 6 was based on the Prince album *Purple Rain.* Why? Well, you can check my notes on the Flamingo's design (reproduced on page 168), although you may be none the wiser after reading them. This may well be the first *pink* Batman cover ever, and it is likely to be the last you will ever see.

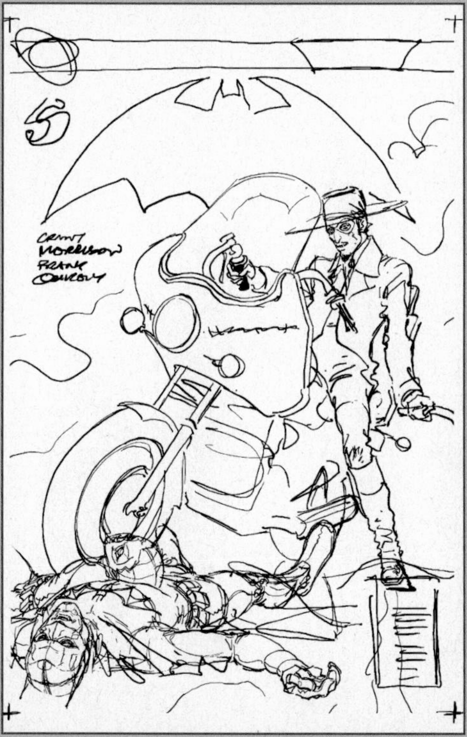

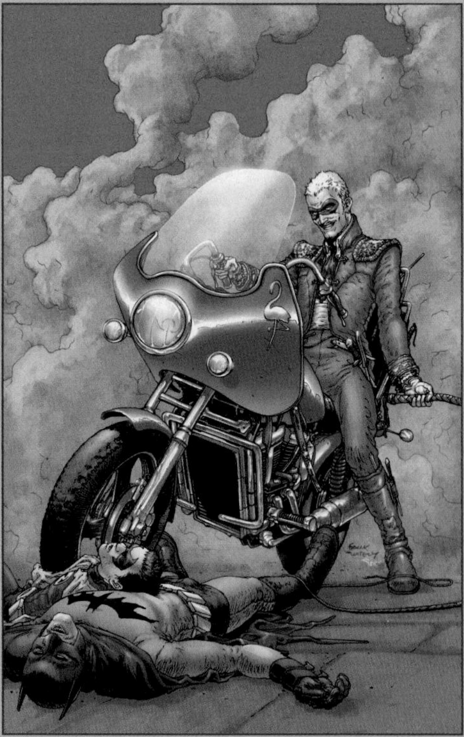

THE DESIGNS

batman & robin

The new Batman and Robin first appeared in a flash-forward scene at the beginning of BATMAN #681, but artist Tony Daniel was asked to draw them in silhouette so as not to reveal any potential costume changes before they'd been approved. I'd suggested some major revisions, including a *yellow* bat symbol in a black circle — the reverse of the traditional chest shield — and a yellow and gray Robin outfit, derived from the uniform of the Earth-2 Robin from the 1960s.

FAO Mike Marts / Tony Daniel
Batman 676 p1
Future Robin wears modernized version of original 'Earth 2' Robin suit
Batman - as Alex Ross' sketch - but add new emblem -
Maybe update belt to be more like movie?
Gold bat in black circle
Grant Morrison

Armoured cowl
Articulated neck, elbows, groin & knees
Armoured suit
Bat-shaped belt buckle with small compartments, getting bigger at sides
Long gloves
Long boots
Long cape
FQ
BATMAN A bit more detail

Batman
#2

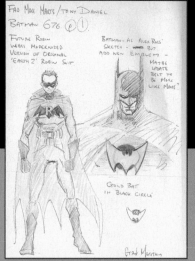

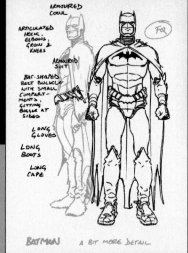

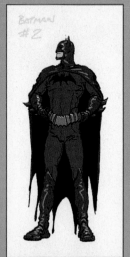

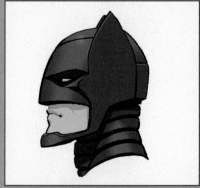

Frank Quitely added his own touches, such as longer boots for Batman and a more articulated, plated hood, but in the end all of these redesigns were regarded as being too "off-model" for the characters and we settled on something a little more familiar.

Frank Quitely B&R GM colours

Frank Quitely B&R DC colours

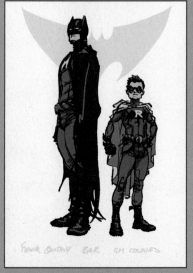

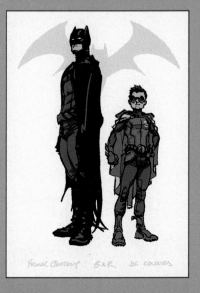

the batmobile

We didn't want our global warming/recession-era Batmobile to resemble the chrome-piped, gas-guzzling, Techno-Deco road leviathans of the past, so the Batmobile of 2009 was created to be compact and curvy. As you can see from Frank's sketches, the new Batmobile comes fully equipped with hydraulic suspension, which enables it to assume various driving configurations.

BATMAN

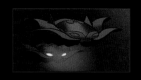

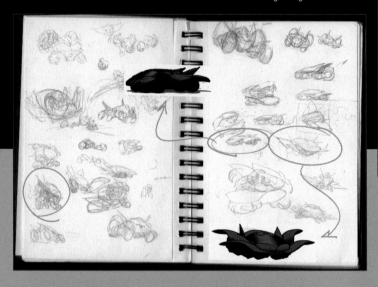

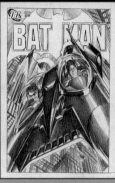

The idea for the flying Batmobile in BATMAN AND ROBIN was suggested by this beautiful and exuberant Alex Ross sketch, done as a potential BATMAN cover in 2007.

the red hood & scarlet

The Red Hood is a venerable Bat-villain name. In 1951 The Hood was introduced as a mystery villain dressed in a tuxedo, a red cape and a red, reflective, pill-shaped dome helmet. The story revealed the unlucky man beneath the Red Hood to be a petty criminal who promptly fell into a vat of chemicals, only to emerge, vastly more famous, as Batman's arch-enemy The Joker. The same story was, of course, woven into the flashback plotline of THE KILLING JOKE.

When a new version of the Red Hood appeared in Judd Winick's "Under the Hood," he was revealed to be the presumed-deceased second Robin, Jason Todd. A leather jacket and jeans replaced the dapper formal wear of the original, while the new red hood itself resembled a motorcycle helmet rather than a crimson bell jar.

-HOOD' CAVE' TRUCK-
-CRIME LAB-
-DOJO-
-LIVING AREA-
MINI-FRIDGE

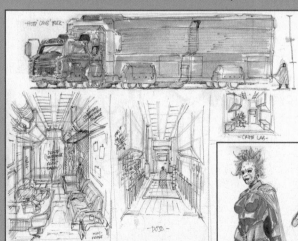

We decided that Jason's second attempt at anchoring the Red Hood identity in the public consciousness would be more self-consciously super-heroic — cape, tights, secret HQ, the lot. In his latest effort to get noticed, the former Boy Wonder would imitate more blatantly the basic look and M.O. of Batman, his mentor. The weird pill helmet and cape were brought back as a nod to the original design.

RETRACTABLE BLADE
-SCARLETT STUDY-

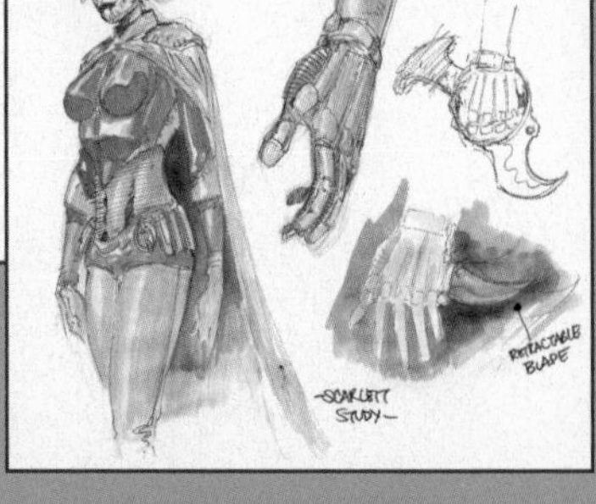

The brief for Scarlet was simple — an *ersatz* female Robin whose beautiful young face was hidden beneath a shriveled mask of horror.

NEW CHARACTERS

professor pyg

Pyg, along with his mind-controlled killer Dollotrons, had appeared briefly as a crucified, upside-down corpse in issue #666 of my BATMAN run with artist Andy Kubert. I didn't think I'd use him or any of the other characters mentioned in the story — Max Roboto, Candyman, Loveless, Jackanapes, the Weasel and Flamingo — again, although I'd concocted detailed backstories for all of them. Some things, however, tend to take on a life of their own, and it became impossible to keep a bad Pyg down.

Pyg's name is derived from the song "Pygmalism," as written by Nick Currie (recorded by Kahimi Karie on her *Tilt* CD and also by Currie's alter ego Momus on the CD *Folktronic*). The name refers, of course, to the Greek myth in which the sculptor Pygmalion falls in love with a statue of a woman he has carved, which is then brought to life by the goddess Aphrodite. *Pygmalion* is the name of the play by George Bernard Shaw which inspired the musical *My Fair Lady* and which tells the tale of Professor Henry Higgins, who makes a bet that he can transform Eliza Doolittle, a uneducated Cockney flower seller, into a convincingly well-spoken society lady as proof of Nurture's superiority to Nature. Like Pygmalion, Higgins is creating his own ideal woman, and like Pygmalion he falls in love with her. The Currie song is from the point of view of the Professor's latest "creation" — *"sometimes in the night I sing the songs Professor Pig has taught me"* — and brilliantly reconfigures *Pygmalion* as a story of mind control and rebellion.

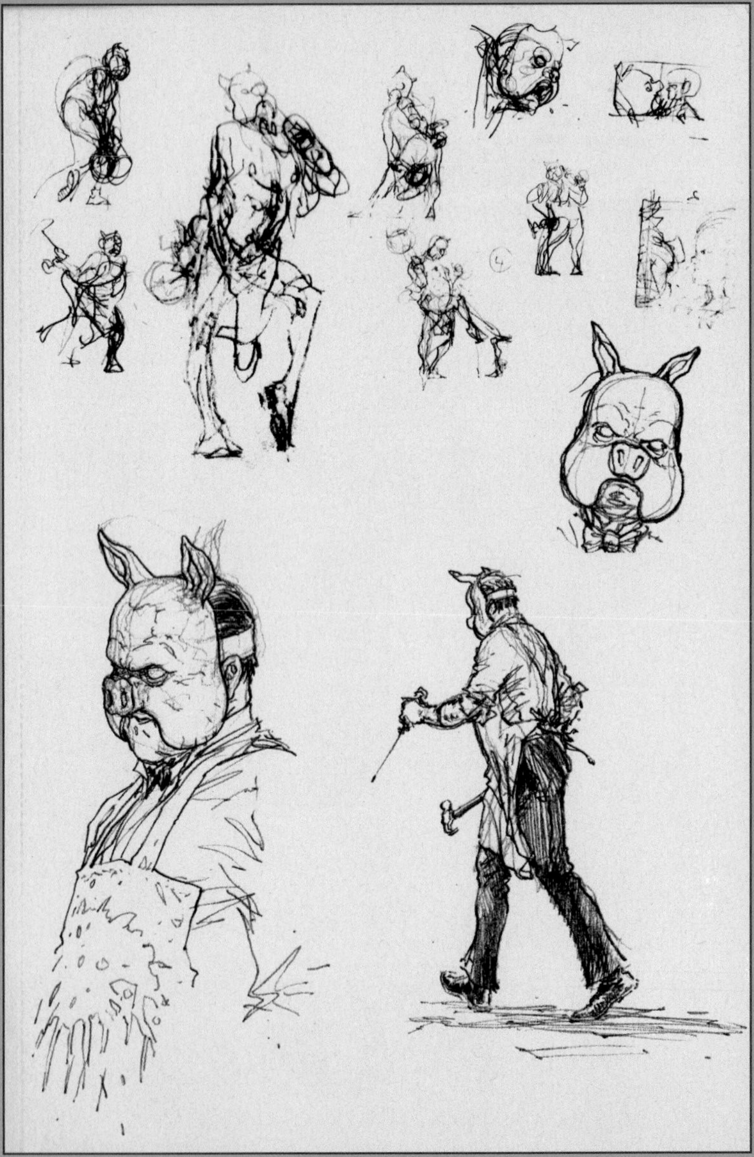

Professor Pyg's wardrobe recalls the Edwardian suits worn by Rex Harrison, who played Higgins alongside Audrey Hepburn's Eliza Doolittle in the 1964 film version of *My Fair Lady*. Harrison, of course, also portrayed *Doctor* Dolittle, who could speak to animals. The attempt to dominate and redefine the feminine principle by forcing biology to conform to the artist's will (*"Why can't a woman be more like a man?"* sings the frustrated Higgins) suggested links to the "wire mother" experiments of Harry Harlow and backwards to the chaotic proto-mother mythologies of ancient Babylon and Mesopotamia. The shattered mind of extreme circus performer Lazlo Valentin has mashed all these connections into a frightening personal *mythos*, constructed to justify his deranged activities as Professor Pyg.

the circus of strange

With Dick Grayson's origins as a circus aerialist, it felt right to pit him against a group of circus-themed villains in his first adventure as Batman. There have been circus criminals before, but rather than the traditional Ringling Brothers clowns and ringmasters, I imagined the Circus of Strange as an "extreme" troupe, more along the lines of the Jim Rose Circus.

The members of the Circus of Strange are all based on classic "freak show" archetypes — the lizard man, the bearded lady, the Siamese twins and... um... the man with his head on fire...

Mr. Toad — half man, half amphibian, all stud — is inspired by the character of the same name from Kenneth Grahame's *The Wind in the Willows*, right down to the opening "wild ride" in his odd car. Several Batman villains have been lifted from Lewis Carroll's books, and the time seemed right to begin the plunder of another beloved children's author.

Phosphorus Rex was mentioned previously in BATMAN #666. His skin combusts in the air. What else do you need to know?

Big Top was originally written and drawn as a more obviously feminine "bearded lady," but it seemed rather ungallant, even for the Damian Wayne Robin, to administer the kind of beating he hands out to a woman, so we made Big Top look more masculine and referred to the character as "he" — all of which served only to compound his strange allure.

Siam was the kind of challenge Frank Quitely loves — conjoined *kung fu* triplets. When not hard at work on BATMAN AND ROBIN, Frank loves nothing more than to while away the hours drawing perfectly constructed anatomical grotesques — people with their torsos reversed so that their heads hang down between their legs, etc. He works out how they would sit, eat, play football or have sex, then draws them doing it. Siam was a breeze for him to draw after some of these creations, but the character design is still a technical masterpiece that fully justifies all those dedicated hours of life drawing classes. Look at the way the three lock together and provide momentum and balance for one another when they fight. No one but Frank could have drawn this villain.

oberon "the gravedigger" sexton

Originally the character was called "Auberon Sexton," but I changed the spelling to link the character to the King of the Fairies in Shakespeare's *A Midsummer Night's Dream* both to underline the Englishness and also to amplify Sexton's "mystery man" feel.

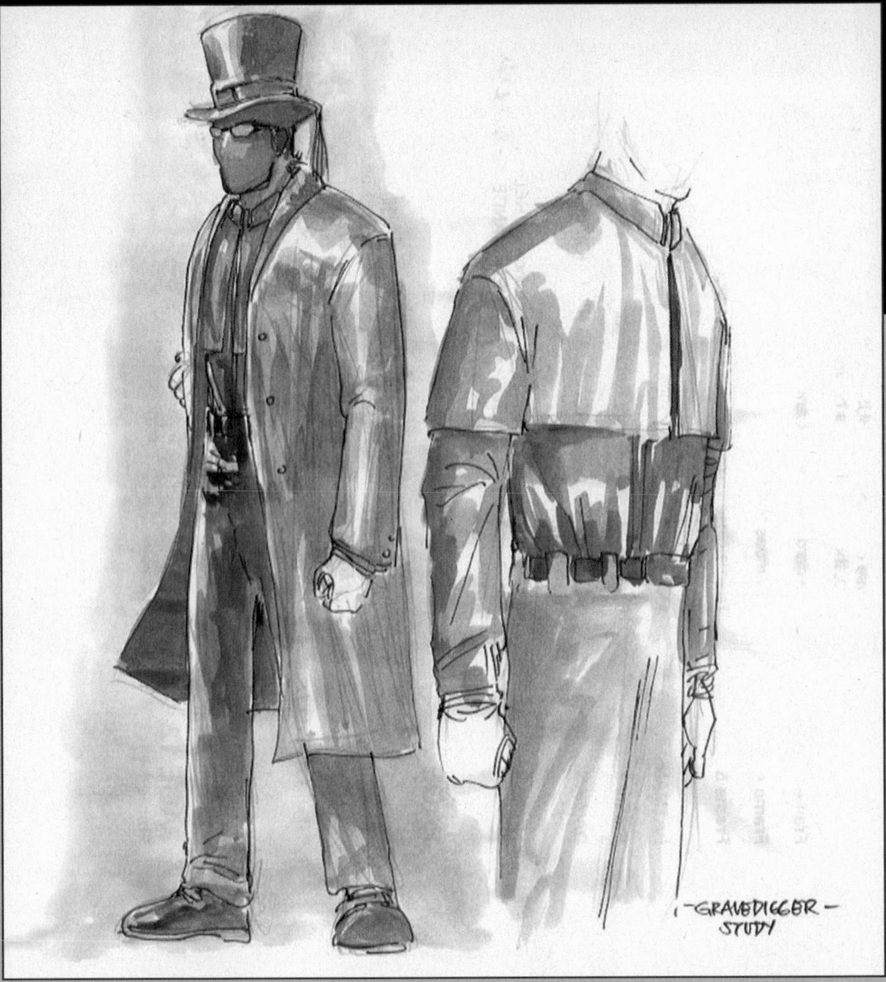
-GRAVEDIGGER-
STUDY

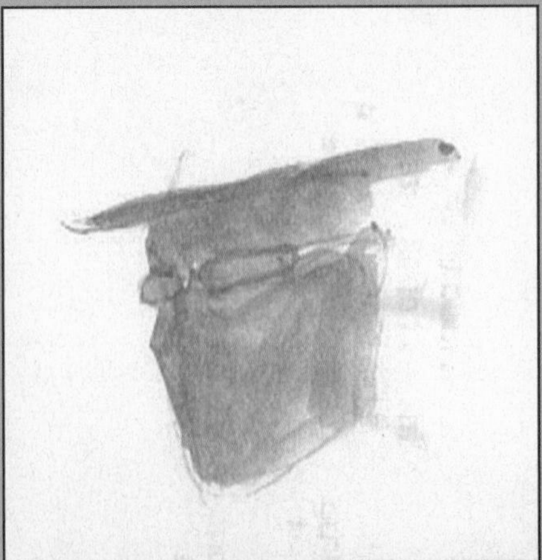

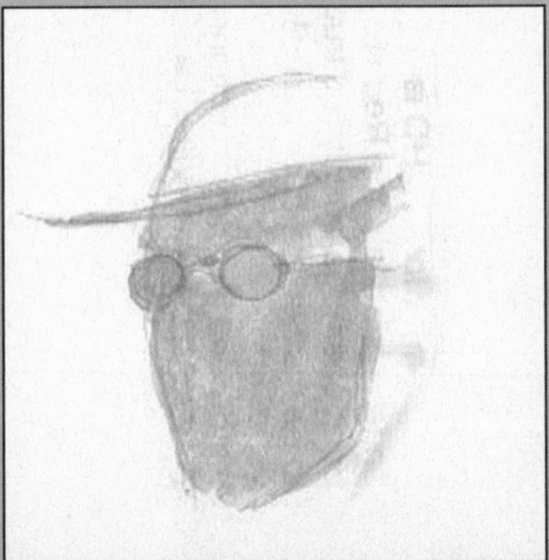

gotham gangsters

When the plot of BATMAN AND ROBIN #4 called for a meeting of several Gotham City crime bosses, nobody wanted to see another faceless crew of mob guys parked round a table. Although most of these characters would only hang around for a couple of pages, it was fun to give them names and a little bit of history, which may or may not be explored in future Batman stories.

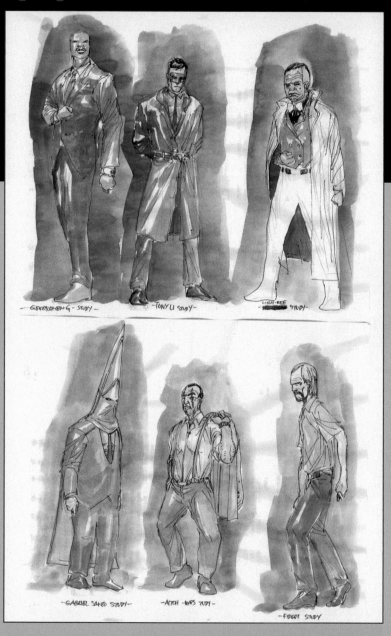

-GENTLEMEN-G - STUDY -
-TONY LI STUDY-
HIGH-RISE [redacted] STUDY-
-GABRIEL SANTO STUDY-
-AITCH -EYES STUDY-
-FIDGET STUDY

Some of Batman's rogues' gallery — particularly the "face" villains like Two-Face, Clayface and False Face — were clearly inspired by Chester Gould's distinctively grotesque bad guys from the *Dick Tracy* strip, so I decided to throw a couple of Gould-style hoods into the mix; hence the double-decker forehead of Romeo "High-Rise" Romero, as well as the vertical facial scars of "Aitch-Eyes." The mob accountant Rodney Fidget suggested a minor Batman baddie from the Denny O'Neill '70s or the Alan Grant '90s. Gentleman-G Merriwether, slick in his Ozwald Boateng suit, was named for the makeover show *From Gs to Gents* while Neon Dragon Triad boss Tony Li has echoes of Hong Kong action cinema and Quentin Tarantino's Crazy 88 gang from *Kill Bill*. Gabriel Santo — emissary of the enigmatic *El Penitente* himself — is wearing the hood and robe of the *Penitente* order of flagellant monks. Every one of these characters opens doors into potential stories.

NEW CHARACTERS

flamingo

Like Professor Pyg, Flamingo was another throwaway character from BATMAN #666 who came alive in my head and demanded to muscle his way into new stories.

One of the big influences on Batman—both in the real world where he was created as a character and in the fictional world of young Bruce Wayne—is Zorro, and the idea of going back to that primal root to create an "evil Zorro" as a new enemy for Batman seemed appropriate and overdue. So the briefly glimpsed Flamingo of BATMAN #666 became Eduardo Flamingo, lobotomized super-assassin for the shadowy *Penitente* cartel, with his own origin story, special abilities and motivations. Where Pyg is dementedly in love with the sound of his own voice, Flamingo first appears as an engine of pure Death and mayhem. There's no discussion, no appeal with Flamingo. He is here to kill you and he *will* kill you. I loved the idea of a terrifying, amoral and brain-damaged monster who was still self-aware and style-conscious enough to dress in pink and choose as his emblem the graceful, ludicrous flamingo.

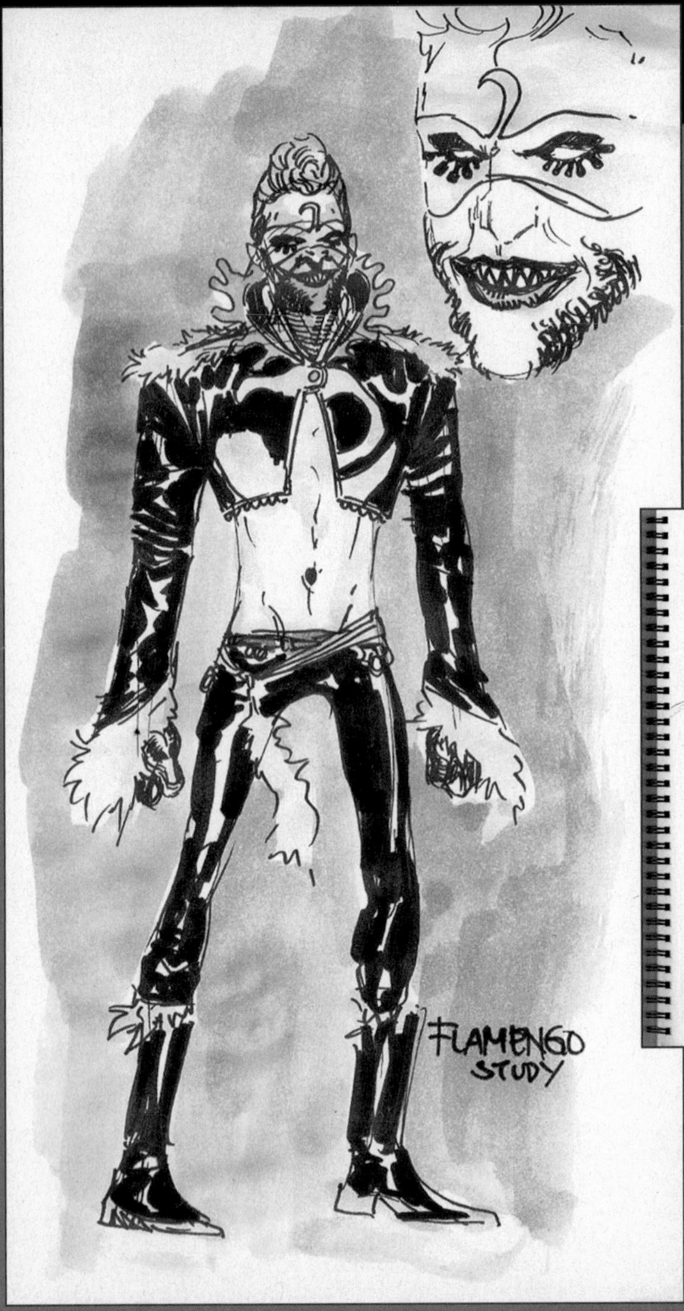

FLAMENGO
STUDY

Another obvious inspiration for the look of Flamingo is the artist currently known once more as Prince—particularly as he appeared on the cover of his 1984 record *Purple Rain*. Don't ask me why but Batman and Robin vs. Prince seemed to make perfect sense at the time.

—Grant Morrison
Los Angeles
November 2009

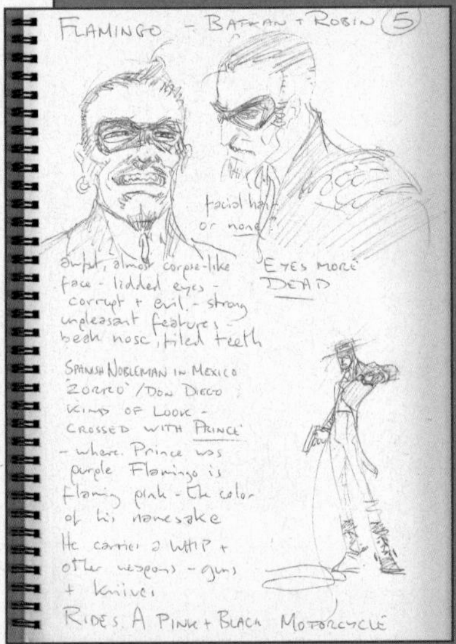

FLAMINGO - BATMAN + ROBIN (5)
facial hair or none
awful, almost corpse-like face - lidded eyes - corrupt + evil - strong unpleasant features - beak nose, filed teeth
EYES MORE DEAD
SPANISH NOBLEMAN IN MEXICO 'ZORRO' / DON DIEGO KIND OF LOOK - CROSSED WITH PRINCE
- where Prince was purple Flamingo is flaming pink - the color of his namesake
He carries a WHIP + other weapons - guns + knives
RIDES A PINK + BLACK MOTORCYCLE